THE VICTORIAN HOUSE BOOK

The VICTORIAN HOUSE BOOK

Robin Guild

With VERNON GIBBERD
and other Contributors

SHELDRAKE PRESS
LONDON

Published in Great Britain in 1991 by
Sheldrake Press Limited,
188 Cavendish Road,
London SW12 0DA.

Second Edition
First published in 1989 as *The Complete Victorian House Book*
by Sidgwick & Jackson Limited

ISBN 1 873329 02 4

EDITOR: SIMON RIGGE
Commissioning Editor: Diana Dubens
Deputy Editor: Antony Mason
Managing Editor: Susan Mitchell
Contributing Editors: Francis Graham, Adam Hopkins
Assistant Editors: Chris Schüler, Frances Kennett, Peter
Brooke-Ball, Wendy Lee
Special Contributors: Gail Cotton, Stephen Hoare, Annie
Sloan, Charles Brooking, Ian Hedley, Angela Burgin
Sub-Editors: Helen Ridge, Amanda Ronan, Marianne Ryan,
Sue Midgley, Judith Hart, Linda Lambert, Valerie Bingham,
Eric Smith, Ruth Burns
Editorial Assistants: Kathryn Cureton, Tracey Stead
Researcher: Kieran Costello
Indexer: Valerie Chandler

Picture Editor: Eleanor Lines
Picture Co-ordinator: Anna Smith
Picture Researchers: Jane Lewis, Philippa Lewis,
Irene Lynch
Picture Assistants: Linda Bassett, Harriet Peel,
Sarah Tudge

Art Direction: Bob Hook, Ivor Claydon
Designers: Caroline Helfer, Nic Bellenberg

Photographers: James Mortimer, Ken Kirkwood, Derry
Moore, Peter Woloszynski, George Ong, Robin
McCartney
Illustrators: Nigel Husband, Stephen Carpenter, Ann
Winterbotham, Sime Baillie Lane

Production Manager: Hugh Allan
Production Controllers: Rebecca Bone, Helen Seccombe

Typesetting by Sheldrake Press Ltd, Caroline Helfer and
DataFlow Graphics Ltd
Colour origination by Columbia (UK) Ltd, London
Printed in Italy by Amilcare Pizzi SpA

AUTHOR

Robin Guild has acquired an international reputation as a
designer of interiors ranging from small studio
apartments and country houses to the cabins of motor
yachts and private jets. During the course of his career he
has worked for many well known clients including the
Rolling Stones, Joan Collins, Desmond Morris, Lulu and
the royal family of Saudi Arabia.

Robin Guild designed the interiors of Browns' and
Ralph Lauren's London clothes stores, and most recently
the Empress Garden Restaurant in London. Co-founder
of Designers Guild, he has restored and designed a wide
variety of Victorian houses. His previous book, *The
Finishing Touch*, has been translated into four languages.

CHIEF CONTRIBUTOR

Vernon Gibberd, RIBA, has run a private architectural
practice in London since 1970; before that, he spent two
years working as an architect in New York.

The practice is very mixed, combining new work with
restoration. Recent commissions include aviaries and a
maze and grotto for Leeds Castle in Kent, work for the
National Trust and the rehabilitation of a wing at
Arundel Castle.

Vernon Gibberd's publications include booklets
written and illustrated for the National Trust, a book on
kitchen design and a history source book of architecture
from Egyptian times to the present day.

CONSULTANT

Charles McKean, FSAScot, FRSA, has been Secretary and
Treasurer of the Royal Incorporation of Architects in
Scotland since 1979. As Architectural Correspondent of
The Times, he was named Architectural Journalist of the
Year in 1979 and 1983. He has written nine books,
including *Fight Blight* (1979), *Edinburgh, An Illustrated
Architectural Guide* (1982) and *The Scottish Thirties* (1987).
He is General Editor of the RIAS/Landmark Trust series
to Scotland.

NOTICE

This book has been written for all who own Victorian houses or are
interested in them. Some householders who are skilled in do-it-
yourself techniques may use the information in the book to carry
out their own projects, but we have assumed that most will use the
professional services of architects, engineers, surveyors and
builders.

The author, editors and publishers have gone to great pains to
ensure that the information given in the book is accurate and
reliable. We cannot accept liability for damage, mishap or injury
caused by anyone attempting to carry out projects described in the
book without professional advice, nor can we be held responsible
for any contravention of building regulations, which must be
checked by the householder before alterations are made to the
fabric of a house.

Half-title page: The main bathroom in a Victorian Gothic
country house has the benefit of space, which allows it to
be used as a comfortable family room. Medicine cabinets
have been created by recessing a pair of Gothic-shaped
cupboards into the wall either side of the main window.

Frontispiece: Built-in cupboards with mirrors have been
added to match the original detailing of this Gothic
house and increase the sense of space in an upstairs
passageway. The walls have been decorated with a faded
stencil effect.

This page: The ceiling rose, a hand-carved luxury in
the 18th century, became a mass-produced novelty in the
19th, when it was often despised by professional
designers. It is now back in fashion as a period feature.

CONTENTS

P R E F A C E

Architecture is a vulnerable art; like the landscape, it is subject to meddling by succeeding generations. In this respect, music and literature are more fortunate, for however much abuse or neglect they may receive, the essential integrity of the original will probably survive. This is not at all the case with buildings, and very few houses over a hundred years old have survived unaltered. In many cases, the effects of weather and pollution and the additions, repairs and extensions made by several generations of inhabitants have changed them to such an extent that their builders would have difficulty in recognizing them.

Not that our forebears were any different. Indeed, before the listing of buildings of architectural importance began in Scotland in 1933, and in England, Wales and Northern Ireland in 1947, ownership conferred the right to pull down anything considered obsolete or which stood in the way of future development. For this change of attitude we must be thankful to William Morris, the instigator in 1877 of the Society for the Protection of Ancient Buildings. True, Morris would probably not have cared much if all the houses of the 18th century had been pulled down, but at least he brought to public attention the state of many medieval buildings which were then suffering serious neglect or were threatened with demolition.

We may think of ourselves as more enlightened today, but our aesthetic vandalism is more insidious. If a roof needed retiling in the last century, the chances are that the replacements would have been made from the same clay – or even the same kiln – as the originals. And although cheap bricks were soon being brought by rail to all parts of the country, and Welsh slates were replacing the old stone and clay tiles, at least they derived from natural materials and blended well with neighbouring buildings.

Nowadays there are countless substitutes on the market, and nearly all of them are visually inferior to the originals. A glance down any Victorian street will illustrate this sad decline. The roofline will probably have suffered most, with slates replaced by interlocking concrete tiles and cast-iron gutters by plastic ones. Nor will the facades have survived unscathed; good brickwork will have been painted over or repointed in coarse cement mortar, and sashes will have given way to aluminium-framed or plastic-coated windows.

Each age works within the cost limits and technology of its time. The industrial components of today's builders' merchants – concrete tiles, plastic rain-water goods, mass-produced bricks and blocks, metal windows, flush doors and building boards – can be seen as the only architectural currency capable of satisfying present housing demands. Houses built of these new materials are

Opposite: The rich glow of stained glass in this imposing Victorian doorway offers a warm welcome and the promise of comfort, security and good cheer – qualities which are leading more and more home buyers to turn to period housing.

Opposite: A new conservatory has been built on to a Victorian detached house. It is an assured and confident construction, while remaining entirely in keeping with the rest of the building. The geometric tiles and the cast-iron brackets bear witness to the upsurge of small firms willing to make authentic reproductions of 19th-century fittings.

truly houses of today, and for better or worse, estates up and down the country reflect their dubious standards.

Unfortunately these same materials are quite unsuitable for repairing and extending the older housing stock in which a large proportion of us still have to live, or choose to live.

The building heritage of Britain may be divided into four periods: pre-1830; the loosely categorized Victorian period, extending from the 1830s to the outbreak of the 1914-18 war; 'between-the-wars'; and the post-war period from 1945 to the present day. Pre-Victorian buildings represent a very small percentage of the private housing stock. A look at the prices in Edinburgh New Town, Bath or Hampstead will confirm that Georgian and earlier houses are highly sought-after and well beyond the reach of most buyers. Even in northern English towns and in many parts of the countryside, they are comparatively expensive.

The housing of the inter-war period continued the themes of the Edwardian era; at its best, it drew on the aesthetics of the Garden Suburb Movement, albeit watered down by faltering convictions and rising prices. This mild vernacular is not without its charms, although the position of these houses, relegated by historical accident to the outer suburbs, makes them unattractive to those who prefer closer contact with city life.

With much post-war housing, these standards have been reduced to the absolute minimum. There will be little in these buildings, one imagines, to interest later generations; it seems inconceivable that historical societies will seek to preserve them or record their details with any pleasure. They house people; they keep them warm and dry, and as such they have a respectable function.

For many people, however, this is not enough. More and more of us are coming to appreciate the character and craftsmanship of older houses, to value the special atmosphere of a place that has been lived in for generations and to take pleasure in the wealth of architectural detail so lacking in more modern homes. And of the earlier housing stock, by far the largest and most accessible proportion will have been built in the 19th century. In Britain alone, almost six million houses were built during Queen Victoria's reign, the majority after 1870.

'Victorian' – the very word that was shunned by estate agents for years – has now become a positive selling adjective. This has its ironic and even absurd aspects, but it is also an accurate gauge of public opinion. Estate agents may like to believe that they lead trends, but in reality they merely reflect the changes in public taste. In Britain, on the Continent, in the United States, the real trend-setters have been artists, followed by architects and craftsmen. Chelsea, the Left Bank and Greenwich Village were all infiltrated by artists and poorer professionals such as architects, who wanted homes with some character and were able and willing to renovate

Above: In an exciting combination of modern spatial planning and period detail, a light well has been artfully let into a first-floor landing to create a feeling of space, and has been fenced with a reproduction Victorian balustrade.

a run-down property. They created a lively atmosphere which attracted the richer professionals and pseudo-artists: lawyers, bankers, advertisers and public relations people. In due course, the new arrivals pushed up the prices, forcing the artists to look elsewhere; in London the move was northwards to Islington, in New York to Soho, and in both these districts the pattern is now repeating itself.

Nostalgia may be an element of the charm which Victorian houses hold for us, but it can be a misleading quality. We can only see Victorian houses through 20th-century eyes, and cannot transport ourselves back to the aesthetic, moral and social climate of a hundred years ago, any more than the Victorians felt empathy with the Georgian era. Their dislike of 18th-century architecture has been echoed in our own century by the condemnation of Victorian taste by almost all 'enlightened' people until quite recently. John Betjeman, for many years a lone voice in his admiration for Victoriana, was held to be at best an eccentric and at worst a fraud.

This was a natural enough reaction. The generation which knew at first hand the darker side of 19th-century life – the grinding drudgery of factory life or the suffocating respectability of a middle-class Sunday – felt little nostalgia for the period. After the First World War, the blueprint for the Modern Movement in architecture – often called the International Style – was drawn up. Its basic tenets – austerity, the absence of ornament and the simple lines created by the machine tool – were the antithesis of everything Victorian architecture stood for. The widespread rebuilding after the Second World War allowed the architects of the International Style to put their ideas into practice on a large scale, and the slum clearances that followed saw much old building swept away as the impractical, squalid survivors of a recent, unloved past.

With the passage of time, however, the art and architecture of the Victorian age can be reviewed in a more sympathetic light. The new theories, case studies and aesthetic polemics have failed to solve the problems of society, and are actually felt by many to have aggravated them. The high-rise building that reached its peak in the 1960s has come to be seen as a regrettable mistake, a hostile and impersonal environment that does little to foster human values or community spirit. Victorian houses, in contrast, no longer strike us as gloomy and forbidding but as cosy and cheerful.

A house must, first and foremost, provide a sound and practical place in which to live. There are people who have turned the restoration of their Victorian house into a rigorously purist exercise, creating something akin to a museum-piece, but in the end they are left in a period cocoon. Their gaslight, coal boilers, tub baths and Belfast sinks may be irreproachable, but nothing will stop the world going on its way outside. Cars will pass in the street, not carriages, and their children will come in wearing jeans, not pinafores.

What is important today is not so much the pursuit of authenticity as finding a balance which reconciles our way of living with what we see as valuable in Victorian style and decoration. Gaslight, with its gentle hiss and mellow tone, is most attractive, but electricity is more convenient; Victorians would not have used a coffee table, but low-level furniture suits the way we live. The degree to which we shape a period house to modern requirements is a highly individual matter; to accomplish this with tact and sensitivity does not require textbook knowledge so much as a feel for Victoriana that can be acquired through familiarity.

This book is intended to give the reader just such an acquaintance with the developments of Victorian style. Our aim has been to show what Victorian houses were like, and why, and to show how they may be adapted to modern living without loss of character. The photographs illustrate houses that have been decorated in a wide variety of Victorian fashions and complementary modern styles. The black and white line illustrations give accurate details of a wide range of Victorian ironmongery, woodwork, plaster mouldings, door furniture and other fittings and furnishings.

The chapters lead you through the house, from its foundations to the decorative details of each room. The information is organized in approximately the order that a householder contemplating a plan of repair and decoration will find useful: background history in Chapter 1, structural and building information in Chapter 2, interior architectural detailing in Chapter 3 followed by decoration of the public and private rooms in Chapters 4, 5 and 6. Finally, Chapter 7 takes you out into the garden. Technical guidance is given in Chapter 8 for those who want to undertake restoration work themselves, or want to be able to talk to architects, surveyors and builders on something like equal terms. At the end of the book there is a technical and reference section, and a bibliography. A list of suppliers provides information on where to find period fittings and decorations, both genuine antiques and authentic reproductions. Nothing demonstrates better the renewed interest in Victorian domestic architecture than the resurgence of manufacturers, craft studios and designers covering virtually every aspect of period restoration.

This book is itself an expression of that renewed interest, and is addressed to all those who, disillusioned by sterile modernism, are seeking to make their home into a haven; not a precious or purist recreation of the past, but a shelter in the best sense of the word, comfortable and welcoming.

Above: This ceramic chimneypiece – a stunning example of French Art Nouveau at its most luxuriant – would probably have shocked the original owners of the English Victorian house in which it has now been installed.

Below: Part of a modern restoration of a Victorian house, this lancet-shaped doorway with its two flanking niches adeptly revives the Gothic Revival – a clever *jeu d'esprit* in the spirit of post-modernism.

Left: The columns and capitals of this beautiful drawing-room chimney piece, executed in three different types of marble, show the Victorian love of Early English Gothic.

Chapter One

THE VICTORIAN
INSPIRATION

All generations see themselves as modern. Our local geography bears witness to this harmless vanity: Newports, Newtowns, New Streets, Newchurches, most of them now as old as New College, Oxford, if not older. Nor are politics, the arts and philosophy immune from this transient fancy. Nevertheless, in looking back over the Victorian age, it is impossible not to be struck by the particular modernism which had been born out of the Industrial Revolution. Change was so profound and irrevocable that it was soon clear that the world was never going to be quite the same again. Mass production and faster communications had not only introduced new goods and processes, it had created new, speeded-up ways of life. A different society was forming: coal-powered, steam-driven, factory-based. Some of the liveliest and most brilliant minds of the time celebrated and revelled in the possibilities of new technologies, men like the engineer Brunel, and Paxton, designer of the Crystal Palace. Others, like Pugin, Ruskin and William Morris, found the prospect of mechanized production appalling. This divergence of intelligent opinion was a Victorian phenomenon and one which has not only persisted but has deepened in our own times, as the full effects of man's crushing superiority over the natural world unravel.

The Industrial Revolution transformed a primarily rural population into a predominantly urban one. Riding on the back of the Agrarian Revolution of the mid-18th century, it drew surplus labour from the countryside into the new towns where industries were being established: coal mining in Yorkshire, Wales and Scotland, iron founding in Shropshire, textiles in Lancashire. By the time Queen Victoria came to the throne in 1837, coal and steam power had made possible the railways which in turn brought cheap coal to those regions where it was scarce, to fuel developing industries.

Britain, saved from the turmoil of revolutionary France and the unstable regimes of Continental Europe, had surged ahead of all her competitors by 1850. Self-confident and rich, her Empire expanded, providing cheap imports and, at the same time, captive markets abroad for home-produced goods. The population grew rapidly. Towns and cities expanded into the surrounding countryside, engulfing villages and small towns. Developments grew by accretion around the perimeter of towns or along their connect-

Opposite: 'The Hall and Staircase of a Country House' by Jonathan Pratt, 1882, depicts the vitality of the High Victorian era. With its Gothic arches, stained-glass windows, elaborate iron balusters, and the clutter of interesting objects from a wide variety of sources, this hall in its day would have seemed the epitome of modern taste.

Above: Transitional well-to-do town housing from the middle of the century continues the stucco Italianate tradition, a style about to give way to the more severe all-brick treatment glimpsed further down the street.

Above right: Built for mill workers, terraces like this raw brick housing in Oldham covered miles of the industrial heartlands of Britain. The facades are functional, for financial reasons. The sole concession to decoration can be seen in chamfered reveals to windows and lintels.

ing roads and railways. With the railway came the rise of the middle-class suburb. The emergence of a defined middle class was the salient political development of the 19th century. This section of society had been slow to recognize its political strength. The 1832 Reform Bill had given it greater political representation, yet in matters of taste and social expectation it was largely content to follow the ruling aristocracy. The new money wanted to copy the aristocracy or, if possible, go one better, but rarely destroy or condemn it.

As land acquired new value for building, the large-scale developer made his appearance. The distinction between builder and architect became defined. Architects, surveyors and engineers formed professional associations to consolidate and protect their interests; conversely, architects were no longer permitted to be property developers, as the Adam brothers had been in the late 18th century. Building regulations were gradually tightened up. The aim of 18th-century regulations had been to control fires; the purpose of 19th-century legislation was to raise standards of health and hygiene. Rules were introduced to improve drainage and water supply and to make buildings structurally sounder.

As the big town became the dominant feature of British life, it bred a longing for a romantic countryside filled with rich allusions to a noble past. The concept of country life as a pastoral pageant was, as always, essentially a fantasy of the middle and upper classes. For them, country life was fused with history to satisfy the romantic hunger of the times, a romanticism epitomized in the novels of Walter Scott, then famous across Europe. They loved the exuberance and non-intellectual styles of an imagined Merrie England. They wanted castles, comfortable, convenient, free of draughts and damp, but castles all the same. In the 17th century Sir Edward Coke had coined the phrase 'A man's house is his castle'. Two centuries later it became 'An Englishman's home is his castle', establishing a new concept, the home, in its way as British an invention as cricket or afternoon tea.

Not since Elizabethan and Jacobean times had quite the same combination of crude vitality been displayed in architecture, not since then had the same naive, half-understood elements been assembled for their historical allusion and picturesque effect. Somehow the Victorians managed to weld together paradoxical, even contradictory, ideals to produce a vigorous architecture uniquely of its time. The love for new technology combined with a longing for a rosier past, a distrust of intellectuals coupled with a reverence for cultural high priests, materialism welded to religious puritanism – all these are evident in any survey of their art and architecture.

Victoria's reign was long, so long that it makes nonsense to talk of any single characteristic style, not at least in the sense that the 'Regency' or 'Edwardian' labels have a precise meaning to us. 'Victorian' remains a style more easily recognized than defined, so that a neo-Jacobean house, for example, however meticulous a copy of the past, remains caught in its period: later generations may imitate historical forms but they can never tap the spirit itself of the age they seek to recapture.

In a simplified shorthand, most 19th-century styles may be labelled classical or Gothic. The classical derived from the architecture of ancient Greece and Rome, and from the re-interpretation of those forms in the Renaissance. The Gothic was based upon medieval church architecture and surviving 16th- and 17th-century

Below: This 1860-ish home in Washington DC, curiously Post-Modern in appearance, owes much to the Italianate tradition of early 19th-century European models, a style that was popular among newly prosperous Americans.

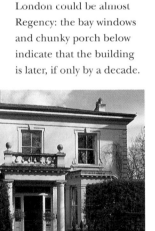

Below: The low-pitched roof and simple upper windows of this middle-class house in South London could be almost Regency: the bay windows and chunky porch below indicate that the building is later, if only by a decade.

Right: The cheerful mixture of Gothic with classical forms in this house from Savannah, Georgia, in no way detracts from its appeal. The dark paint against a light background is unexpected but effective.

Above: Sunlight is an essential ingredient for this generous American verandah. The mixture of wood and cast iron combine to create a deck like an ocean cruiser's, with complementary furniture. The deep overhang is only practicable for hot summers.

Right: As a contrast, this High Victorian interior in Castell Coch, Cardiff, is completely inward-looking. Designed by the extraordinary architect William Burges for Lord Bute, this bedroom for Lady Bute was never used. Understandably perhaps, for while the conception is dazzling, the end result is hardly cosy. It is an interior which represents the very peak of medieval fantasy, all paid for out of the profits from the Cardiff docks.

domestic architecture. Taking a broad view of the changing fashions, the three main periods are Late Regency (1830s and 1840s, with classicism still in the ascendant), High Victorian (roughly 1850 to 1870, Gothic, Elizabethan and Jacobean ascendant) and Late Victorian (1870 to the turn of the century, eclectic experimentation, including Arts and Crafts and Queen Anne revival, dominant).

In the United States and British colonies, most of the 19th century was dominated by European influences, modified by a different climate and local materials. However, this aesthetic traffic was not all one way: in India, for example, craft tradition embellished the more decorative aspects of classical and Gothic revivals, sending oriental ripples back to England in the form of bungalows, verandahs, furniture and cottons. The warmer climates of Australasia and the southern states of the United States encouraged features such as the balcony and porch, which were enlarged to provide protection against the sun and make cool sitting places on summer evenings. Although cast-iron buildings were exported in kits to the colonies, architectural styles were largely dependent on local materials. In the United States wood was often the cheapest, sometimes the only material available, so that European styles became translated into a more light-hearted and colourful technology than their Old World models. Each wave of immigrants brought homeland styles with them: Irish in Boston, German in Baltimore, Swedish in the Mid-West and Spanish on the western seaboard. The architectural independence of the United States was fired by the Centennial Exhibition of 1876, which sent Americans off in search of a native American idiom. At the same time indigenous architects such as Louis Sullivan (the father of the skyscraper), Frank Lloyd Wright and H.H. Richardson were producing distinctive and personal architecture which today seems the authentic American form.

The early 19th century saw the beginning of the Battle of the Styles. This was an intellectual and moral war as much as a contest of architectural aesthetics. Each camp, classicists and Gothicists (there were lesser opinions fighting for other fashions) claimed that their style of architecture could supply the basis for an authentic 19th-century architecture. It was the re-appearance of Gothic as a respected architecture, firstly as a decorative style then as a moral force, that supplied the Battle of the Styles with its lasting intellectual fascination. The first signs of Gothic are seen in the gentle, almost frivolous, leanings towards the romantic which erupted as early as Walpole's 'Gothick' Strawberry Hill at Twickenham of 1766. Even though this was essentially a dilettante exercise by a gifted amateur in the 'Picturesque' (an idea currently much in vogue for gentlemen's parks), it remains all the same an interesting forerunner of much that was to follow. 'Gothick' (as it was then spelled) was still a pejorative term for what was generally considered the rude and barbarous architecture of the Middle Ages. It was not until an architect called Thomas Rickman categorized the period into 'Norman', 'Early English', 'Decorated' and 'Perpendicular' (terms so convenient it now seems astonishing such an analysis had not been made long before) that much of the stigma against the old architecture lost its force.

Gothick, then, was chosen for its picturesque qualities. Stylistically close was 'Rustic', the style John Nash chose for the delightful Blaise Hamlet, a collection of cottages outside Bristol, in 1810. Other even more exotic styles came and went: Chinese, Egyptian, Italianate, Hindoo, Moorish. As always, experimental and exotic architectural ideas were tried out on garden buildings or in interior decoration before they became serious styles to be used in street architecture.

Not all architects – and by no means all their clients – welcomed the Gothic Revival, choosing instead to remain within the comfortable classical tradition, or staying with the 'Old English' or 'Scottish Baronial' styles. Though Gothic was suitable to churches and free-standing public buildings, it was less readily adapted to domestic architecture. So often, the writings of Victorian architects blind us to the fact that these men had livings to earn and that the client had his own idea of a proper style. An architect had to please his patron or lose a potentially profitable commission. Thus, there are architects – Edward Blore, Salvin, William Burn, among others – who have a foot in both camps and whose works do not fit neatly into either category. The extraordinary Harlaxton in Lincolnshire, the product of the owner Gregory Gregory (*sic*) and his architects William Burn and the young Salvin, is an example of a client's idiosyncratic demands, a mixture of Gothic, Baroque and Jacobean styles. Eastnor Castle, in spite of its romantic silhouette and Gothic detailing, is a building that shows the architect Robert Smirke's essentially classical sympathies. Smirke was obviously happier when building the British Museum, which is impeccably neo-Greek. The stable and monumental tradition of 18th-century classicism retained its hold over the Establishment right through the first half of the 19th century. The palazzo or Palladian villa remained the standard model for clubs, banks and grand town houses; as well as providing continuity, the palazzo fitted perfectly into street facades.

In the middle years of the century, it was undoubtedly Gothic which made the greatest impression on building styles. The difference between the new serious Gothic and the preceding Gothick is whole and absolute. To its promoters the chosen style was nothing less than a moral crusade. The hard core of the new movement is to be found in architects like Augustus Welby Pugin and Gilbert Scott. Here one has to distinguish what they wrote and the buildings that they built. Their writings reveal dogmatism; their best buildings have all the qualities of the freshness, toughness and

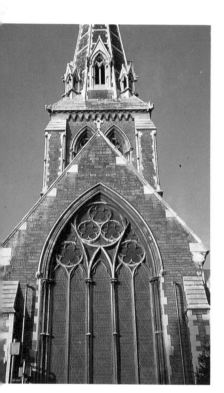

Saint Giles, Camberwell, in London is one of the first and most muscular Gothic Revival churches by the young Gilbert Scott, built in 1844. This serious and committed return to Gothic form (here Early English) coincides with two decades of religious turmoil and renewal among the English middle classes.

Above: As early as 1750 Horace Walpole was contemplating ideas for one of the first Gothick houses (as opposed to garden buildings or follies) in England. Strawberry Hill, Twickenham, was the result. The vaulting, based on Henry VII's chapel at Westminster (but translated into plaster) is enchanting: indeed the early 16th-century masons might have found its flamboyance nearer their taste than Gilbert Scott's severe exercise opposite.

Top: Unravelling the details of this wooden confection in Georgia, one discovers elements of classical, Gothic, Saracenic and oriental precedents.

Above: John Rylands Library, Manchester, built by Basil Champneys in 1890–1900, is an unapologetic and persuasive *envoi* to the Victorian Gothic tradition.

Left: Heywood, Wiltshire, dates from 1869, an assured neo-Jacobean house with intricate gables and chimneys which create a lively skyline.

innocence so often to be found in the exciting first phase of radical new movements. Significantly, it was the Early English period which was *de rigeur* for these early medievalists, that pure but austere style in which the first English Gothic churches and cathedrals were constructed in the 12th and 13th centuries. The quest for a 'national' style was always at the back of the theorists' minds.

The first great public success of the Gothicists was the new Palace of Westminster. The old building had been destroyed by fire in 1834 and designs for the new Parliament were put out to competition in 1835. One of the conditions was that it was to be built in the 'Gothic or Elizabethan' style. The competition was won by Charles Barry, who, though happier in the Renaissance style favoured by the Establishment, was able to turn his hand to another discipline if required. As his assistant he employed the 24-year-old A.W.N. Pugin. The exact contribution Pugin made to the designs has been debated: what is certain is that he had almost complete control over the interior furnishings and exterior detailing.

Pugin introduced not only the Gothic public building but also the Gothic domestic building; his St Marie's Grange, built for his own use outside Salisbury, was finished in about 1835. For such an archetypal Victorian building this is an astonishing date: it could well have been built, without arousing comment, at any time over the next 50 years. In it are combined all the major characteristics of the new style: asymmetry, picturesque silhouette, texture and

Above: The Egyptian House in Penzance, by the Plymouth-based architect, George Wightwick, is a Regency excursion into one of the exotic styles which so entertained both architects and patrons in the early part of the century. By contrast the fantasies of the Victorians tended to more traditional influences.

Right: The rectory style is given a thoroughly ecclesiastical treatment at Holly Lodge in Highgate.

Above: One of the most charming manifestations of early 19th-century romanticism resulted in these estate cottages at Blaise Hamlet, near Bristol, designed by John Nash for a local landowner. Some are thatched, others like the example here, tiled in stone. Many of these vernacular features were rediscovered later in the century by Voysey and Lutyens.

Left: This neo-Norman castle was built by Sir Robert Smirke at Eastnor, Herefordshire, in 1812. Although picturesque in outline, a classical discipline is evident beneath: not surprising from the hand which designed the British Museum, although Smirke seems to have retained a special fondness for the romantic in country commissions.

Above: The door to a kitchen garden, heavily embellished with Gothick detail, provides an unexpected touch of romance and history to intrigue the visitor on a tour of the grounds.

A later colonial mansion in South Africa exploits a mish-mash of styles using mass-produced ornaments from the builder's catalogue to decorate the wide verandah. The design is intended to provide an interior coolness and shaded sitting areas.

This typical Victorian embellishment was made of stucco or artificial stone, and painted. Precedents for these features are obscure, but probably derive from plates taken from one of the many mid-century copy books.

Above: Bedford Square, London, built in 1775, may be described as high-quality developer's Georgian. The vermiculated quoins and voussoirs round the door are in Coade Stone. The 18th-century squares and terraces of Bloomsbury were admired by many Victorians for the quality of the construction and interior detailing.

Osborne House on the Isle of Wight was designed by the Prince Consort and built in 1850 by Thomas Cubitt, the London builder. Prince Albert chose to employ the famous builder rather than an architect in order that he himself should have a free hand in the design and decoration of the royal home. The Italianate style remained popular with the Establishment for country houses and public buildings.

variety of material. It was, according to its architect, 'the only modern building complete in every part in the ancient style', that is, of the 15th century. In one sense this is true, in another absurd, for the social gap between the centuries defies comparison. To modern eyes St Marie's Grange looks like a rectory or gentleman's residence and not an ancient manor, however scrupulous its detailing.

Much of the attraction of the Gothic Revival was that so much of work-a-day classical architecture was banal. Pugin never tired of pointing this out. In contrast to the endless rows of London terraces, a dramatic Gothic building had a lot to be said for it. This contrast may be a clue to why Scotland never took the Gothic Revival so seriously: the streets of Edinburgh and Glasgow are filled with exciting classical buildings. And more often than not, these terraces are designed by talented architects; this was rarely the case in Southern England, where the developer employed a tried and tested formula of house building. English architects were ever keen to bemoan London's dreary streetscapes; they were missing out on a lucrative market! Yet London housing was run up to meet an ever greater demand, and while some London terraces are wanting as architecture, judged as commercial ventures to meet a public need, they often may be rated a success.

London building practices had changed in the second half of the 18th century with the invention of Coade Stone. It was a complicated formula devised to make an artificial stone which could be applied outside and would last without damage from the weather. In other words, it served outside as plaster had done for many years inside. Stucco followed close upon Coade Stone. Since Roman times, walls had been rendered, that is, coated with layers of a mixture of lime and sand, the ingredients of brickwork mortar. In about 1800 Roman cement, much stronger than traditional lime, was introduced and Portland cement, a much stronger material still (later used in concrete), followed in 1825. These new materials made possible stucco rendering, a finish which could be painted and was taken up enthusiastically by many architects, including John Nash, famous for his grand terraces round Regent's Park. A contemporary jingle ran: 'John Nash, that very great master, who found us all brick and who left us all plaster'. Though an out-and-out Regency figure, Nash in his work and methods did in many ways anticipate Victorian practices.

While he, Decimus Burton and the builder Thomas Cubitt exploited the advantages of stucco to good effect, later and lesser men succumbed to the ornamental temptations of the new material. The appetite for ostentation and ornament was irresistible, particularly to the newly rich. Coade Stone slowly went out of production, for the new cements made cheaper decorations possible in stucco. This led to a deterioration in quality, for Coade was fine and hard and the patterns had been taken from originals modelled

Above: Carlton House Terrace, London, was built in the 1830s and 1840s by John Nash. The use he made of stucco was bold and individual. Many of his contemporaries frowned on the material, yet his skill in creating dramatic monuments out of brick and plaster bequeathed terraces of lasting distinction to London.

Opposite: Details of the Speaker's House in the Palace of Westminster reveal the hand of A.W.N. Pugin who was responsible for much of the interior design.

by sculptors and designers of talent, whereas lesser talents were now in demand to turn out ornament by the yard.

The Gothicists, naturally, detested stucco, denouncing it as a sham, which in a sense it was, purporting to be stone (it was painted in a stone colour, not white, as today). For them, the true materials were brick and stone, wood and tile. They perceived something which either escaped the classicists or simply did not interest them, which is that stucco was taking the craftsmanship out of building. Mass production had come in, cheap, new and exciting, but only the more thoughtful spotted the dangers ahead for the old intrinsic character and grain of architecture and craftsmanship.

For us today, used as we are to the lowest common denominator of industrialized building elements, materials like Coade Stone, stucco and terracotta, which supplied many characteristic decorative fillips, seem the very epitome of crafts long vanished. The fact that a street of Victorian houses may have the same repeated decorations seems to us a relief after our own dismal heritage of picture windows and the ubiquitous range of standardized entrance doors.

To Pugin, Gothic represented the culmination of craftsman and builder working together for the glory of God. The Renaissance, based on pagan forms and heartless geometry, was anathema. Pugin himself had assisted his father in the production of books of measured drawings, *Specimens* and *Examples of Gothic Architecture,* and followed this up with fanciful cityscapes depicting classical forms opposed to Gothic ones, the former miserable, ugly and debased, the latter beautiful and flourishing, with men free to work together for the common good. It was all, of course, a delightful self-deception, a wilful and sentimental misinterpretation of building in the Middle Ages.

There was, in reality, little real craftsman freedom for the men quarrying and carrying stone, or for the masons shaping standard shafts for cathedral columns. In all architecture there is much repetitive work and even more sheer hard labour, the drudgery of which is overlooked in the glory of the completed statement.

In the end, a movement which had sought to re-create Gothic as the only true architecture, turned out to be just another fashion like any other. This revelation would have dismayed Pugin, but it does not detract from his work as a valid architecture, worthy to stand with that of other periods. Pugin had come out with the extraordinarily modern statement that 'form follows function'; Gothic architecture obeyed this injunction. The structure of a Gothic building was expressed on the outside; classical architecture was indeed a sham in this respect, for the conventions of symmetry caused whole sections of buildings to be put up with no regard for purpose or structure. Though the Modern Movement discarded Pugin's delight in individualistic decoration of parts, it took up Pugin's 'form follows function'.

A deeper inspiration behind the Gothic Revival was the need to integrate man and society by means of a purposeful activity. The point of the celebration of an idealized medieval past was that it should give moral guidance to the present. The Christian-Gothic school of history was always attractive to men who could not believe in Macaulay's Whig notions of progress. It is a cliché of 19th-century history that eclecticism is but an expression of doubt. Even before Darwin's *On the Origin of Species* (1859) threw the idea of God into question, the 19th century was always on the look-out for an idea to hang on to. For Pugin, and Ruskin and Morris after him, this would be the ideal of craftsmanship.

More than in our own time, writing and critical polemic were second nature to the architectural profession. John Ruskin was foremost a writer and critic; his one sally into architecture proper was confined to the unfinished Oxford Museum. Ruskin never openly acknowledged his obvious debt to Pugin, because of the latter's strident Catholicism, but he continued the same medievalist line none the less. In 1849, the year after his marriage, he went on a second honeymoon to Venice. He fell in love with the city and from this visit resulted, in 1851, *The Stones of Venice*. It is curious to reflect how a chance foreign trip could change the face of English architecture, but that is what happened.

Ruskin was acute enough to realize that the outward features of Gothic were not, by themselves, important. 'The shape of the arch,' he wrote, 'is irrelevant.' What mattered was that the craftsman should be free to express himself unfettered by outworn classical orders and ornaments which were based at many removes on natural forms. This, in a sense, is unarguable. The craftsman working on his own, or as a participant in a small studio, is generally considered to be happier, more fulfilled than his counterpart at a factory bench. The mistake the Ruskinians made was to believe that the whole accelerating process of industrialism, well under way by mid-century, could be reversed by dogma: that a half-understood picture of medieval society could actually turn back, let alone withstand, the pressures of mass production. The truth was that artist – craftsmen were a dying race and were to survive only as a gifted few, patronized by an elite and for the most part ignored by the masses except at second and third hand. This indeed is the unhappy situation which has continued unchanged to our own day.

Ruskin's painstaking drawings did not have the hoped-for influence. Manufacturers fell on them and travestied them in cheap imitations to stock every builder's yard in the country. The irony of this is poignant: what Ruskin had meant as an incentive to greater personal involvement in building craftsmanship merely resulted in convenient patterns for the ignorant and unimaginative to copy. *The Stones of Venice* became a cheap and profitable trade catalogue for the speculator and local builder.

Left: Rows of late Victorian houses like this may be found in any British city. Though despised by architects and many Victorian critics, these streets fulfilled a social and economic need, making cheap housing available for the ever-expanding middle classes.

Far left: A plate from Ruskin's *Stones of Venice* illustrates an arch he describes in detail over three pages. Not only a persuasive writer of prose, Ruskin was also a fine draughtsman; many of the plates from *The Stones of Venice* are by his own hand.

Left: An example of mass-produced decoration in a London street owes its origin to *The Stones of Venice.* Ruskin spent much of his middle life in the suburbs of South London surrounded by middle-class terraced housing finished with this kind of ornamentation, copied from illustrations to his books.

29

EARLY VICTORIAN SEMI-DETACHED

Cottages of *c*.1840s. Classical tradition still dominant. Rectangular box-like form follows the standard Regency villa, now divided into two semi-detached dwellings. Simple play of solid and void in keeping with Georgian architectural ideas. Applied decoration in artificial stone around windows and doors.

FLAT-FRONTED TERRACE

Standard labourers' housing. Brick the commonest material in southern Britain and coal-mining districts; stone traditional in Scotland. Run up cheaply to meet housing needs of the workforce; front door alone allows for any individual treatment.

DETACHED ITALIANATE VILLA

Italianate styles popular in 1830s – 40s; J.C. Loudon's influence made brick Italianate villa the suburban style *par excellence*. Stuccoed ground floor highlights the equivalent of a *piano nobile* of the Italian palazzo. Roof-line given a picturesque emphasis.

DETACHED BRICK VILLA

Standard house with Tudor dressings and Gothic asymmetrical plan. Roof given steep pitch and spiky details to suggest the vertical lift of medieval domestic architecture. Again, most of the character is contained in historical detailing selectively deployed.

THE NEW YORK BROWNSTONE

Standard form of mid-century speculative housing on eastern seaboard of the United States. Italianate palazzo integrated with the British terraced town house. Fenestration in Central European Baroque idiom.

THE MANSION FLAT

Apartment buildings, traditional in Scotland and on the Continent. English were reluctant converts to self-contained flats. Known by the nick-name Pont Street Dutch, these terraces of red brick and white-painted Queen Anne windows began to appear in newer estates after 1870s.

CARPENTER'S GOTHIC

Native New World style of building dependent on the plentiful timber and invention of cheap nails. Decorative Gothic forms, often taken from pattern books, re-interpreted in wood. High standard of joinery, idiosyncratic display of individual talent.

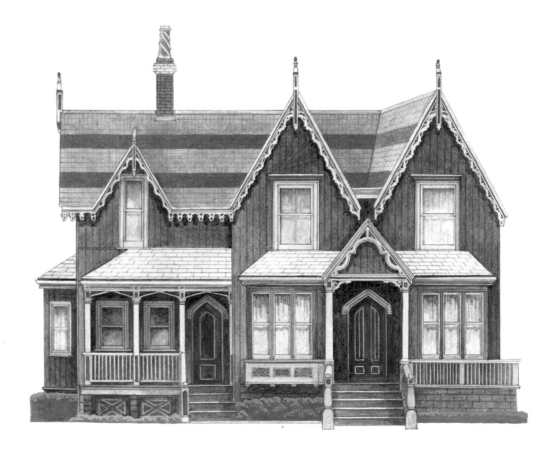

MIDDLE-CLASS TERRACED HOUSING

1880s onwards, following success of Utopian London suburb of Bedford Park. Queen Anne style dominant: red brick, white woodwork, smaller panes for upper part of windows, Dutch or Flemish door surround. Flemish strapwork on gable end.

THE ARTS AND CRAFTS COTTAGE

As developed in further suburban zones and garden cities. Pebbledash walls with stone dressing used, not least for its relative cheapness. Strong horizontal lines create an artificially low, cottage look. Given artful informal character by its incomplete symmetry, supplying both prestige and homeliness.

19th-CENTURY AMERICAN TOWN HOUSE

The new American vernacular. Influence of materials and climate more important than academic styles. Details borrowed from all ethnic traditions. Bold paint colours give consistency to a house that could be endlessly extended or modified.

Top: Stepped brickwork supports the curious bay window in the Red House, designed for William Morris by Philip Webb. The windows themselves are plain: some have pointed heads or Gothic relieving arches set flush in the brick. This is an English manor house look: somewhere between medieval and Queen Anne.

Above: One of the beautiful wallpapers designed by Morris is still hand-printed by Sanderson from the original blocks.

All great art is subject to plagiarism and dilution, none more so than architecture. The original and lively minds in any generation provide the direction and, eventually, a kind of accepted grammar. The grammar of the 18th century, based on simple rules of proportion and scale, resulted in a coherent architecture guided by the taste of an educated few and limited by contemporary building technology. Mass production and mass communication in the 19th century changed all this. To the consumer, any underlying theories were unimportant: what was new was, by definition, the best.

Naturally, the majority of houses to which this study is addressed are those which descended at second or third hand from the original models thrashed out by leading architects of the day. To unravel each stylistic history a study must be made of individual parts, to which end later chapters of illustrated details will be useful.

Many Victorians were concerned that no essentially Victorian style was emerging, and it is true that their architecture up to the middle of the reign relied almost entirely on interpretations of classical or Gothic forms. In the second half of the century, a new influence emerged, resulting in an architecture which was genuinely different, eclectic and one which was, by the end of the century, to flower briefly in stylized forms which were adapted on the Continent into Art Nouveau or, in Italy, *il stile liberty* (named after the London department store).

The first major figure in this new phase was William Morris. He was one of the greatest Victorians: designer, artist, poet and socialist, he worked tirelessly to improve the standards of everyday design which, as a young man, he had so despised at the Great Exhibition of 1851. 'Have nothing in your home which you do not know to be useful or believe to be beautiful,' he proclaimed.

Morris continued the Pugin-Ruskin line of extolling the work of the artist-craftsman but more realistically in that he set up craft workshops to put his principles into practice, so establishing what

Opposite: Morris & Co.'s Strawberry Thief, although unmistakably 19th-century, has a bold and simple treatment that comes near to Gothic wall and tapestry designs.

Left: At the Great Exhibition of 1851, held in the Crystal Palace in Hyde Park, many designs of High Victorian taste at its most ostentatious were on view. To the young Morris, as to many other minds, the display of bad design was a grave cause for concern.

Left: 'When Adam delved and Eve span' is a Morris design with a Pre-Raphaelite flavour. The naturalism is in contrast with the bird design shown above.

Far left: This excellent design was produced by Watts & Co. of Westminster, a firm still in existence.

Top: A contemporary lithograph of Queen Anne Gardens, Bedford Park, London, was produced from a painting by H.M. Paget. Pictures like this were used to advertise the benefits of life on the new garden estates.

Above: Built for the first Lord Armstrong by Norman Shaw, Cragside in Northumberland was an extraordinary venture, built on a barren hillside outside Newcastle. The building is an extravaganza of eclectic styles, adapted to late Victorian comfort.

became known as the Arts and Crafts Movement.

Morris and his collaborators searched for pre-industrial forms of furniture and tapestry which they developed with their own distinctive idiom. Many of their styles were 16th- and 17th-century in origin. Although the English Renaissance style had been popular for country houses of the 1840s, with Morris and Webb and later E.W. Godwin it became the starting point for the radical simplification of form that took place in the 1870s.

Morris's own house, The Red House, Bexleyheath, was built by his friend Philip Webb in 1856. It follows the designs of the vicarages that Webb had drawn up while working in the office of G.E. Street. The Red House, like these vicarages, can best be described as architect-designed vernacular, employing classical and Gothic features to accentuate the facade and skyline. The detailing of The Red House was broadly utilitarian, providing the casing for the decorative art that Morris installed inside. Webb's architecture is most often seen in conjunction with Morris & Co. interiors – he designed furniture for the firm as well as being the chief animal and bird draughtsman for their tapestries and fabrics.

In Philip Webb there is a link between Arts and Crafts and the Queen Anne style which grew in popularity in the late 1860s. Webb built a number of houses in Chelsea to complement the original Queen Anne housing by the Thames.

Like the Arts and Crafts Movement, the Queen Anne revival was born in reaction to the constricted ethos of the 1850s and 1860s. Queen Anne revival gave architect and client greater freedom of plan. The architecture had a friendly aspect and the interior lent itself to an 'artistic' lifestyle; indeed, Queen Anne revival was the style most commonly commissioned by working artists.

The leading figure of the Queen Anne revival was Richard Norman Shaw. An approachable and gifted architect, his large office produced designs for buildings from Chelsea to Hampstead as well as the Utopian garden suburb of Bedford Park in West London. Shaw's success and facility in turning out these fashionable houses led to criticisms that the architecture lacked thought. Morris himself was a critic of Shaw, but nevertheless, Morris & Co. accepted the commission to decorate the interior of Shaw's Old Swan House on the embankment in Chelsea. The success of the Old English cum Queen Anne style – warm red brick, generous amounts of painted woodwork and a telling amount of individual detail – led to its extensive use in England to well into the 20th century.

Other architects developed the Queen Anne style, notably George and Peto, whose Harrington and Collingham Gardens in South Kensington represent the best of the Queen Anne style for visual excitement. The more relaxed architecture of Queen Anne mirrored the more relaxed social arrangements of the 1870s and 80s. The so-called 'Freestyle' of the 1890s borrowed heavily from

Baillie Scott was the architect of this house at Knutsford, built in 1895, a typical 'Artistic' house in an informal garden suburb. Baillie Scott continued the Voysey tradition which itself stemmed from Godwin and Philip Webb. Garden cities were popular at the turn of the century for their Utopian socialist charms as well their new, fashionable architecture.

Opposite: This Voysey house, The Orchard, Chorley Wood, was sensibly adjusted to the needs of contemporary families. The high stylization of interiors such as this had a profound influence on the architects of the Modern Movement in Germany.

Standen, at East Grinstead, West Sussex, was built by Philip Webb in 1891. Designed as a weekend house for a successful London solicitor, Standen shows Webb in his typically unpretentious manner. The careful assemblage of vernacular details stands in the way – albeit intentionally – of any grand or even coherent architectural statement. Standen and its fine Morris & Co. interiors has been miraculously spared by the 20th century; it is now open to the public.

the vernacular traditions of British building. Vernacular architecture was not bound by rules of proportion or archaeological niceties, and this meant that elements could be adapted from all dates and styles and then blended into a convincing whole by the plan and purpose of the building. Vernacular freedoms allowed architects to develop their own idiosyncratic styles, Voysey and Mackintosh being two late examples.

C.F.A. Voysey was an architect who, once he was established, became as obsessive and demanding as Philip Webb had been. Owing to a recession and a scarcity of jobs at the time when he started practice on his own, he was advised by Mackmurdo, his senior by a few years, to try his hand at decoration and interior design, which he did with great flair. When architectural commissions came in later, he took as his inspiration the English small manor house and cottage, and in a sense he reduced all his designs, however big, to this simple model. One feels with Voysey that his deep respect for the traditional domestic building of the past never degenerated into sentimentalism or nostalgia. He was designing houses for his time, for sensitive and educated clients who wished to be housed comfortably but without ostentation. The pebbledash walls made the exteriors relatively cheap, and the interiors, which would be designed by Voysey down to the tea-spoons, follow his paradoxical maxim of 'richness from simplicity'. The siting of the house, he maintained, should always be subordinate to nature. In his respect for the site, he draws comparison with his American counterpart (ten years his junior) Frank Lloyd Wright. Of course, Wright's talents were unquestionably greater, but Voysey with quiet integrity was the unhappy and unwilling forerunner of much of the better modernism now associated with the 1920s and 1930s.

Voysey was a revolutionary with a distaste for revolution: both Art Nouveau and the Modern Movement admired and annexed Voysey's ideas; this he resented. An austere, religious man, he had deplored the *décadence* of Art Nouveau; and living until 1941 he also came to detest the Modern Movement for its lack of soul.

Two other architects symbolize the period at its close: Charles Rennie Mackintosh and Edwin Lutyens. Both were immensely gifted. Mackintosh, the more passionate genius, had only a peripheral influence on domestic architecture outside Scotland, which derives from the particular version of Art Nouveau decoration which he developed with his wife Margaret Macdonald. His architectural works, mostly in his native Clydeside, are an eclectic mixture of the Aesthetic Movement's adaptation of Japanese forms and mostly traditional Scottish architecture, distilled through the vision of a powerful if idiosyncratic designer who was born at a time when Glasgow was experiencing a cultural Renaissance unparalleled elsewhere in the British Isles, save Dublin. His influence on suburban houses lingers on in watered-down stained-glass panels and fireplace

A black and white house by C.R. Mackintosh owes more to English models than his native Clydeside.

Above: A studio house that Voysey built in the 1890s has horizontal windows, wide eaves and pebbledash that mark it as distinctly 'Modern'; indeed there is more than a passing likeness to the Chicago houses of Frank Lloyd Wright.

Below: A middle-class interior of *c.* 1900 recalls an earlier taste in its general clutter; more modern fashions are reflected in the display of china and the classical revival chimneypiece.

Above: Hill House, Helensburgh, was built by C.R. Mackintosh for clients on a hill outside Glasgow overlooking the Clyde. Everything in the house was designed by the architect, or his wife, down to the humblest fittings and fabrics. The term 'Art Nouveau' may be applied, but cannot begin to convey the intensely personal genius of this striking house and its extraordinary interiors.

Top: Lutyens's house at Munstead Wood, Surrey, built for Gertrude Jekyll in 1896, takes Tudor a step further towards simplicity. Any mannerist fussiness has been subordinated to pure form and textural contrasts.

Above: Little Thakeham is an impeccable exercise in symmetry, demonstrating Lutyens's versatility in harnessing romantic styles to classical discipline.

Left: A typical country bedroom of the end of the period at Lindisfarne Castle has a wide-board floor with rugs, unpainted furniture and functional fittings.

designs, but interiors such as those of Hill House, Helensburgh, or Miss Cranston Tea Rooms are inimitable. Largely unnnoticed in England, he was feted on the Continent where a joint exhibition with his wife in Vienna in 1900 caused a sensation. His influence has leapfrogged several generations, providing inspiration, much of it sadly imitative, to the young of our own times. What his effect on British architecture would have been if he had continued his practice into middle life can only be conjectured from one or two small sketches. As it was, he declined into professional inactivity and we have only the exquisite watercolours of his later years as compensation for a genius who had run out of talent.

Lutyens, born the year after Mackintosh, was a very different figure, the urbane Anglo-Saxon as opposed to the imaginative Celt. Like Shaw, his sympathetic and witty character endeared him to his clients, but rarely to fellow architects. As with Shaw, one suspects there lay hidden an organized, even ruthless nature which kept his practice profitably busy. He started off with small houses and alterations around his native Surrey. His collaboration with Gertrude Jekyll, the garden designer, enlarged his practice. He was never addicted to movements nor apparently was he much interested in current trends. Clearly influenced by the Webb-Morris-Shaw architecture of his youth, he nevertheless went his own way, evolving through Old English and Arts and Crafts and finally arriving at a classical idiom in the first decade of the 20th century.

Marriage into the aristocracy served him well and the commissions for country houses became larger, followed by public buildings. Somehow, in domestic architecture, the vernacular always seems his happier inspiration, more personal and idiosyncratic, and in close harmony with his interior arrangements of space which are unrivalled for their flair and excitement. The country houses in his later classical manner were equally inventive but more staid, making them easily and often imitated by other architects, who usually reduced their wit into pallid milk and water neo-Georgianism.

Lutyens presided over the end of an era. His extraordinary and subtle Castle Drogo, built in local granite on the edge of Dartmoor, is the most remarkable example of the dying tradition of the large country house. With his conversion to the fashionable Baroque classicism, the so-called 'Wrenaissance' of the Edwardian era, Lutyens rounds off the return to the very historicism that the Victorians had worked so hard to shrug off. Interestingly, Voysey had also returned to historical styles in the first decade of the century, in his case Gothic. Just at the moment when Victorian England had discovered the self-confidence to break free of historical revivals, a new revivalism broke out. Perhaps presciently enough, the Edwardian Classical Revival tried to hold on to a stable and monumental tradition which was, as we know, and many Edwardians suspected, to prove illusory.

Above: Castle Drogo on the edge of Dartmoor marks the end of the era. The Victorian castle tradition might have seemed to end with the neo-Gothic Arundel, Sussex, in the 1890s, but less than a decade later Lutyens began sketches for Drogo. The contrast with earlier castle design is absolute: embellishment is confined to the entrance, with only mullioned windows to modify the stark granite walls.

Winslow House, River Forest, Illinois, was built by Frank Lloyd Wright in 1893. Wright was influenced by the British Arts and Crafts Movement and by the great Chicago architect, Louis Sullivan, in whose office he had worked. Also, Wright was interested in the idea of a Mid-West vernacular architecture which was subservient to the surrounding landscape. These influences, as well as pre-Columbian decorative forms, he quickly assimilated to produce a style uniquely his own, of which this house is a striking example.

Chapter Two
EXTERIOR
FEATURES

Architecture is always a compromise between style and technology. Whatever the period, whatever the school of thought, the fierce aesthetic arguments of the protagonists are tempered by the available materials and their intrinsic properties, however unwelcome this limitation may be. In ancient Greece and Rome, and in northern Europe during the Middle Ages, great architecture could be said to have grown out of the material technology of wood and stone, 'honest' materials seized upon and celebrated by men such as Ruskin and Pugin. By the Renaissance, building materials such as stucco were known to have allowed a certain degree of fakery, that element of deception which so offended the Gothic revivalists. Modern archaeology has since shown that even in the ancient world, thin marble veneers and painted plaster were in widespread use. But the structural limits of natural materials remained unsurpassed.

Sometimes, as we have seen only too clearly in our own century, doctrinaire aesthetics run ahead of technology. The Modern Movement made demands which could not be met by the existing construction methods. By the time technology had caught up, an irony of taste decreed a return to the old, despised traditions, and pitched roofs, pediments, ornament and colour have all made a strong come-back.

Although great strides were made in civil engineering and industrialized building in the 19th century, domestic architecture remained, in structural terms, relatively unchanged. Houses continued to be constructed of load-bearing walls of brick, stone or sometimes wood. Across this basic frame wooden joisted floors provided essential lateral bracing. Roofs were made of wood trusses which were generally clad with tiles, slates, thatch or shingles. Foundations slowly but surely improved, mostly as a result of new building codes, although footings were still only taken down to plain earth or, at best, compacted rubble mixed with lime. F. P. Cockerell first used concrete for footings in 1850, and the first building to be constructed from poured concrete, Down Hall in Essex, dates from 1871, but with the notable exception of Scotland the material was not considered suitable for ordinary domestic use until late in the century. At this stage it was often employed in barrel vaults supported on steel joists. Ground floors were sometimes constructed in this way over basements, and the improving technique made

The crisp, well-proportioned architecture of this American shingle house makes a focal point of the main entrance. The colour scheme gives due prominence and dignity to the front porch, bringing it forward from the body of the house.

42

Left: Illuminated from behind by stained-glass windows, this Federation verandah, with its florid cast-iron brackets and balusters, becomes a welcoming exterior living space for long summer evenings.

possible larger and stronger spans which were needed for the popular mansion flats and high-rise charitable dwellings.

More obvious changes resulted from improvements in transport. Whether these can be judged beneficial is open to argument; what is unarguable is that the face of Britain was changed for ever by the expansion and improvement of the railway and canal systems and the subsequent accessibility of building materials hitherto considered too cumbersome to move. In the United States the general availability of timber produced a coherent translation of current European fashions into frame and clapboard, leading, for a few decades at least, to that homogeneous domestic architecture of honest distinction that gives such grace to the towns of the East Coast and southern states. In Britain it meant only that much of the intrinsic character of local building became blurred. Slates, produced by the million in North Wales and Cumbria, were transported by rail to all corners of the country. Being much less heavy than tiles, they made possible shallower pitches and lighter roof construction. In the same way, brick buildings turned up in what had hitherto been stone country or among the wood and plaster towns of East Anglia. Identical terracotta ornaments were now incorporated in houses as far apart as Penzance and Inverness. The new Midlands brick fields turned out the harsh red facings so favoured by architects such as Butterfield, who positively delighted in their raw appeal and decorative possibilities when mixed with blue engineerings or ochre terracotta.

Improvements in glass manufacture brought radical changes to window designs. Panes grew larger, and if this did not always enhance the proportions of the facade, it was not yet as destructive as the production of cheap plate glass in the present century.

In perspective, Victorian architecture can be seen as the bridge between the hand-crafted building that went before and the bleak but eclectic houses of the post-war West. Today's buildings may be superior in terms of stability, insulation and convenience, but the constituent parts are applied without love or understanding. It would be frivolous to pretend that the Victorians were substantially different in attitude, but they caught the tail-end of a centuries-old tradition of craftsmanship that ensured a certain solidity of construction and a generosity of joinery and finishes.

With their sublime lack of self-consciousness about class, the Victorians openly distinguished between the social status of different house types, categorizing them as Class I, II, III or IV according

Exterior details make a statement about a building: the ornamental keystone at Burlington Mansions in St Martin's Lane, London (*left*), confidently exudes neo-classical grandeur, while the simple but elegant lancet window of a Sussex farmhouse (*above*) unpretentiously signals a solidity of craftsmanship within.

Above: Foot scrapers were an important fixture at the entrance, marking the transition from the muddy outdoors to the cosy Victorian interior. They were usually of cast iron, and were often embellished with charming ornamental details.

Right: The overhanging roofs, elaborate corbels, cast-iron balcony rails and exuberant dormer of this house in Washington DC present a distinctly Spanish aspect to the world.

to their prospective owners or tenants. A Class I house is what would now be called a small estate, with a substantial villa standing on its own in maybe 50 acres of land. Smaller Class II houses stood in a modest acre or half acre, served by a short drive from the road, forming part of a development of similar houses. Inner suburbs of most towns (formerly the outskirts, of course) have many examples of such houses set in leafy avenues, groves and crescents: Castle Park in Nottingham, Sneyd's Park, Bristol, and King's Park, Stirling, to name just three. Today the gravel of the drives is probably invaded by weeds, the house itself a little down at heel and divided into flats.

Next down the scale came the semi-detached villa. Although such houses had been built in the Georgian era, their development and popularity dates from Victorian times, as did the bay window, which became such an essential ingredient of their design.

Class IV was the terraced house, so called because the ground was terraced flat before building. Mr Pooter, readers of *The Diary of a Nobody* will recall, lived in such a house in Brickfield Terrace, Holloway, itself a reminder that bricks were often fired on site from local clay in temporary kilns. The great glory of the 18th-century terrace declined over the early decades of the 19th century. As the cost of road frontages increased and building regulations discouraged basements, single- and double-storey back extensions

became common, housing the new bathrooms and closets as well as the servants' quarters. The removal of rooms to rear extensions reduced the height of the house and concentrated the architectural treatment on the facade; anyone travelling through the suburbs by train cannot fail to notice how plain and even brutal the treatment of the backs of these houses is in comparison with the fronts.

In the United States, cheaper land deferred such economic measures except perhaps in the city centres. In the suburbs the concept of a house sitting in its own plot of land was possible to realize for much longer; indeed the American suburbs today still continue this tradition, though the architecture grows meaner and the backyards smaller.

It is always difficult to assess the extent to which social changes have influenced the architecture of a previous age. What may seem to later generations to have been eras of modesty and taste may not have appeared so to contemporaries. Seen through late 20th-century eyes, the snobberies, enthusiasms, revivalisms and aesthetic battles of the Victorians have dulled with the passage of time. We can only judge their buildings on our own terms, and our judgements are tinged with our own peculiar nostalgia, that mixed emotion which our Victorian forebears would surely have understood and, above all, condoned.

Above: This richly-ornamented door handle, with more than a suggestion of Art Nouveau about it, gives the visitor an impression of artistic flair.

Left: Many Victorian town residences had a door plate such as this. A sliding brass panel – now missing – would have indicated whether the occupants were in or out.

T H E
D E T A C H E D
V I L L A

Underlying the almost infinite variety of Victorian houses were a few basic structural forms, repeated millions of times over by builders following well established principles.

Of the three types illustrated on the next six pages, the first is the detached suburban villa, or Class II house, built of load-bearing brick or stone with a cross-wall and wooden stud partitions. From the early part of the century the foundations were a series of brickwork steps laid directly on to the excavated trench, diminishing as they rose to the width of the wall.

The first part of the wall above the ground is the plinth, generally a few courses of different-coloured brick or perhaps a different finish of stone. Above the plinth, there rises the rest of the wall, in this instance ashlar facing (chosen for economy) bonded into a masonry backing which provides structural stability. Then comes the cornice, consisting here of a stone coping, to throw water away from the wall, and finally, to complete the composition, the roof.

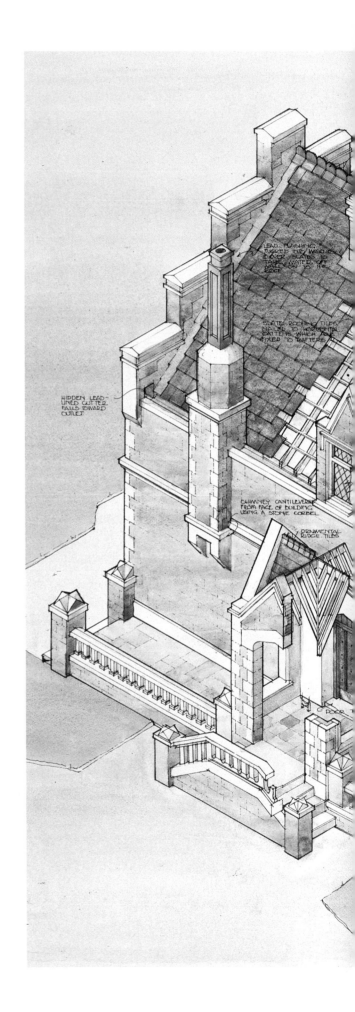

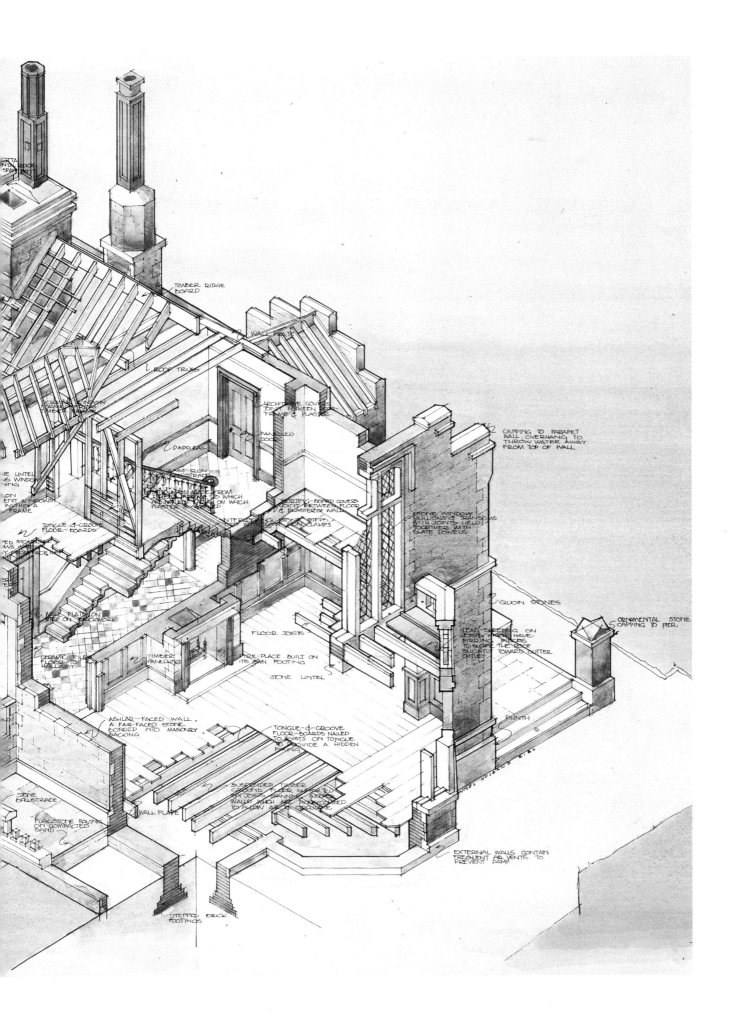

TIMBER RIDGE
BOARD

WALL PLATE

ROOF TRUSS

ARCHITRAVE COVERS
JOINT BETWEEN DOOR
FRAME & PLASTER

PANELLED
DOOR

CAPPING TO PARAPET
WALL, OVERHANG TO
THROW WATER AWAY
FROM TOP OF WALL

DADO RAIL

CAST-IRON
BALUSTRADE

STONE WINDOW
MULLIONS & TRANSOMS
WITH JOINTS HELD
TOGETHER WITH
SLATE DOWELS

SKIRTING-BOARD COVERS
JOINT BETWEEN FLOOR
& PLASTER OF WALL

TONGUE-&-GROOVE
FLOOR-BOARDS

INTERNAL STONE STEPS,
HELD WITH IRON CRAMPS

WALL PLATE ON
STEP ON BRICKWORK

QUOIN STONES

ORNAMENTAL STONE
CAPPING TO PIER

FLOOR JOISTS

LEAD SHEETING ON
JOISTS WHICH HAVE
FIRRING PIECES
TO SLOPE THE ROOF
SLIGHTLY TOWARD GUTTER
OUTLET

CERAMIC TILED
FLOOR TO
HALLWAY

TIMBER
PANELLING

FIRE-PLACE BUILT ON
ITS OWN FOOTING

STONE LINTEL

ASHLAR-FACED WALL,
A FAIR-FACED STONE
BONDED INTO MASONRY
BACKING

TONGUE-&-GROOVE
FLOOR-BOARDS NAILED
TO JOISTS ON TONGUE
TO PROVIDE A HIDDEN
FIXING

PLINTH

STONE
BALUSTRADE

WALL PLATE

SUSPENDED TIMBER
GROUND FLOOR SUPPORTED
BY JOISTS SPANNING SLEEPER
WALLS WHICH ARE HONEYCOMBED
TO ALLOW AIR TO CIRCULATE

FLAGSTONE PAVING
ON COMPACTED
SAND

EXTERNAL WALLS CONTAIN
FREQUENT AIR VENTS TO
PREVENT DAMP

STEPPED BRICK
FOOTINGS

49

THE TERRACED HOUSE

The terraced (in America, the row) house was rarely designed for an individual occupier. Most of these Class IV houses were built, often streets at a time, by speculative builders using the cheapest convenient wall materials and details purchased from a catalogue.

Terraced houses were only rarely over three storeys tall, and inherited their basic characteristics from their Georgian predecessors, including stylistic patterns that continued to be built right up to the 1850s. Constructed with load-bearing external walls and internal cross-wall, terraces generally had only two main rooms on each floor, divided by internal partitions of lath and plaster. Basements and semi-basements provided a service area at the bottom of the house, giving way as the century progressed to back extensions. This house has both.

Save in the very late Victorian period – and then often only for the poorest rows intended for miners and factory workers – terraced houses north of Derby and west of Worcester were built of stone. In the Midlands and the south-east, the long tradition of brick building led to levels of craftsmanship every bit as accomplished as the fine masonry to be found in the stone terraces of Cardiff or Bristol.

Terraces were frequently designed to be read as a whole from a distance, with prominent buildings at either end and often in the centre. External details – such as whether a bay carried up to the first floor or was, more economically, restricted to the ground floor – gave a precise indication of status. Stone lintels, brick voussoirs, pillars, capitals and terracotta details all played their part in announcing the social standing of the occupants. Many of the rows that still make up much of Britain's inner-city housing stock represented the lower end of the social scale.

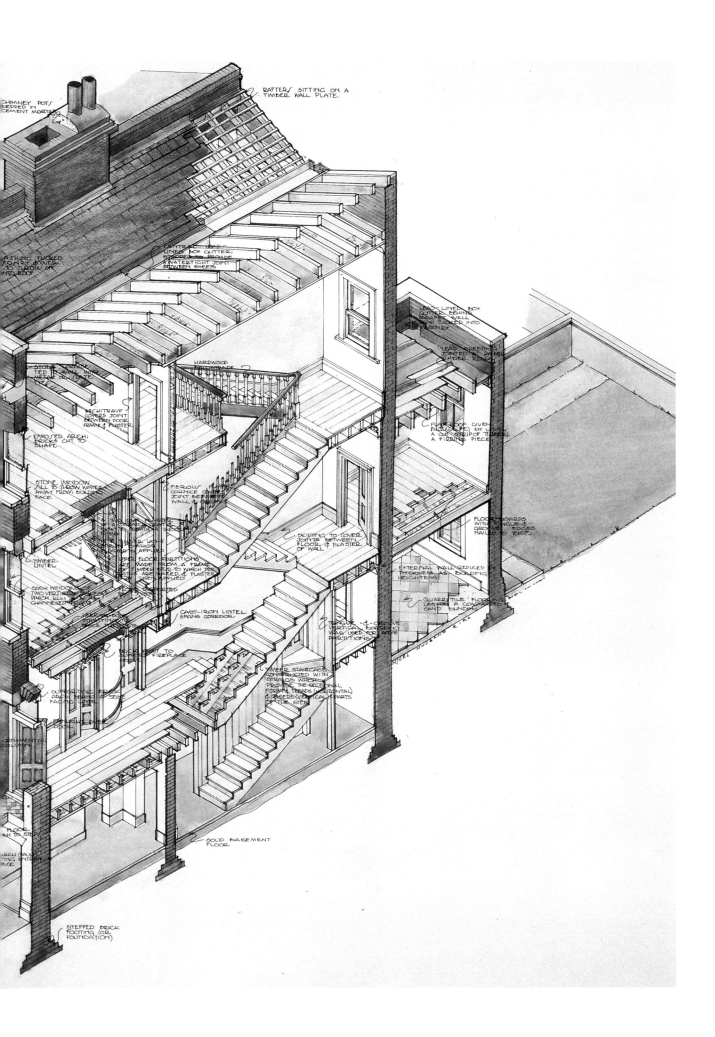

CHIMNEY POTS
BEDDED IN
CEMENT MORTAR

RAFTERS SITTING ON A
TIMBER WALL PLATE.

FLASHING TUCKED
INTO WALL OVER
TO THROW OFF
INTO ROOF

CENTRAL LEAD
LINED BOX GUTTER
STEPPED TO PROVIDE
A WATERTIGHT JOINT
BETWEEN SHEETS

LEAD LINED BOX
GUTTER BEHIND
PARAPET WALL
LEAD TUCKED INTO
MASONRY

STONE CORBEL
TIED IN WALL WITH
METAL CRAMP TO
TAKE

HARDWOOD
HANDRAIL

LEAD SHEETING
JOINTED AT ANGLE
TIMBER ROLL

ARCHITRAVE
COVERS JOINT
BETWEEN DOOR
FRAME & PLASTER

EXPOSED ARCH,
BRICKS CUT TO
SHAPE

FLAT ROOF GIVEN
FALL (SLOPE) BY
A CUT STRIP OF TIMBER,
A FIRRING PIECE

FIBROUS
CORNICE COVERS
JOINT BETWEEN
WALL & CEILING

STONE WINDOW
SILL TO THROW WATER
AWAY FROM BUILDING
FACE

FLOORBOARDS
WITH TONGUE &
GROOVED EDGES
NAILED TO JOISTS

TIMBER FLOOR
PROVIDE SMOOTH

SKIRTING TO COVER
JOINTS BETWEEN
FLOOR & PLASTER
OF WALL

EXTERNAL WALL REDUCES
THICKNESS AS BUILDING
HEIGHTENS

UPPER FLOOR PARTITIONS
ARE MADE FROM A FRAME
OF TIMBER STUD TO WHICH
LATHS ARE NAILED & PLASTER
IS THEN APPLIED

QUARRY TILE FLOORING
LAID ON A COMPACTED
SAND SUB-BASE

TIMBER
LINTEL

SASH WINDOWS WITH
TWO VERTICALLY SLIDING
SASHES WHICH RUN IN
CHANNELLED FRAME

CAST-IRON LINTEL
SPANS CORRIDOR

TONGUE & GROOVE
VERTICAL BOARDING
WAS USED FOR SOME
PARTITIONS

TIMBER STAIRCASE
CONSTRUCTED WITH
STRINGS WHICH
PROVIDE THE SECTIONAL
FORM OF TREADS (HORIZONTAL)
& RISERS (VERTICAL PARTS
OF THE STEPS

BRICK ARCH TO
SUPPORT FIREPLACE

SUPPORTING BRICK
ARCH HAVING STONE
FACING TO

FLOOR TILE

ORNAMENTAL
COLUMN

SOLID BASEMENT
FLOOR

FLOOR
FINISH TO STEPS

ARCH VAULT
FORMING ENTRANCE
SPACE

STEPPED BRICK
FOOTING (OR
FOUNDATION)

THE BALLOON FRAME HOUSE

The balloon frame was a method of building unique to America and perfectly suited to the expanding Mid-West states where it originated. Reflecting the innovative, experimental and completely uninhibited attitude of a wealthy young country in a hurry, with unlimited supplies of timber, it was a cheap, easy-to-erect system using a wood frame of simplified construction and factory-made nails.

Unlike other houses with load-bearing walls and primary and secondary joists and rafters, the balloon frame – no doubt so called because the houses went up like balloons – consists entirely of standard-dimension timbers nailed together with standard-dimension nails. No one part of the structure supports any greater load than any other. There are no corner posts or heavy load-bearing timbers to cut by hand. Instead of this principal members are made of two or more standard timbers nailed together. The walls are then clad in timber and the house is finished off with a roof usually of mansard design.

This streamlined system put construction of houses within the reach of ordinary occupiers at low cost and with foolproof methodology. First used in Chicago in the 1830s, it became the dominant building method in the Mid-West by the time of the Civil War, and developed its own aesthetic which was christened stick architecture, and later Carpenter's Gothic or wood-butcher's art. With slight modifications, it is still the most common construction method in America.

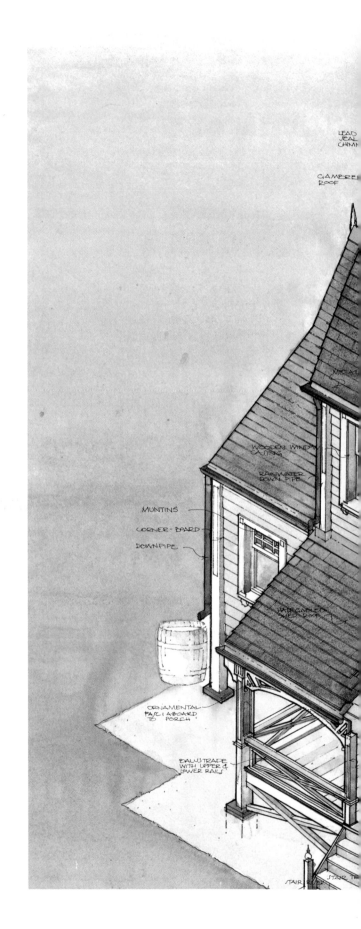

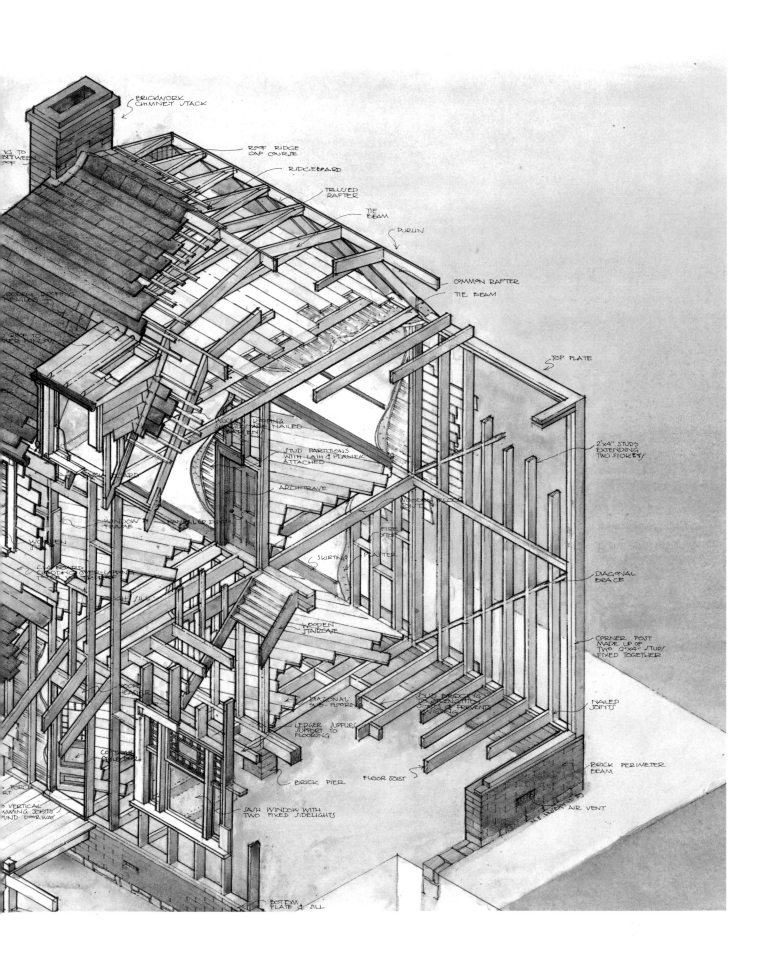

BRICKWORK
CHIMNEY STACK

ROOF RIDGE
CAP COURSE

RIDGEBOARD

TRUSSED
RAFTER

TIE
BEAM

PURLIN

COMMON RAFTER

TIE BEAM

TOP PLATE

2"x4" STUDS
EXTENDING
TWO STOREYS

STUD PARTITIONS
WITH LATH & PLASTER
ATTACHED

ARCHITRAVE

DIAGONAL
BRACE

FIRE
STOP

PLASTER

SKIRTING

CORNER POST
MADE UP OF
TWO 2"x4" STUDS
FIXED TOGETHER

WINDOW
FRAME

PANELLED DOOR

WOODEN
STAIRCASE

DIAGONAL
SUB-FLOORING

STUD BRIDGING
TO STRENGTHEN
JOISTS & PREVENT
MOVING

NAILED
JOINTS

BRICK PERIMETER
BEAM

LEDGER SUPPLIES
SUPPORT TO
FLOORING

BRICK PIER

FLOOR JOIST

SASH WINDOW WITH
TWO FIXED SIDELIGHTS

AIR VENT

BOTTOM
PLATE & SILL

T H E   F R O N T   E N T R A N C E

Before the Victorians, only a rich minority were able to pay for an imposing doorway or porch: now the growing middle classes could afford them too. As long as the materials had been just wood, brick or stone, a certain homogeneity had been assured: the introduction of stucco, decorative tiles, cast iron and cheap coloured glass led to a confusion of design and ornament. Early entrances continued the classical themes of the Regency, somewhat coarsened in detail. Later, the medieval revival played a part, though classical grammar was generally found to combine the requirements of public presentation more satisfactorily than Gothic. In the lower echelons of the urban terraced house, such niceties of style were usually ignored or misunderstood, resulting in a cheerfully eclectic marriage of the two leading schools.

Left: A lace-like double staircase and entrance, from Queensland, Australia, shows how colonial architecture often went one further than the home product, employing cast iron fittings exported as ballast in the holds of ships. The nearest to such exuberance in Britain was usually confined to the seaside or health resorts.

Right: Nothing could better exemplify the upper-middle-class town houses of the 1850s than this grand parade of Tuscan columns. The relatively modest doorcases of the previous century have been replaced by heavy stucco entrance porticos. Above, the walls are so ornamented with architraves, cornices and balustrades that the brick is dominated by the applied decoration.

RAILINGS AND GATES

In early town houses, the front door opened directly on to the street; railings came in the 18th century to define the property and protect the strip of land in front, as well as to add another touch of elegance. In the 19th century the wish to enclose the property became stronger, reflecting the growth of private ownership and the simultaneous transformation from a rural to an urban society. The new owners of suburban villas wanted to mark out their territory, just as the landowners of the 18th century had done. Gates and railings afforded another opportunity for decoration and display. Whether the enclosure is of iron or wood, the gate should generally be of the same material. Delightful hybrids were concocted, however; the railings to the right are made of a wood frame with twisted wire panels. In cases where dwarf walls and piers are made of brick or stone, iron railings usually look best. They should be 18 inches to 2 feet (45 to 60 cm) high.

In general, cast iron was popular in the early years of the century while wood and wrought iron, beloved of the Arts and Crafts Movement, came into their own later, to persist into Edwardian designs.

Right: A classical revival entrance, wrought-iron railings and grandiloquent overthrow and lantern all derive from English baroque models, but seen through later eyes.

Left: The wood and wirework fence, with ornamental gate, casts its pattern upon the pattern of the tile path which leads up to a porch in which classical and oriental styles have been shamelessly blended together.

Below: These cast iron railings show Victorian design at its everyday best; the interplay of curves and straight lines has been skilfully handled.

Left: Porch and railings combine in an artless but charming ensemble of decorative ironwork. Classical features and nearly Gothic ones have been gloriously mixed up.

Left: Though at first sight elaborate, this front gate is made up of simple rails decorated with standard finials and rosettes from the ironwork catalogue; the white paint is effective against the dark background.

PATHS, TILES AND ORNAMENTS

The strip from front gate to entrance door provided another chance to proclaim the status of a house. Traditionally the materials had been, in descending order of quality, stone flags, brick, gravel and beaten earth. Horse traffic alone provided sufficient reason for keeping dirt out of the entrance hall, necessitating pathways that were hard, clean and good to look at. The new tessellated tiles, recently reintroduced through the rebirth of interest in medieval flooring, met this need. Made of dense clays baked hard, they either drew their colour from the clay itself, giving dull reds, browns, ochres and near blacks, or were artificially coloured by more elaborate techniques. Glazing produced tiles which, too delicate for flooring, gave ample opportunity for pictures or patterns on adjacent walls. Many of these showed pastoral scenes of hunting, shooting and fishing, accurately reflecting the aspirations of the new surburban middle class.

Above: An Australian tiled path is a good match for the bright sunlight and a luxuriant border.

Left: A typical and aggressive tiled entrance of the second half of the century looks like a hall floor which has been rolled down to the gate.

Right: This sphinx is an example of the new range of cast sculptures made possible by advances in cements and mass production techniques.

Above: The quality of Victorian clays and glazes is shown by these tiles with their sunshine motifs.

Left: The plant forms in the small roundels betray the familiar influence of William Morris.

Far left: A popular place for tile pictures was in the return of an entrance wall, no doubt to impress and divert the waiting visitor.

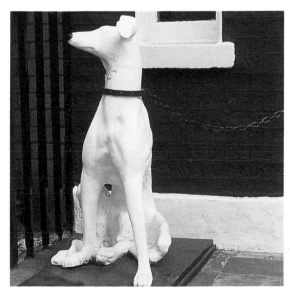

Far left: This dog shows some of the lighter touches a little imagination can lend to an entrance.

Left: Door scrapers came in a variety of cast-iron patterns of which the harp was a favourite, and one which remained in production for decades.

PORCHES

The porch has always had a dual function, to call attention to the entrance door and at the same time provide temporary shelter for the visitor, both simple attributes sadly neglected in our houses today.

As might be expected, urban examples tend to the grandiose, even pompous, while those in the country are noticeably more relaxed.

The Victorians understood the importance of bravura around the entrance, from garden gate into the hall itself. However discordant some of their material juxtapositions may seem to us – violent tile patterns against stained glass, for example – one cannot but admire their enviable self-confidence. What has to be remembered, from our present more egalitarian century, is the added effect that servants had on the Victorian entrance. Brass was polished regularly, often daily, and similar treatment was accorded to the step and tiled pathway. Everything sparkled and shone: those who for reasons of poverty or sluttishness did not comply would have been regarded by their neighbours with contempt. Nor was this attitude merely a middle-class fetish; such pride in appearance could be found in working-class terraces up until the last war.

Old photographs of city streets, taken in the days of horse-drawn carriages, show how the impact of urban facades have been compromised by the ubiquitous motor car, parked outside as a kind of temporary portal, symbol of the householder's status but, unlike the porch, capable of replacement as means or fashion dictate. In detail too, the entrances to Victorian buildings have been spoiled by the intrusion of modern plastic signs, entry phones, burglar alarms, bells, lights, and so on, to say nothing of unsympathetic, often brutal, alterations to the doors themselves. But, as the examples on these pages show, reinstatement and sympathetic painting can restore much of the original effect.

Top: This deep porch in East Hampton, Long Island, beautifully complements a New England clapboard house.

Above: The classical components of a Texas house assembled unconventionally, nevertheless have an agreeable sense of scale.

Right: These doors were doubtless made up by a local joiner, but their simple carpentry is very effective.

Above: The Victorian porch was not entirely for show, but had a protective function too, to shelter visitors alighting from carriages. The invention of large sheets of glass made glazed arcades possible for the first time.

Above right: The balustrade of this American porch has been cut from softwood using new woodworking machinery, after the manner of some 17th-century staircase balustrades in Britain.

Right: Echoes of the Queen Anne movement, which became popular in the United States, are evident in a Rhode Island porch.

Far right: This delightful porch is greatly enhanced by the simple use of trellis in the side panels, betraying its rural origins. A standard iron cresting gives it a fretted roofline.

Above: Porches-cum-bays like this were popular at the seaside. The Regency tradition of slim panes of border glazing has lingered on, filled with coloured glass to provide a decorative frame round the windows. The square corner panes were usually picked out in a strongly contrasting colour or, as seen here, with decorative rosettes.

Left: A projecting porch was a social signal, implying that a house was occupied by a wealthier family than one would expect if the porch were recessed. Some of the richest self-made men regarded an elaborate Gothic house as an advertisement for success.

Above: There is a whiff of the sea about this porch, and it is no surprise to find that it comes from St Columb Major in Cornwall.

FRONT DOORS

There can be no denying the importance the Victorians placed on first impressions: the visitor had to be left in no doubt as to the owner's position in society.

However charming the gate or imposing the porch, it is the entrance door which captures the eye of the visitor as he waits to be admitted. Up until the Regency, front doors had all been solid, made up of panels of wood held together by framing called styles (vertical) and rails (horizontal). The only way of introducing light into the hallway was by means of graceful semi-circular fanlights. Fanlights of this kind continued into the 19th century, particularly where the accent was classical. With the introduction of cheaper, stronger glass, it became possible to

Left: The door becomes a work of art at Old Swan House, on the Chelsea Embankment in London, designed by Norman Shaw. Traditional fielded panels are limited to tiny inserts at the bottom of each door. It is not too fanciful to see how Art Deco grew out of such precedents; indeed the sculptured panels already seem to be in advance of their time.

Above: Colour is an integral part of this jolly Australian entrance, more suited to a public house, perhaps, than a residence. Whether the colour is original or not it looks appropriate for the folksy baroque woodwork and decorative glazing.

incorporate large panes into entrance doors.

With this new plate glass came glass engraving, seen at its voluptuous best in public houses of the day, stained glass and, for the first time, obscured glazing of all kinds.

Gothicists brought back pointed doors to some houses, but the practical difficulties of their geometry meant that the new medievalism was usually confined within the old and convenient rectangle. As a tribute to the past, however, many of these doors were given leaded lights, the only method by which early Elizabethan windows could be put together from the small glass sizes then available.

Decorative fun could be had, too, with baroque treatment of the door panels themselves and the adjacent columns and supports, elaborations made easier by new machinery.

A Queen Anne door surround is embellished with fine brick and terracotta detailing.

Ruskinian capitals decorate plain columns supporting a top-heavy surround.

Paint has given an icing-sugar effect to this variation on the same theme.

Cheap but effective mouldings decorate these handsome doors in San Antonio, Texas.

A Queen Anne revival doorway makes rich use of mixed window panes.

A sense of scale is apparent here, with elaborate door panels and railings.

NUMBERS

As Victorian architecture grew more ornamental, so did typography and graphic design. In the 18th century classicism had provided the basic grammar for lettering and numerals, but the interest in medievalism brought new influences to typefaces; William Morris, among his many activites, turned his hand to typography for his Kelmscott edition of Chaucer. Elaborate variations were played on the old Roman founts, expanding and condensing the letters and enlarging the serifs to create fanciful and often bizarre styles. Most people will be familiar with the typical Victorian poster or billboard, each line set in a different type and weight, producing an effect which is both chaotic and vigorous. New techniques of engraving and painting on glass enlarged the scope for signing and lettering buildings, as can be seen here.

These examples show the variety of design and material used on Victorian doors and their surrounds. No. 71 shows a standard number and knocker which would have been familiar to Dickens. No. 42 is straightforward signwriting on glass, while 5 and 23 are in tailor-made metalwork. The blue and white enamel is an appropriate modern alternative.

DOOR FURNITURE

The fitting out of hundreds of thousands of front doors provided great opportunities for the foundries and engravers of the day, and one is struck by the sheer fertility of ideas and excellent craftsmanship of these quite humble artefacts. Some were undoubtedly one-offs, commissioned by an individual client, but the majority were made to fill those extensive catalogues which are one of the pleasures of Victorian manufacturing.

Early Victorian knockers repeated the classical themes of the previous century, such as shields, lion heads and medusas. Later there are clear influences of Morris & Co.; later still and perhaps most beautiful of all, the sensuous and slightly sinister forms of Art Nouveau.

Letter boxes (more properly called letter plates) only became widespread after the introduction of the penny post in 1840. The addition of 'Letters' or 'Newspapers' was perhaps more a symbol of literacy and self-importance than any instruction for tradesmen. Materials for this ironmongery were brass, gun metal and bronze. Cheaper models were made of cast iron, a material unsuitable for delicate design.

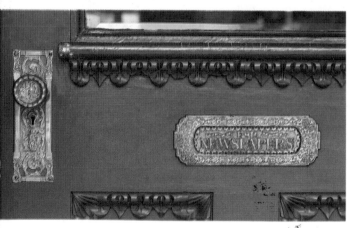

The invention and quality of Victorian ironmongery is exemplary. These designs range from Georgian classical through Arts and Crafts to Art Nouveau. One of the most beautiful (*opposite, bottom right*) is a purely functional bell pull which would have won the admiration of the Modern Movement. The cast iron letter plate (*above*) is coarse by comparison, but more suitable to a Victorian door than a plain modern design in newly cast brass.

TYPES OF ENTRANCES & BOUNDARIES

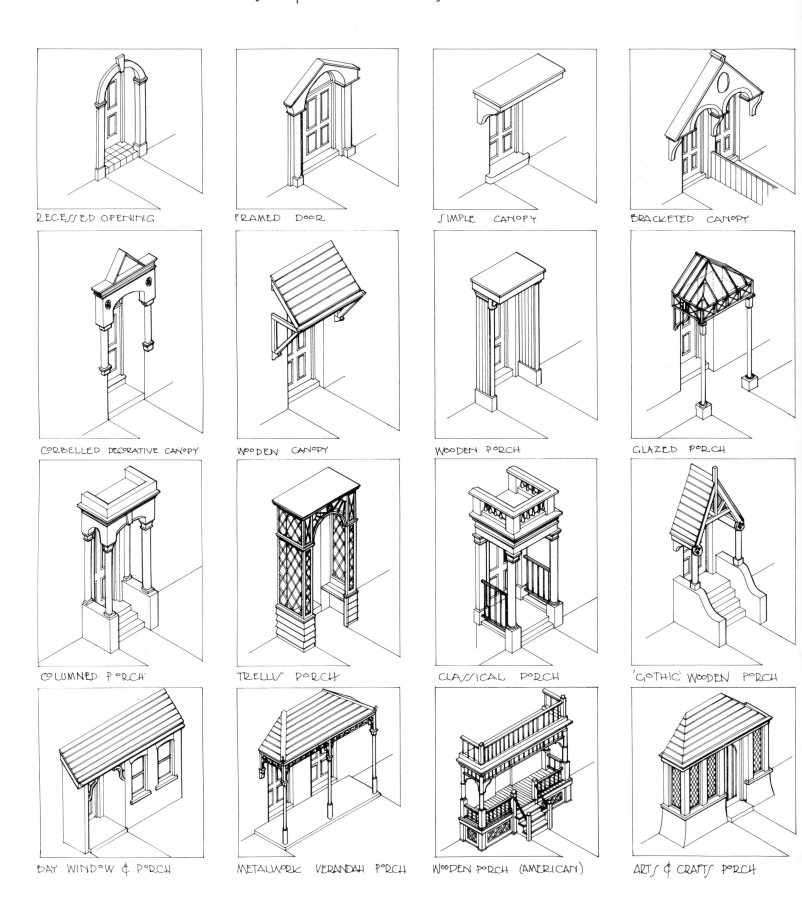

RECESSED OPENING

FRAMED DOOR

SIMPLE CANOPY

BRACKETED CANOPY

CORBELLED DECORATIVE CANOPY

WOODEN CANOPY

WOODEN PORCH

GLAZED PORCH

COLUMNED PORCH

TRELLIS PORCH

CLASSICAL PORCH

'GOTHIC' WOODEN PORCH

BAY WINDOW & PORCH

METALWORK VERANDAH PORCH

WOODEN PORCH (AMERICAN)

ARTS & CRAFTS PORCH

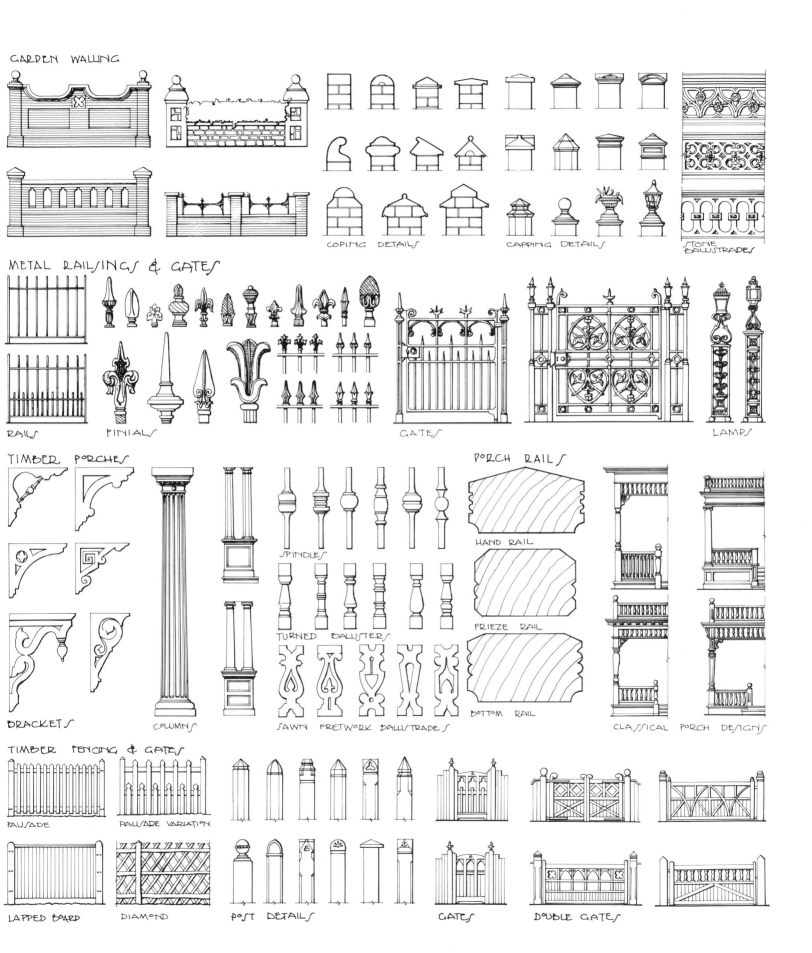

GARDEN WALLING

COPING DETAILS   CAPPING DETAILS   STONE BALUSTRADES

METAL RAILINGS & GATES

RAILS   FINIALS   GATES   LAMPS

TIMBER PORCHES

PORCH RAILS

HAND RAIL

FRIEZE RAIL

BOTTOM RAIL

BRACKETS   COLUMNS   SPINDLES

TURNED BALUSTERS

SAWN FRETWORK BALUSTRADES   CLASSICAL PORCH DESIGNS

TIMBER FENCING & GATES

PALISADE   PALISADE VARIATION   POST DETAILS   GATES   DOUBLE GATES

LAPPED BOARD   DIAMOND

71

EXTERNAL WALLS

The three most popular Victorian building materials were brick, stone and wood. Each developed its own subtleties, variations and character, and, except when a wealthy client wished to impress, the material used would be local. With the growth of the railways, however, more of the materials were transported and local characteristics became indistinct.

Of all these materials, brick probably offered the greatest variety, both in methods of bonding and the types available. London stock brick is yellowy in colour, Cambridge brick is white and the hard engineering bricks of the North deep red, blue or purple.

When the details surrounding doors and windows were also in brick, better or more ornamental bricks would be deployed. The use of stone to highlight details – cornices, arches, capitals, quoins and sometimes plinths – was customary in brick buildings with grander pretensions. Later in the century, brick and faience decorative tiles became available, usually in floral patterns or animal heads.

All Victorian brick houses were built with walls deep enough for a brick to be laid crosswise on the wall, showing only its end face or 'header'. This allowed for variation between header and 'stretcher', a brick laid lengthwise along the wall. The characteristic variations of bond were thus composed of varying mixtures of header and stretcher, their syncopation giving a wall both character and strength.

The most attractive bonds are considered to be English and Flemish (see page 300). If you are building an extension to your Victorian house, try to match the original bonding. The outer skin of a modern cavity wall is almost always built in stretcher bond with no headers as variation. The effect of Victorian bonds can be recreated, however, by the use of 'snapped' headers, bricks broken in half by the bricklayer, though at an additional cost in labour.

The next most important detail of brickwork is the treatment of the joint. Accurately made bricks such as engineerings fitted together so snugly that the Victorians often managed to get away with using very little mortar; bricks could also be rubbed together (a brick called the red rubber was a great favourite for this) until they fitted. For uneven hand-made facings, like

Right: Moulded brick tiles were made out of dense clays burnt hard, and were very durable, as can be seen from their precise profiles after a century of use. These dark reds provide a sharp contrast to the soft yellow stocks of the main wall, which has been unsympathetically repointed during the 20th century.

Below left: These decorative lintels are ultimately derived from Venetian and Oriental sources. The unusual pointed keystones tie in with the central mullion.

Below: A simple diamond (or diaper) pattern was a favourite device to liven up large areas of brickwork. Colour variations were achieved by using headers, the smaller end faces of the brick, which often came out darker than the stretchers, or long sides.

the splendid reds of Sussex, Kent and Berkshire, extra mortar was needed; it was usually finished flush and excess mortar cleaned off with a rag.

Lime was commonly used for the mortar; it looks better than cement, is softer and easier to work. For normal work today, the best mortar is a 1:1:6 mixture of cement/lime/sand.

Today, pointing rarely matches 19th-century standards. The main types used are flush pointing, level with the face of the bricks, and recessed pointing where a recess is formed between the joints with a special tool. This can look attractive with fairly regular bricks but does not weather well, as it allows water to penetrate the joint. The all too popular 'weathered' or 'struck' joint, although excellent in rejecting water, is hideous in appearance and should never be used. The trouble occurs where horizontal and vertical joints meet, creating ugly breaks.

Stone continued to be used for economy where it was locally available, and elsewhere for effect. Ornamentation is naturally expensive in stone, but remarkably elaborate work can be found where quarries produced stone soft enough to be easily worked. In regions such as Cornwall and Aberdeen, the intransigence of the local granite allowed only simple cutting, and ornament was restricted to incised decorations or chamfers, made by cutting away the corner of a stone block at an angle of about 45°. Rubble walls of irregular stones fitted together as closely as possible were often contained by brick or dressed stone quoins at the corners of the building, and sometimes by horizontal string courses too.

At the beginning of the Victorian period, exterior plastering, or stucco, was popular. It could provide columns, cornices and false stone walling at a fraction of the cost of the real thing, and was either painted or left to revert slowly to the natural colour of its basic constituent, sand.

Gothic architects, however, deplored stucco as a sham, preferring terracotta. Like brick, terracotta is made of fireclay. It could be

Above: Ogees over the windows and a mock-Jacobean pediment give this early 19th-century Cotswold house its playful 'Gothick' charm.

Centre: An American Queen Anne house in Newport, Rhode Island, incorporates numerous elaborate patterns in decorative shingles and carved panels.

moulded to virtually any form and fired to give a vitreous finish. Terracotta could be used as a simple facing block like brick, as well as for moulded features such as cornices, swags and sculptured panels. Only large houses used this costly material extensively, but for developers of cheaper housing it provided a decorative fillip, serving the same function as a fibreglass pediment on a modern 'Georgian' estate.

Timber frame walls in the Victorian period really have American copyright. Some clapboard houses were built in the south of England, but it was the Americans who invented the stick or Carpenter's Gothic style by taking the timber-framed house and filling in the panels with timber patterns.

Left: This American house, if executed in brick and stucco, would not look out of place in a British suburb, but its timber construction has allowed a lightness and exuberance impossible in other materials.

Above: Careful examination of these rusticated quoins shows them to be mass produced. The squiggly incisions, or vermiculation, give strength and character to the corner stones.

Left: Some cheaper examples of Victorian decoration, like this pierced balustrade, were made up from ready-made components.

ROOFS AND GABLES

With the exception of a few great houses, the Georgians never took roofs seriously. Palladianism had greatly reduced the accent on roofs as part of the architectural composition, and in terraced houses in particular Georgian designers often suppressed them as far as they could, reducing their pitch and tucking them away behind stuccoed parapets. The picturesque revival led to an increase in the importance of skylines, with a reappearance of towers, turrets and battlements, but it took the Gothic revival to rediscover the architectural opportunities and bring a return, a celebration, even, of the steep and picturesque roof lines of the medieval past. Gables became prominent, with the walls rising to the level of the top of the roof not just at either end of a building but on other elevations too. This led to complicated roof plans with a delightful confusion of hips and valleys.

Nothing was left unembellished. Ridges were fretted and crested; the apex of the gable often had square wooden posts like balusters,

Right: The inspiration for this lodge cottage is Elizabethan, but the carved bargeboards, bay windows and decorative roof tiles are typically Victorian.

Above left: The influence of Second Empire France is apparent in this American house. The almost vertical mansards are clad in thin metal tiles.

Left: A wedding-cake house in Connecticut blends classicism with hints of colonial and oriental styles.

Above: The crow-stepped gable of this neo-Elizabethan building has stone dressings and dark headers forming diaper patterns in the brickwork. This rather aggressive effect is common in Victorian buildings, improving durability at the expense of homogeneity.

both rising upwards and extending downwards. Bargeboards suspended underneath the gables met centrally at the downward-pointing post and were frequently elaborately carved, providing further opportunities for romantic posts, balls and finials.

The building's silhouette became all-important. Often the age of a house can be told by a glance at its outline, a Victorian house positively identified by a fragment of roof or a chimney rising above the trees. For the Victorians, chimneys were a source of the greatest pleasure. Their Georgian predecessors had taken a more sceptical attitude; the Greek temples they admired so intensely had had no chimneys, and even the precedents of Palladio's villas were unhelpful. But in the twisting, soaring chimneys of the Elizabethans, the Victorians found an answer to their craving for the picturesque, not to mention draughts for the fireplaces below.

Victorian taste also ran to chimney pots, and they did much to refine the quality and design of the rather crude versions of the late 18th century. Whether pots are needed at all is a matter of debate. Some maintain that properly built chimney stacks are adequate on their own. But pots provide an easily weather-proofed wind protector at the end of the flue and increase flue height without the cost of extra brickwork. More important still, perhaps, from the Victorian point of view, they made a distinctive contribution to the roofscape. The Victorians sought out their models with enthusiasm and some of these, castellated like chess pieces or twisted in Elizabethan chevrons, are now collectors' items.

The main roofing materials were the clay tile, stone, thatch, and, increasingly, slate. Though it came to be used without much discrimination throughout England, Welsh slate seems in retrospect much kinder to any area

Right: These astonishing bargeboards, conveniently dated to 1892, have suspended decorations which hang like icicles from the gables.

Far right: The tall roofs of 19th-century houses provided ample opportunities for decoration, as in this polychrome example from New England.

Right: A high standard of workmanship was needed to make a success of this ornamental detail, applied like a frieze under the eaves.

Far right: Pointed slates, called fish scales, had to be trimmed by hand, but help to break up the monotony of a tall roof.

than its ugly present-day equivalent, the ubiquitous interlocking concrete tile. In Scotland, Ballaclinish slate was popular, while wooden shingles or thin metal tiles were widely used in America.

Not content with plain slates or tiles, the Victorians invented patterns, introducing courses of rounded tiles to break the rhythm of an otherwise unbroken roof pitch. Surprisingly, they never competed with the extraordinary decorative roofs of France and Belgium, where elaborate patterns were created with vari-coloured slates and parts of the roof were sometimes gilded. But in any event, the full-blown Victorian roof was a splendid affair.

The roof space and attics provided useful accommodation for servants, and their quality slowly improved. The rooms were generally reasonably lit and provided with simple fireplaces. Skylights were normally confined to internal roof slopes invisible from below and were simple in construction – a pane or two of glass set in a hinged wooden frame or, more basic still, metal-framed and fixed, the whole arrangement set into the roofing material and flashed with lead. They would probably have been more widely used if there had been a foolproof way of making them watertight.

Where central roof lighting was needed, for example above an internal staircase, a flat roof with a solidly constructed lantern light or dome would have been usual, like a miniature greenhouse or conservatory. Fortunately for servants, high gables provided space for upper windows in detached houses. High roofs provide immediate opportunities for modern loft conversion (see page 297), but wherever possible dormer windows should be used in preference to the efficient but bleak proprietary skylights which are available on the market today. In cheaper

Above and top: Rain-water heads often carry the date of the building, while the pipes could be elaborately decorated.

Far left: Comparatively restrained bargeboards complement the Gothic gable of this row of East Anglian almshouses.

Left: Harder bricks and stronger cement allowed the Victorians to produce bigger and better chimneys.

Below far left: Striped chimneys enliven an otherwise undistinguished roofline.

Below left: Elaborate chess-piece chimney pots harmonize with the finials, hood moulds and castellations of the rest of the building.

Victorian dwellings the dormer window was the norm. Each had a little pitched roof of its own, and afforded further scope for ingenious decoration.

Drainage of the roof was achieved by a wide variety of external cast iron gutters and downpipes, with hidden gutters behind the parapets of terraced houses. Where an external gutter met a downpipe, it often debouched into an ornamental collecting sleeve or basin called a hopperhead, wider than the downpipe itself. The new and higher roofs, however, brought problems of drainage. Their steep pitches increased the area of the roof and added to the catchment rate of rain-water, in turn increasing its discharge rate into the gutters and hopperheads. Downpipes were often far too narrow, 3 inches (60 mm) or less. They looked elegant, but were quickly blocked with leaves in the autumn.

Many such details of the Victorian house only functioned well if regularly inspected and maintained. In large houses, gutters were checked regularly by the gardeners. In smaller homes the householder no doubt took responsibility, while in cottages, clearing of gutters and downpipes was a continuous necessity since water supply was often by means of water butts filled from the roof. Nowadays, however, we tend to wait for a disaster to occur before attending to roof drainage.

As is common today, except in towns with mains drainage, rain-water was taken to soakaways. Sometimes, in an excess of medievalism, gargoyles were used to throw the rainwater clear of the building, a pleasant idea in principle but one not much respected by high winds.

As in earlier centuries, hopperheads were used decoratively, often carrying the date of the building and the initials of the owner. They were usually made of cast lead, although cast iron became increasingly common during the 19th century. Fine hopperheads can be seen on Queen Anne Revival buildings such as the Willing House in Grays Inn Road, London.

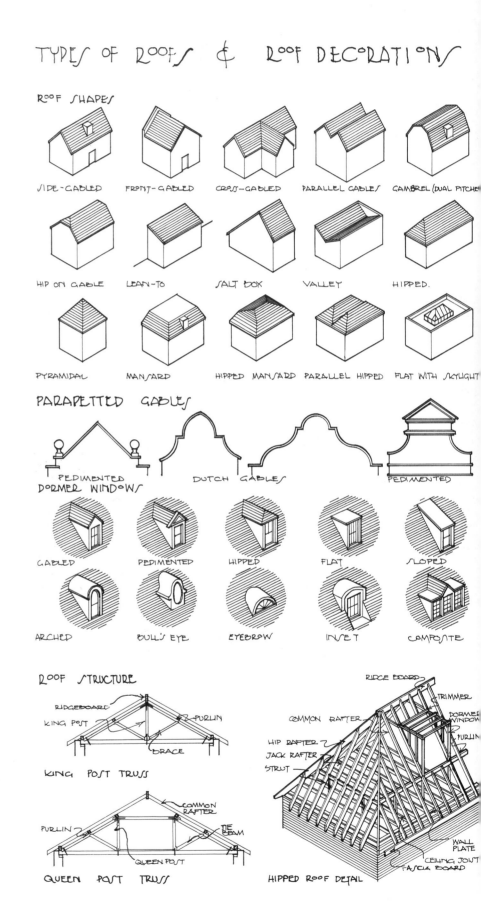

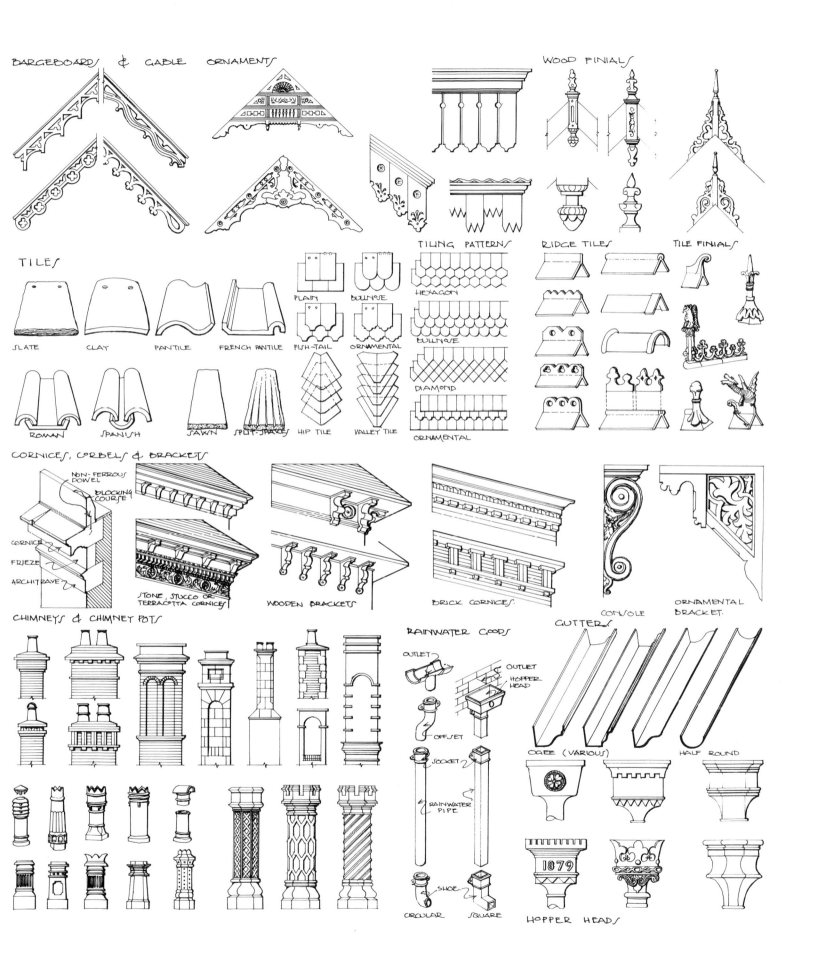

BARGEBOARDS & GABLE ORNAMENTS

WOOD FINIALS

TILES

SLATE   CLAY   PANTILE   FRENCH PANTILE   FISH-TAIL   ORNAMENTAL

PLAIN   BULLNOSE

ROMAN   SPANISH   SAWN   SPLIT-SHAKES   HIP TILE   VALLEY TILE

TILING PATTERNS

HEXAGON
BULLNOSE
DIAMOND
ORNAMENTAL

RIDGE TILES

TILE FINIALS

CORNICES, CORBELS & BRACKETS

NON-FERROUS DOWEL
BLOCKING COURSE
CORNICE
FRIEZE
ARCHITRAVE

STONE, STUCCO OR TERRACOTTA CORNICES   WOODEN BRACKETS   BRICK CORNICES.   CONSOLE   ORNAMENTAL BRACKET.

CHIMNEYS & CHIMNEY POTS

RAINWATER GOODS

OUTLET
OUTLET
HOPPER HEAD
OFFSET
SOCKET
RAINWATER PIPE
SHOE
CIRCULAR   SQUARE

GUTTERS

OGEE (VARIOUS)   HALF ROUND

1879

HOPPER HEADS

81

EXTERIOR PAINTWORK

We know that the Victorians loved colour, texture and pattern in their buildings, but it is hard to be dogmatic about the actual colours they applied to their external stuccoed walls and woodwork. Photographic records, of course, are all in black and white and scrapes (the method by which layers of paint are methodically exposed down to the bare wood) are not always reliable because undercoats can be mistaken for surface finishes. Contemporary paintings are a useful source of information, as are books and magazines of the time. Most valuable are the colour charts and sample paint schemes, printed in colour, which were issued as advertisements by paint manufacturers beginning in the 1860s.

White was widely used both in Britain and America, particularly in the earlier part of the century. By the 1840s, however, people were beginning to regard it as too painful to the eye, and one American writer thought that its use showed a 'puritanical hatred of colours'. Other handbooks pointed out that it rapidly became discoloured, particularly in the polluted air of the 19th century. As a result, white paint was quite often 'lowered' by adding lamp black to produce a silvery grey, or ochre to produce a creamy stone colour.

Pastel tints such as grey and cream were sometimes applied to stucco during the Regency and early Victorian periods and made a comeback with the Queen Anne revival. The last coat was often 'dusted' with fine white sand to imitate stone, an effect that can be reproduced quite easily with modern textured exterior paints. At

Right: The olive green and cream of this San Francisco house has an authentic air and conforms to the colour schemes suggested by contemporary trade catalogues. Sometimes a third colour, usually dark, would be applied to the window sashes in order to recede and so emphasize the large expanse of glass.

the time, all stucco was painted in limewash, which had to be renewed once a year. When, inevitably, the moment of repainting was postponed, the finish wore thin and the pigment of the underlying stucco started to show through, streaking many a facade in otherwise handsome terraces and streets.

For woodwork, the range of external paint colours was more restricted than it is today. According to Webster and Parkes' *Encyclopaedia of Domestic Economy* (1844), the tints most frequently employed were grey, pea, sea and olive green, and fawn. Originally, these tints would have been mixed on the spot from a narrow range of basic pigments, such as Prussian blue, yellow ochre and burnt umber. As the century progressed, manufacturers started to produce ready-mixed paints, and the range of colours widened. These were still limited, however, by a shortage of colour-fast pigments: bright reds, purples, yellows, blues and blue-greens faded too quickly to be practicable (even today's blues and purples are notoriously fugitive). The later Victorian range included black, white and cream, dark reds, browns and ochres of all shades and a wide variety of greens.

Graining, the painting of ordinary wooden surfaces to imitate hardwood, was a favourite Victorian technique, commonly used on front doors and also on window joinery and other external woodwork. Although graining fell out of favour towards the end of the era, when more 'honest' real woods were preferred, it did not die out completely until the 1930s, and is today enjoying a modest revival.

The ideas of Michel Eugène Chevreul, who was Director of Dyes at the Gobelins tapestry works, were widely influential. His *Principles of Harmony and Contrast of Colours*, translated into English in 1854, pointed out that some colours change their values when put alongside other colours. Charts of compatible colours soon appeared in manufacturers' catalogues.

Some examples of original Victorian paint

can still be found, even outside, and this longevity is almost certainly due to its high lead content, in proportions not permitted today but which certainly extended the life of the material considerably. Country panelling which has survived with its original paintwork is almost always in brown or green and is likely to be a good guide to the colour of an exterior. Right up to the 1930s most suburban houses were painted green or brown, some of the browns approaching red. There was a kind of 'bull's blood' which was very popular, as was Indian red.

External frescoes, murals and painted decorations, where these existed, were often executed in creams, ochres, terracotta, dull blues and olive

In a scheme published in Philadelphia in 1887, the body of the house is painted in drab and the trim in brownstone, with a third colour for the sashes and the door and shutter mouldings. The colours could be reversed, to give a light trim on a dark body. Both effects were considered superior to the earlier tradition of white for the body and green for the shutters.

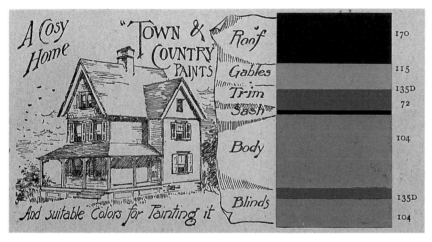

A manufacturer's advertisement of about 1890 helps customers resolve the choice of colours by suggesting how to paint the different parts of the house and achieve a harmonious result using related tones.

a paler tone for the body of the house and a slightly deeper tone of the same colour for the trim, including window frames and sashes. From about 1870 to 1900, colours became deeper and more varied, with the addition of full browns, rich reds and dull greens, and Queen Anne houses were painted in particularly complex, multi-coloured schemes, with different tones for each storey, and window sashes in one of the deep, almost black tones. Finally, around the turn of the century, pastel tones returned to favour for the body of the house, and all the trim was painted white.

The owner of a Victorian house today who wishes to be correct, if not pedantic, about appropriate schemes might consider some of the colour ranges described here. The almost ubiquitous use of white, or off-white, in recent years does tend to provide too harsh a contrast for many houses of the period. Green can look well against some of the harsher red bricks and ochres and dark browns go well with stone. The 'earth' colours favoured by the Victorians are not only among the cheapest and most readily available pigments but are also fast, retaining their colour for decades without noticeable fading (a factor which has remained influential in paint manufacture right up to the present day). Beautiful greens and browns can be obtained by taking the time to add small quantities of black or umber to everyday trade colours, and the extra time spent in experiment can be well worth while when the result is something which is to last for five or ten years or more. To make sure of the colour, a small window round the back can always be painted as a sample. Also try to imagine the effect that any new painting may have on the building in years to come.

greens; durability must have been a consideration in selecting these colours.

Today, railings are usually painted black or white; in Victorian times, however, the range would have been greater, and generally followed the colour scheme of the rest of the house.

Stone and unrendered brick walls were never painted, and it is worth noting that the modern habit of painting stone window surrounds or the entire brick frontage of a house brings with it an unnecessary expense, for once painted, a facade will require regular repainting.

Wooden walls have to be painted, of course, and consequently it was in America that some of the most elaborate colour schemes emerged, with differing treatments for walls, trim, gables and shutters. Up to about 1840 colour use was simple: a white house body, white trim and green shutters. Later, softer earth tones became popular. It was generally considered fashionable to use

Top: The pure white trim of this West Coast Italianate house contrasts sharply with the dark body colour. This cocoa red was a Victorian favourite, and traces can still be found on houses all over Britain.

Above: A typical Italianate house has been demurely painted in lavender and white. If the fondant treatment is judged to be too genteel, it is still kinder than the neighbours' scheme to the right.

Left: Victorian colour schemes, such as the Neapolitan paint effects of these houses in San Francisco, can come as something of a surprise, so strong is the impact of black and white and sepia photographs on our image of the period. Both schemes are successful in their own way, and show what can be achieved by reviving original ideas of exterior decoration.

Below: A traditional, early 19th-century colour scheme adds dignity to this cheerful confection from the States. While bright colours look well in city streets, the presence in suburban settings of neat green lawns makes white paint, a classic foil, always hard to better.

Right: A simple combination of sandpaper brown and white is perfect for the unpretentious classicism of this facade.

Far right: The purplish-brown woodwork of the Mark Twain House in Hartford, Connecticut, relieved by thin red bands, echoes the tone of the brick.

Right: The colour scheme for this window surround has been very carefully selected, the lilac and pink restrained by bands of darker grey.

Far right: This red and white scheme brings life and accent to a plain facade, enhancing the architecture without undue jokiness.

Above left: The green detailing brings this ordinary bay window to life.

Left: The blue and cream colour scheme gives maximum support and dignity to another fairly commonplace bay window.

Top: The decision to use light orange against a powder blue background shows the delicate wrought iron of the balcony to fine advantage.

Above: The quiet colour scheme of this Victorian bay is probably close to the original, although the terra-cotta decorations would have been unpainted.

DECORATIVE IRONWORK

The art of wrought-iron working reached its peak in the 18th century, but some of its refinement was carried over into cast iron in the 19th. Wrought iron, as its name suggests, is iron hammered into shape while hot, the traditional art of the blacksmith. And it was the blacksmith who was called upon to make the hinges, latches, nails and gates for the builders of early Victorian houses and cottages. Some of these craftsmen became distinguished artists, called upon by leading patrons and architects to provide the railings and gates for the grander homes.

The introduction of casting, the pouring of molten iron into moulds, meant that gates and railings could be replicated by the thousand. Wrought iron continued to be cheaper than cast for one-off jobs, just as it is today. But casting was naturally adopted for the large-scale production necessary to meet the swelling demand in the Regency and early Victorian period for balconies, railings, grilles and so forth. Coalbrookdale in Shropshire became the centre for this new industry of cast ironwork.

The greatest English ironwork is undoubtedly wrought, yet the standard achieved in Regency cast iron balconies was probably higher than could be achieved by local blacksmiths using traditional methods. The hardness of wrought iron is excellent, while cast iron is relatively brittle and will break if dropped. On the other hand, cast iron often develops a patina which inhibits rust. It also has a grainy quality, caused by the coarse sand used in the moulds, which gives it a pleasingly robust character.

The bulk of Victorian production was in cast iron. The Victorians saw in the new technology almost infinite possibilities for decoration, and used it to embellish the features of a house; balconies, roofs and porches were bedecked with cast iron cresting, valances and finials, windows dignified with balconets, and front doors with elaborate scrapers, knockers and letter boxes.

As the period wore on, the designs became ever more elaborate, culminating in the curvilinear exuberance of Art Nouveau. Much of this design was, inevitably, repetitive, and all of it was, of course, mass-produced, but this caused little concern until the Arts and Crafts Movement called for a return to the hand-made and a reassertion of the nobility of labour. Some cast ironwork had undoubtedly grown coarser and heavier, but in the hands of a sensitive designer the medium could be refined and attractive. Many fine conservatories and interiors of the period, such as the Oxford University Museum, bear witness to its potential. The fantastic ironwork of New Orleans rightly has many admirers, as does that of colonial Australia, much of it shipped as ballast from Coalbrookdale.

Much cast iron was scrapped during the Second World War to help the war effort, and more has been destroyed since. At the same time, faced with falling demand, manufacturers cut down their range and hundreds of foundries closed. Modern interest in old buildings has changed this trend; long-established manufacturers like Ballantine in Scotland publish specialist literature devoted to traditional ranges, and many new foundries will turn out replicas from original samples at modest rates.

A final point on the maintenance of cast iron: after the application of a few layers of paint its characteristic grain becomes invisible. Removing the paint with liquid strippers is a long and arduous process. Sand-blasting produces none of the deleterious effects associated with its use on stone or wood and is generally the best method. Ideally it should be carried out off-site, under workshop conditions, and care should be taken to employ the appropriate size of grit.

Right and above right: The repeated panels of these Australian balustrades show how mass-produced cast iron components could be used with grace and delicacy.

DECORATIVE METALWORK

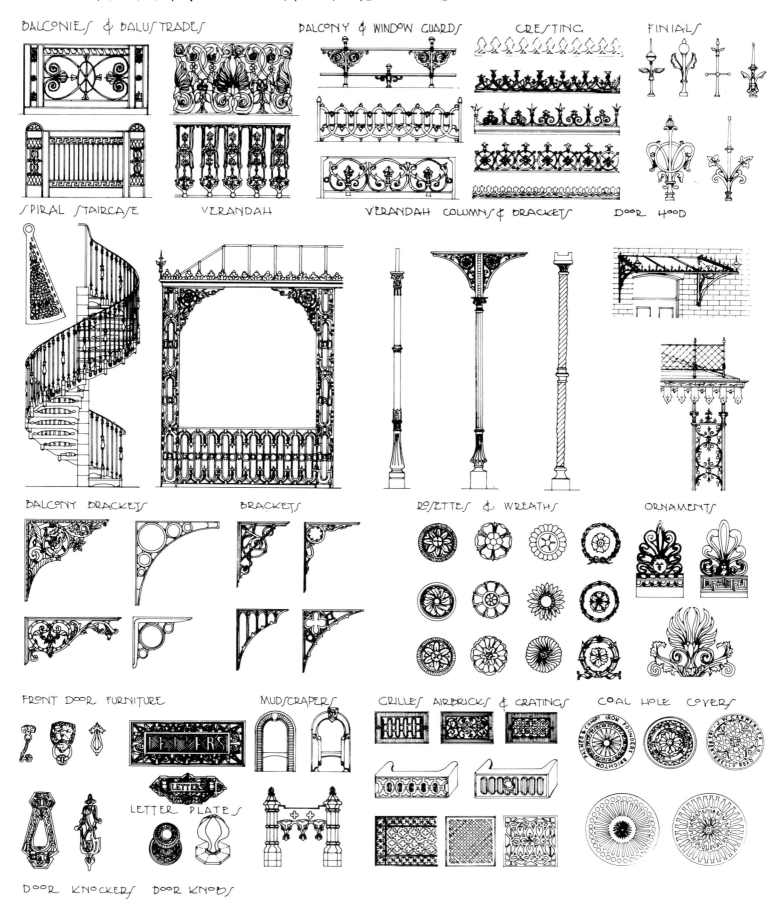

BALCONIES & BALUSTRADES

BALCONY & WINDOW GUARDS

CRESTING

FINIALS

SPIRAL STAIRCASE

VERANDAH

VERANDAH COLUMNS & BRACKETS

DOOR HOOD

BALCONY BRACKETS

BRACKETS

ROSETTES & WREATHS

ORNAMENTS

FRONT DOOR FURNITURE

MUDSCRAPERS

GRILLES AIRBRICKS & GRATINGS

COAL HOLE COVERS

LETTERS

LETTERS

LETTER PLATES

DOOR KNOCKERS DOOR KNOBS

Far left: Delicate railings in Charleston, South Carolina, harmonize perfectly with the foliage that trails around them.

Left: Dark paintwork sets off the exquisite tracery of this cast-iron balcony in Savannah, Georgia, against the white walls and matching shutters.

Above: Commercial pride and advertising are combined in this decorated coal-hole cover.

Overleaf: The juxtaposition of plain uprights and louvres set against highly ornate brackets and railings has produced a sophisticated abstract composition, enhanced by the chic dark green and white colour scheme.

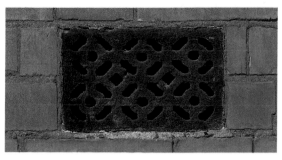

Above: Robust cast-iron window box guards were popular in the mid-Victorian era.

Left: Cast-iron vent grilles are more attractive than those in brick or terracotta, and worth emphasizing.

WINDOWS

The range and variety of windows increased dramatically during the 19th century, though essentially all derived from two main types: sash and casement. In medieval times and down almost to the end of the 17th century, the casement was the universal model, a window hinged vertically to the window frame and opening inward or outward like a door. The sash window is believed to have originated in Holland and arrived in Britain at about the time of William and Mary. It consists of two framed sections, one above the other, which overlap at the dividing transom bar, and slide up and down in grooves instead of opening in or out. Their movement is controlled by weighted pulleys hidden behind the sides of the window frames.

Some windows, particularly in country cottages, had sliding sashes which moved horizontally rather than vertically, without need for counterbalancing weights, and others, notably stair windows, were not designed to open at all, consisting simply of fixed panes. Outbuildings often had fixed cast-iron windows with many small panes.

Sash windows replaced casements on the main facade of more formal houses during the 18th century, although casements also continued in use in dormer windows, basements, and for most cottages and houses of few pretensions. Casements are cheaper to produce than sashes, particularly by less skilled joiners. With the Gothic revival, the casement made a comeback, but in most houses the sash window remained very much the norm.

New ways of incorporating sashes were devised early on. The most obvious of these was the bay window, by no means a Victorian invention, but one which was revived with great enthusiasm. Georgian and Regency bay windows may have included an element of ostentation but one feels they were built for people to look at a particular view, such as the sea or a busy high street. The enjoyment of views, it should be remembered, was a recent phenomenon, starting round

Right: More expensive suburban houses had double-decker bay windows, often with sculptural panels between the storeys.

Far right: When the roses round this cottagey gable fade, the terracotta quoins and polychrome string course will ensure that the house still looks pretty. The casement windows are simple but appropriate.

Opposite: Thatch and wood combine in this example of country Gothic: short branches (from which the bark has long since dropped) set diagonally and studded with oval sections nailed round the edge.

about the 1760s when the growth of romantic sensibility lent a new importance to the picturesque. It is hard not to see the arrival of the mass of Victorian bay windows, at a time when towns were becoming decidedly less picturesque, as being mainly a mark of the status and value of these houses.

New glass-making technology – combined with the abolition of the window tax in 1851 – made larger and larger panes a possibility and transformed the look of Victorian windows. Innumerable arrangements of glazing bars appeared as each joiner developed his own personal style. Glazing bars are worth a study in themselves. Somehow the mullioned lights of Tudor or Jacobean windows seem just right, as do the blunt wooden sections of Queen Anne and early Georgian. Again, the extraordinary delicacy of most Regency bars (usually deemed impossible to reproduce by today's joiners)

Right: This window in 'Victoria Cottage', more Georgian than Victorian, was built when the Queen was only two years on the throne. The shaped Gothic tracery has been comfortably taken up within a round-headed sash, and the rubbed brickwork joints are particularly fine.

Far right: Grey brick headers were a common device to create pattern interest in brickwork, and provide an attractive foil to a simple classical window.

Right: Narrow side panes, which came in with the Regency, are also found on Victorian windows.

Far right: The medievalists hated large panes of glass and sought to decorate their windows like everything else.

impeccably suited their facades; but after that selection depended as much on fancy as on style. Large panes were sometimes incorporated by architects such as Sir George Gilbert Scott even in supposedly Gothic buildings in which one would have expected leaded lights. At the same time, more 'classical' architects were perfectly willing to indulge in a proliferation of glazing bars enclosing small panes, to say nothing of leaded lights. The arch-Victorian compromise was the window with numerous glazing bars in the top sash – for looks – and a plain sheet of plate glass in the bottom – for looking through.

The shape and size of a window went hand in hand with its importance. The bay, the bow, the oriel, french windows, tall stair windows, portholes all had their position in the hierarchy of the facade. Windows usually became smaller the higher they were, or the more humble the occupant of the room they lit.

Above left: The use of steel and concrete allowed window openings to become larger. To fill the wide span created here, four simple sashes have been grouped side by side with decorative fanlights above.

Left: This bay shows how the development of larger panes of glass made large, unobstructed windows possible; the starkness of the window voids is offset by the strength of the surrounding architecture.

Above: This remarkable terrace with vaguely Venetian arched windows crowned with semicircular dormers, each with a spiky finial, reflects the influence of Ruskin. The dormers are new, and much superior to most efforts produced by modern builders.

The junction of the window frame and the wall provided the opportunity for all kinds of decorative treatments. The Regency period's abstract counterpoint of solid and void was too bleak for later tastes. Instead the lintels, arches and hoods surrounding the window frames were embellished with carefully cut bricks, carved stonework with flower motifs, and keystones in the form of animals or fantastic human heads.

The Victorians were inclined to use differing historical reference for buildings of differing type and purpose. Rectories tended to be Gothic, banks were often classical, villas Italianate and warehouses Venetian. But Gothic was the central frame of reference for houses and the evolution of the Victorian Gothic window is of particular interest for today's householder.

The Gothic revivalists, in the full flood of their initial enthusiasm, were all for making the windows in the pointed form of the Gothic arch itself. The style originally favoured was Early English Gothic; its simple lancets, trefoils, freestanding columns and stiff-leafed capitals may be seen in many Victorian railway stations, public buildings and suburban houses. But after a time the benefits of Perpendicular became apparent to the Victorians as they had done to their medieval predecessors. In this severely rectilinear style, sometimes known as 'businessman's Gothic', the arch is squashed flat at the top of each pair of mullions, creating a larger glazed area and allowing more light to penetrate.

For reasons of cost the windows in Gothic facades were often set in rectangular openings which were decorated with Tudor hoods or pointed mouldings. The windows themselves could then be either casement or sash. Gothic arches in flush brickwork were also quite easy to form and after the publication of Ruskin's *Stones of Venice*, many wore a distinct air of the Grand Canal. Fancy had run riot, and perhaps we should enjoy Victorian windows for this very quality, rejoicing in the glorious variety of their manufacture and decoration.

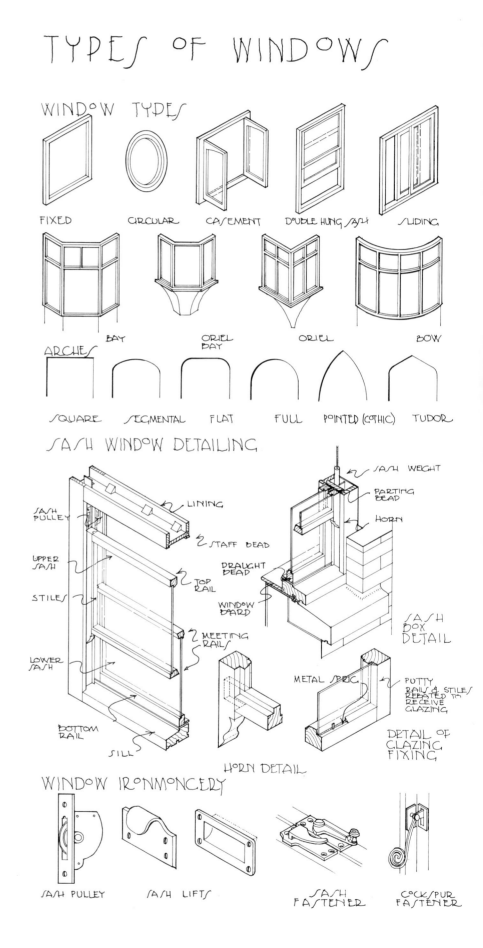

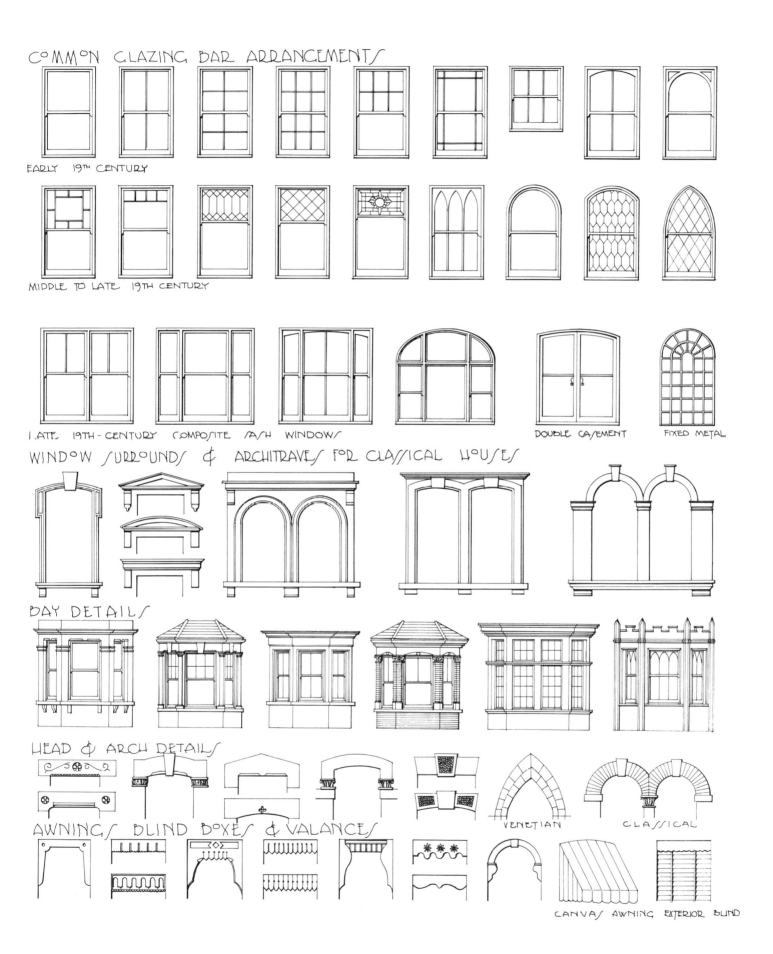

COMMON GLAZING BAR ARRANGEMENTS

EARLY 19TH CENTURY

MIDDLE TO LATE 19TH CENTURY

LATE 19TH-CENTURY COMPOSITE SASH WINDOWS

DOUBLE CASEMENT

FIXED METAL

WINDOW SURROUNDS & ARCHITRAVES FOR CLASSICAL HOUSES

BAY DETAILS

HEAD & ARCH DETAILS

VENETIAN

CLASSICAL

AWNINGS BLIND BOXES & VALANCES

CANVAS AWNING

EXTERIOR BLIND

FIXTURES AND FITTINGS

Much of the character of a Victorian house lies not in the furnishings, nor even in the furniture, but in the fixtures and fittings with which the Victorians embellished the internal features. Fixtures and fittings are, as anyone who has dealt with leasehold property knows, quite distinct both in law and in practical terms. There is no hard and fast rule for distinguishing between the two categories, but in general fixtures are the immovable features such as decorative plaster and tiling, fireplace surrounds, mouldings, doors, sanitary and kitchen installations, the staircase, fitted cupboards and shelving. Fittings arc thc light fittings, door scrapers, curtain fittings, stair rods and numerous other easily removable items.

Most of the architectural details of a house are functional in origin. To take an example, the often glorious architraves and plaster mouldings around doors serve the humble need to conceal the junction between timber and plaster. It is interesting to find that, whatever the style, similar devices have been designed all over the world and at many different times to answer the same functional needs. Similarly, skirting-boards have the practical purpose of protecting wall plaster from damage by furniture and feet; they also hide the awkward gap between the wall and the floor-boards. In the same way a cornice hides the cracks that inevitably appear at the join between ceiling and wall. Dado- or chair-rails were intended to protect walls against being knocked by furniture (in the 18th century it was customary to place chairs and tables round the perimeter of a room, leaving the centre more or less free). The picture rail's purpose is self-evident.

In addition to fulfilling a distinct function, ornamentation was used to alter the proportions of a room or accentuate its features. Ceiling-roses, wall brackets and plaster wall frames introduced additional elements within which different decoration could take place. Dado-rails came to serve a double purpose as it was found that they adjusted the scale of a room, allowing contrasting colours and patterns to be applied above and below. The same is true of the picture rail which, together with the dado, created a tripartite division of the wall which was much favoured by decorators towards the end of the 19th century.

The fixtures and fittings in even a modest room can add up to

Opposite: Flintham in Nottinghamshire, built by T. C. Hine between 1851 and 1854, is a fine example of the High Victorian grandeur to which many lesser homes aspired. The Corinthian columns that frame the library would be out of place in all but the most generously proportioned rooms, but many of the fixtures such as the corbels, brackets and plaster mouldings were echoed in countless humbler dwellings.

Right: With its
magnificently panelled
walls and spirited plaster
moulding on the ceiling,
the drawing-room at
Wightwick Manor near
Wolverhampton draws its
inspiration from the
Elizabethan and Jacobean
periods.

Below: This charming early
Victorian hob, with its
unpretentious overmantle,
shows how simple fixtures
can be put to elegant use
today. Later in the century,
more elaborate register
grates came into
widespread use.

a surprising number. Imagine a small Victorian sitting-room or parlour. The floor may be of simple pine boards, probably wider than most modern examples, or it may be wood strip or parquet. The hearth to the fireplace may be stone or tile, and the fireplace itself will have a surround and a basket grate of some kind, most probably of some mass-produced pattern in cast iron. Close to the fireplace may be the remains of an old bell system with a cranked handle. Then there is the door to the room, its architrave, the skirtings, a dado perhaps, and the window and shutters, if any. There will almost certainly be a cornice in any principal room and possibly decorative ceiling plaster as well.

Despite the stylistic changes that occurred over the century, the basic pattern of the Victorian house remained remarkably consistent. Whatever the size or status of the house, the focus of the building remained the stairwell, hall and upper landings off which the many, often small rooms led. In the great country houses and shooting estates of the landed gentry, the hallway was a grand affair boasting a magnificent fireplace, and possibly an elaborate beamed ceiling with decorative painting. At the other end of the scale, terraced houses had a narrow entrance hall, with a door opening immediately to right or left into a drawing-room or parlour. This arrangement was intended to give the visitor an immediate view of the most impressive room in the house, finished with the finest cornices, fireplace and skirting-boards. The staircase led up straight ahead and past it ran a passage leading to the dining-room and kitchen at the rear. In some of the earlier terraces, a large panelled double door was often used to connect the two principal ground-floor rooms, but this arrangement became less frequent as the century wore on.

Staircase, doors and fireplace were supplied by the builder. Indeed, most of the fixtures of the house including cornices and ceiling roses formed part of the builder's finish. The majority of householders were happy with this ornamentation, which was updated in line with the latest technological advances and supplied an air of fashionable elegance. At the lower end of the scale, ornamentation served to hide the skimped construction of the cheaper houses. As today, ornamentation or 'design' was cheaper than good, solid construction, and since it was to the financial advantage of each member of a production line to follow a tried and tested formula, the finish of many houses was monotonously repetitive. Some features were straight shams. The ubiquitous arch in the hallway and the corbels supporting it were both made of plaster and served no structural purpose. Influential writers and artists decried this trend, but to little avail.

Like 19th-century society, the fixtures and fittings followed hierarchical, not to say patriarchal principles. Decoration was concentrated in the hall, drawing-room, dining-room and the first

Below: As the density of urban housing increased, stained glass was used to ensure privacy and to disguise the proximity of other buildings.

Above: This illustration from the Edinburgh decorators Purdie and Lithgow's 1856 catalogue shows how elaborately the divisions of a wall, from skirting to cornice, could be treated.

flight of stairs. These were the public parts of the house where guests were received and impressions made. The remaining family rooms, such as the bedrooms, were not seen by people that mattered and were furnished and decorated at little expense. In many cases the height of the bedroom storey was sacrificed to achieve a spaciousness in the drawing-room below, and the architectural detailing was reduced. Main bedrooms might have a much simpler cornice than the public rooms, and children's and servants' rooms generally had none at all. The fireplaces shrank in size and were less ornate on the upper storeys, reducing to simpler cast-iron and tiled versions in the main bedrooms and to bare and humble grates in the attic rooms.

The dining-room – often facing west to catch the evening sun – was traditionally 'masculine'. The sombre tone was set by the standard black fireplace; dark, family portraits were traditionally displayed on the walls and dark wood predominated in the furniture. The drawing-room had a white or white-veined marble fireplace, and was decorated in a so-called feminine idiom. 'Feminine' was a licence for ornate cornices and even more ornate furniture and an array of soft furnishings which were felt to exemplify elegant comfort and cosiness.

In Victorian times the services of the house were always of the simplest nature. Electricity, first laid on at Cragside in Northumberland in 1880, was not available to most houses until well into the next century. Some houses may retain the original piping for gas lights, usually concealed in the plasterwork and covered by layers of wallpaper. Plumbing is likely to have been skeletal. Water, in lead pipework, was introduced from the street into the basement or ground floor, to serve the kitchen sink and closet. Piped water was rarely taken above this level until bye-laws made the provision of

water storage in the roof mandatory in 1880. Most existing services found in Victorian houses today are therefore Edwardian or later in origin.

Central heating was found only in the larger and more expensive houses, and reflected the Victorian enthusiasm for invention. Books and magazines of the time reveal a strong market for patented inventions for radiator systems, back boilers, warm-air under-floor heating, and new types of boilers. None, however, supplanted the traditional open fireplace, for that had functions far more significant than the simple process of heating. The Victorians recognized the emotional significance of the hearth as the centre of the home; it is hardly surprising, therefore, that the tiled cast-iron register grates of the period are among the most prized items of architectural salvage today.

PLANNING AHEAD

A Victorian house always has character. It is a quality that comes first and foremost from age, and from the pleasure of rediscovering the past. Anyone walking along a street in any city or town will see examples of buildings awaiting the restorer's hand. Often they have lost the status they once enjoyed, especially if they are no longer lived in as family houses. Many delightful villas set back off the road in wide avenues, now enjoying planting in full maturity, advertise the plight of multi-occupation with six bells by the front door, uncherished drives choked with weeds and parked cars and gates rotting or removed. Inside they may have lost many of their original fixtures and fittings, and acquired unwanted partitions and sinks on the landings. But their original status as a gentleman's residence remains indestructible.

To decorate a Victorian house and make it a comfortable place to live, a great deal of forethought is required, much more than when moving into a modern house. Structural alterations may be needed to adapt the interior layout to modern requirements (see Chapter 8 for the technical aspects). Decisions will be required on which fixtures and fittings to restore or reinstate. Heat, light, power and plumbing facilities may have to be relaid. Even the colour scheme, and whether to paint or paper a wall in one colour, two or three, will be strongly influenced by the architectural detailing of the house.

It is extremely difficult to visualize how a house will be used when all the work has been finished. Surprisingly few decorators and designers use any methodical system for working out the requirements of everyday living. My own method is to prepare a full interior design plan (opposite) before calling in the builders. It can be used both to plan a scheme for fixtures and fittings – the subject of this chapter – and to think ahead to the decoration of the house, discussed from Chapter 4 onwards.

Many people delay in getting builder's estimates because they do not know how they will decorate. This is an unnecessary worry. It is best to think of work on a house as a two-stage operation: building first and decoration second. The first phase takes the house to what may be termed builder's finish, with the interior ready to receive the chosen coat of paint or wallpaper. Decoration can be thought about – and costed – separately. The only important decision to make in advance is whether a room is to be papered or painted, because the sub-preparation will be different in each case.

Before getting down to detail, a question of priorities must be decided. How much importance should be placed on the structure of the building and the internal fixtures, and how much on decoration? My own answer is a simple one. Everybody, whether carrying out their own plan for a house or using a decorator to help them, inevitably has to set themselves a budget. Somewhat against myself, I always argue that the major part of the cost should be spent on the architectural fabric, and that includes the internal architectural detailing. Decoration is secondary. Get the architecture right, and even the simplest decorative schemes work.

The guiding principle in all decoration is, do not do anything that destroys the proportion and form of the original architecture. In a Victorian house the interior architectural features reflect the character and period of the building and are nearly always worth preserving however humble or simple they may be. They are as much an integral part of the architecture as the structure itself. Anyone first viewing a house will find it is prudent to ask the vendor which are fixtures which will go with the house, and which are fittings to be taken away by the owner. Needless to say, doors should come complete with door furniture, but with the rise in value of antique ironmongery the temptation to remove it and

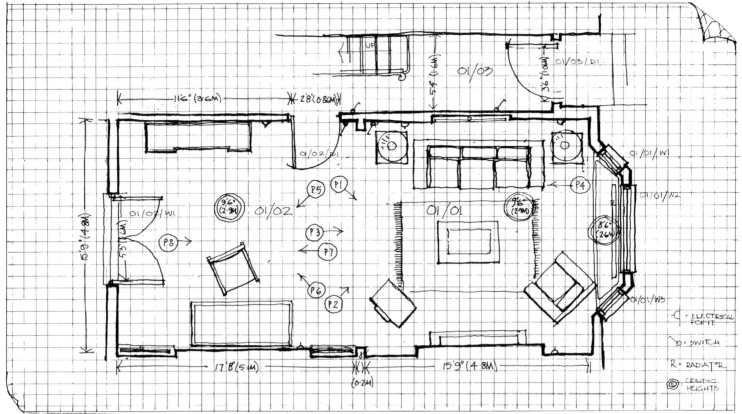

The key to good interior design is a complete floor plan and furniture layout. By working out what furniture you want and where you plan to put it, you will be able to form a fairly exact idea of how you intend to use the house. Once there is a furniture layout, it can be used to work backwards, to plan the infrastructure which will be needed, the wiring, heating, plumbing and all the rest of the 'mechanicals'. At the same time the layout will enable you to look ahead to the final goal, the fully decorated house.

My own approach to any house is first to draw up a proper floor plan, with measurements marked on it. The simplest method is to use graph paper, first setting a scale. In the centre of each room, I put a circle with the ceiling height on it. If the ceiling height alters, say under a bay window, I note that fact in the appropriate spot. Next I mark any existing electrical points and radiators. I also like to note which way the doors are hinged, and whether they open inwards or outwards.

Once I have completed the floor plan, I photograph every room, numbering each shot and marking its direction on the plan with a small arrow. I take a photograph of each window for the curtain-maker.

Then I number each room, door and window on the floor plan, so that I have a quick method of reference. A number of systems will do equally well. My own is to number floor level first, then give each room its number, rather like the system in many hotels – basement 00, ground floor 01 and so on upwards. This might yield the number 02/01 for the master bedroom and I would add the number of each window and door to the same series: 02/01/W1/W2/D1 and so on. Alternatively, start with the basement B, the ground floor G and number on upwards from there.

Once the house is mapped out on paper, with doors and windows numbered, and room sizes, ceiling heights, electrical points and radiators noted, I make three lists of furniture. The first contains items that will definitely be used: furniture to be moved from the owner's old house and pieces that have been bought specially for the new home. The second list is more tentative: items that may be used if they fit and seem appropriate. The third list covers items of furniture that will need to be acquired.

Now I mark on the floor plan the kind of furniture layout that might be expected, using a different colour for items from each of the three lists. Then I can see at a glance what is available for a particular room and what is still needed. This layout phase requires the most detailed thought.

Now, on a separate set of plans, I mark the intended position of electrical services and wiring, and on another I make the radiator plan. These drawings are not intended as great works of art but purely as an *aide mémoire* for the householder which may later be passed on to builder or architect. But they do have the great merit of tightening up one's view of the house.

A carefully prepared plan should also help with decisions about changing the structure of the house or altering the fixtures and fittings. Does a door need to be moved to accommodate a fitted wardrobe? Should the swing of a door be reversed? Is a door needed at all? What will the circulation patterns be when the house is occupied? Would it be a good idea to provide an additional exit into the garden? The answers to all these questions become much more evident when you are able to look coolly at a piece of paper.

Now, and only now, you can begin to think in detail about decoration.

replace it with cheap new fittings may be irresistible to the greedy. The same is true for taps, shower fittings, cupboard furniture, curtain fittings, even fireplace surrounds and decorative tiling. Some vendors are quite unscrupulous and have been known to remove handles, knockers, door scrapers and so on just before they leave, to the irritation of the incoming householder.

Of course, today it is increasingly rare to find a house with very many original interior details still in place. Either they were swept away by 'modernization' during the 1950s and 1960s or they have been badly mauled during past conversions into flats or bedsitters.

Before carrying out any extensive repair or restoration work it is a good idea to use the interior design plan to catalogue, room by room, what remains that is worth preserving and what missing features might reasonably be replaced. Think of the relative ease or difficulty of replacement: replacing broken stained glass in a door or window, for instance, may be done at leisure, whereas the repair of broken cornices, worn flooring or wood panelling will only cause disruption if delayed until the house is occupied.

Deciding which features to restore is not simply a question of cost or practicality. Some kind of cornice, however simple, is important to get the best out of a room; likewise a fireplace, which gives a focus and personality to a room. The reinstallation of a handsome chimneypiece is a good starting point and, with the cornice, will establish a character from which all other decoration will ultimately derive. The standard, Victorian four-panelled door is also an essential feature of a well finished house. Such doors are frequently found in skips, or can be bought from salvage yards. Sometimes they were made of pitch pine, which when stripped has a wonderful grain and retains its characteristic pine smell.

The other fittings that formed an integral part of a Victorian interior, such as door furniture, handles, locks and escutcheons, can be reinstated at a later date. The perfectionist will even want to go into such details as door hinges, window handles and remnants of old curtain fixings. Attractive finger plates, for instance, may be found quite by chance in an antique shop. Whether the list leans to the practical or decorative side will vary with the individual: many houses are bought for impulsive reasons, and what may seem frivolous to one buyer may be crucial to another. There are no rules in restoration, only a few guidelines which may be of help to the inexperienced. It is important above all that the design should be essentially personal.

ALTERATIONS

The Victorians were more formal in their social habits than we are today. They preferred many small rooms with different purposes whereas we are often more at ease in an open, multi-functional living space. Nevertheless, in spite of the arrival of the motor car, the television and modern kitchen gadgetry, our lives have not altered all that much, and a Victorian house will meet most of our needs extremely well with only minor alteration. We still need a living-room, bedrooms, kitchen, bathroom and garden. We no longer need a scullery (it vanished along with the scullery maid), but we can convert it into a utility room; nor do we need a parlour, but we can knock that into the living-room. Instead of having wardrobes, we fill in corners and alcoves with fitted cupboards. We need another bathroom, so we convert one of the bedrooms.

The chief problem in adapting Victorian houses to modern living occurs in small terraced houses and some larger ones where, in an effort to create an air of spaciousness and light, the wall between the front and back rooms on the ground floor is often removed to create one through room with large windows at either end. The result is generally a long thin space with two doors, which is not infrequently difficult to heat and awkward to decorate. Attempts to give two dissimilar rooms some contemporary homogeneity are frequently unsuccessful. In the section below on the styling of through rooms I have suggested solutions to some of these problems. Not unusually the wall that has to be removed is the principal structural cross wall of the house, and considerable engineering work is necessary to provide a replacement (see Chapter 8).

Less drastic is a change I often advocate in reception rooms, where the swing of the door may be reversed. Victorian doors always opened inwards into rooms, and swung not back towards the nearest wall, but out 'against' the room, blocking the view so that servants could withdraw

if unwanted, before they could see what the occupants were doing. In bedrooms this practice is retained today, but in other rooms many now prefer to open the door against a wall and so provide a more spacious feel to the house.

Sometimes the position of a door may need to be changed, especially if it is close to an end wall where a built-in cupboard could be installed. By moving the door along 2 feet (60 cm) space can be obtained for the cupboard, but the skirting-board and dado-rail, if there is one, will have to be moved too, as will any light switch. This is just the sort of decision that must be taken early, before building work begins.

THE STYLING OF THROUGH ROOMS

Knocking through the two ground-floor rooms in a terraced house is the most drastic departure we are likely to make from the original architecture of our Victorian forebears (see the technical discussion in Chapter 8). By using the architectural detailing of the period, however, it is possible to make the opening look an integral part of the house.

Victorians generally had double doors in the opening between the two reception-rooms. These tend to be most inconvenient. When folded back there always seems to be a piece of furniture standing in the way. If major work is to be done to the house, and double doors seem suitable between two rooms, then a solution may be to build a false wall with a new cornice around it in one of the rooms, so the doors can slide into the

space created between the old and new walls.

If doors are not wanted, the opening may still be constructed like an enlarged door frame, with architrave to match the other door openings.

Sometimes, the two rooms to be linked are so small that there is a strong desire to make the opening as large as possible. It is very difficult to take an arch right up to the ceiling. Because space has to be left for a supporting beam, the arch generally stops about 1 foot to 18 inches (30 or 45 cm) below cornice level, so the cornices in each room stay separate. This is preferable since normally they do not match; the room at the front will generally have the grander fixtures and fittings.

An arched opening may be embellished with plaster corbels. Although serving no structural purpose, they *(continued on page 112)*

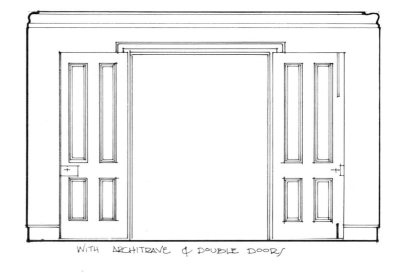

WITH ARCHITRAVE & DOUBLE DOORS

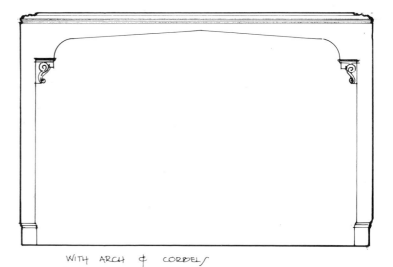

WITH ARCH & CORBELS

SERVICES

The provision of plumbing, central heating and wiring in a Victorian house requires just as much forethought as the fixtures and fittings. Not having been included in the house originally, these services are likely to have been installed in a piecemeal fashion, at the whim of various contractors and owners over the years, and they may well not suit the patterns of use now envisaged.

There is no reason to attempt to preserve the old plumbing and wiring found in an un-modernized house. Most of it will be post-Victorian, and either in poor condition or unsafe. Where cast-iron radiators have survived, flushing and cleaning can extend their life, but the old steel large-bore pipework should be discarded and replaced with copper.

Original gas piping, if intact, may be restored and used, though such a relish for authenticity is likely to attract only the most fervent period enthusiast. Gas provides a very agreeable light source, soft and white, and is accompanied by a faint hissing; but in terms of convenience it is no rival for electricity. There is no reason, however, why a single room or perhaps two should not be provided with this form of illumination, run as an occasional pleasure in much the same way as an open fire.

(continued from page 111) are no more false than the corbels found 'supporting' the arch in the hall. For the sake of symmetry, care should be taken to ensure that any brick pillars supporting the cross beam project equal distances from the side walls. In large houses it may be possible to give extra style to an opening by introducing pilasters or even slim cast iron columns with decorative capitals.

When two rooms have been knocked through into one, many people choose to seal up the door between hall and front room and use instead the door to what was the back room. Usually the hinges will be on the side of the door nearest the back of the house. As the door opens it offers a wide view towards the front of the house and the main fireplace.

An alternative is to seal up the door to the original back room and then, in place of the ordinary-sized door from the hall into the front room, open up a big double doorway. The new door space can be left open so that on entering the house the visitor sees the whole of the hall and sitting-room.

Each room originally had its own fireplace, but it scarcely seems worth keeping two in what has become a single through-room. If the chimneypiece in the back room has gone, one solution is to cover the whole wall with shelving, including the chimney breast. If shelves are made deeper than the recesses, they cross the chimney breast; with skirting taken through at the bottom, and a cornice at the top, there will be a sense of continuity. Another alternative is simply to shelve the recesses and leave the chimney breast bare. A large piece of furniture serves the same purpose as a fireplace in providing a focal point.

Generally through rooms are best treated as a single unit when decorating, with floor and wall surfaces the same. Apart from that, symmetry may be ignored. Hang a chandelier in each room – they do not have to match – or in one and not the other. Chimneypieces, area rugs and seating styles can also be different.

WITH DECORATIVE GRILLE

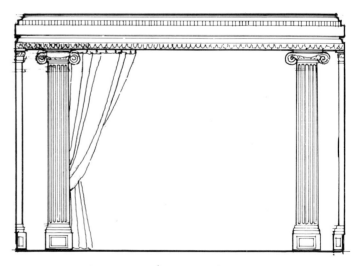

WITH PILASTERS & COLUMNS

WIRING

The wiring plan for a house should be worked out from the interior design plan and furniture layout. The positions of beds, sofa, easy chair and kitchen table will determine where reading and working lights ought to be.

Many people believe their problems will be solved if they put in enough 13-amp power points, but this may not be the answer. Apart from the vacuum cleaner, television, washing machine and electric blanket (and, of course, kitchen equipment) not many appliances today need to be run off 13-amp plugs. My preference is to limit the number of plugs and increase the number of switched lighting points. These are normally five-amp sockets on one continuous circuit controlled from the door of a room. If the circuit is to be dimmed, add up the number of lamps that might be used on one of these circuits and tell the electrician what the load is likely to be, as dimmers do vary in size.

The best place for the lighting circuit is behind the skirting-board. This low-level arrangement allows table and standing lamps to be connected at the most convenient points. Later, if a wall or picture light is needed, the wiring can be run straight up the wall and chased into the plaster with a minimum of damage. For replica Victorian light fittings, brass ducting fixed to the surface of the wall is practical and effective.

Even with a properly prepared furniture layout, it is difficult to foresee all necessary wiring. To decide where to put switches, and which lights have to turn on where, try walking around the house at night, torch in hand, and see where you have to turn the torch on. That is where you need a switch. If you are uncertain where the television will go, cater for every likely position. The cost of wiring at the outset is not prohibitive, but the cost of alterations later can be. The same is true of the sound system. For the sake of flexibility and neatness, it is well worth running concealed speaker cables to several spots.

The doorbell is one of the easiest items to overlook. It should probably ring in the kitchen as well as at the front door so that it is not drowned by the noise of kitchen machinery.

It is also worth giving attention to the placing of controls. An electrician, acting without instructions, is likely to site the central heating thermostat at eye level in the middle of the drawing-room wall and to put the doorbell in the most visible place in the hall. Many burglar alarm control panels are in impossible places because they have been sited as an afterthought. Door entry-phones, and even more so the new TV door entry-phones, should be tactfully placed. The fuse box should be a system of modern circuit breakers placed at eye level in a cupboard with its own separate lighting supply that comes on when the door is opened.

The following people and perhaps some others besides may all need to put in wiring: an electrician, telephone engineer, heating engineer, sound system engineer, security firm and intercom expert. To avoid the constant lifting of floorboards or the confusion of a multitude of different tradesmen on site simultaneously, it is possible – if wiring runs are planned early – to install plastic ducts down which wires may be threaded by each individual expert in turn.

By avoiding unsightly cables and power points, the effort that goes into good architectural detailing in a Victorian house will not be wasted and the result will be modern facilities with period charm.

HEATING

By using an interior design plan, it is possible to work out the best positions for radiators in advance. Pipes can then be laid when other works are being carried out.

The traditional cast iron radiators were handsomely designed and well suited to Victorian interiors. Modern replicas are available in both pressed steel and cast iron. Cast iron has a marvellous grainy finish and looks better, but pressed steel is half the price. These radiators closely resemble the originals, but they run on modern small-bore heating systems.

Radiators should not generally be boxed in unless there is a functional reason for doing so, such as their position under a window seat. Where radiators are placed under bookcases in a recess, they would look strange if not boxed in.

All Victorian houses with central heating had the boiler at the bottom of the house close to the point of coal delivery. This remains the usual site for boilers, but with gas-fired heating other positions are possible.

Equally there is no good reason to run the whole of a house on the same central heating system. In most homes the heating runs all day in cold weather and is turned off at night. But some people prefer to keep their bedrooms warm at night. The answer is to have the upper floors of the house on one circuit and the lower floors on another, with two separate pumps (or alternatively a single pump with two sets of motorized valves), two thermostats, and two time clocks. In this way the house can be zoned so that the heating goes on and off upstairs or downstairs when required.

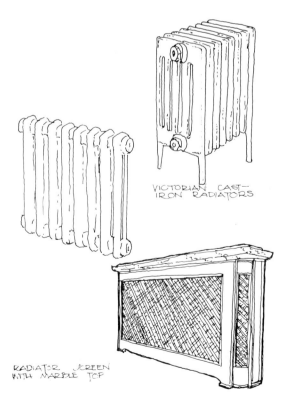

VICTORIAN CAST-IRON RADIATORS

RADIATOR SCREEN WITH MARBLE TOP

HALLS, STAIRS AND LANDINGS

Opposite: A grand newel post at the foot of an otherwise mean staircase provides a strong and unmistakably Victorian accent in an American hall. North America, under French influence and the native woodworking tradition, produced halls that were brighter and much more elegant than their British counterparts.

Below: In this generously proportioned hall the staircase turns three times between ground and first floor, and the Gothic-style door closes into a standard square-arched frame to which a shaped header has been added. Parquet flooring was a common alternative to encaustic tiles in larger hallways.

Today, with our less visible pollutions, we forget that a hall once had to act as a *cordon sanitaire* between a comfortable indoors and a horse-driven, pea-soup fog world outside. A hall also had to impress the visitor and set the tone for entry into the public rooms. Despite the fact that many hallways in terraced houses were poorly lit, often only by a fanlight above the door, dark colours were widely used. They lent an air of authority to what were often thin party walls and, along with the encaustic tiles and marbleized papers, gave an impression of security to resident and visitor alike.

For the walls of the urban terraced hall, Victorians favoured hard-wearing materials. The most common mid-19th-century covering for the hall dado was a series of marbleized paper slabs which were stuck on to scored plasterwork in blocks. These paper oblongs could be replaced singly if any damage occurred. Not all Victorians favoured this effect, however; Charles Eastlake's

Hints on Household Taste of 1865, which was a compilation of articles that had first appeared in the women's journal the *Queen*, attacked this aping of palatial marble panels as an ugly and unnecessary delusion of grandeur in the hallway of an ordinary house. Eastlake favoured encaustic tiles, which were washable and hard-wearing, both for the floor and also as a wall covering to a height of about three or four feet. The most common dado covering in the second half of the century was leather-paper or anaglypta, an embossed and strengthened paper.

The fact that a hall is not a room where you spend much time gives you a little liberty to decorate with extravagant colour schemes, using a profusion of colours and patterns that is exciting when passing through but would become infuriating in a room in which you wanted to work or relax. Another difference is that the wall divisions in a hall are related to people standing.

Given the narrowness of some halls, it is questionable whether any furniture is needed beyond hat-and-coat-rack and umbrella-stand. The hall table of the Victorians with a salver for visiting cards and a drawer for a clothes brush flanked by two chairs, or a bench with a wooden seat for waiting tradesmen, may not quite tally with a modern lifestyle. Nowadays a shelf over the radiator with a looking-glass above may serve for all purposes.

Relatively narrow halls were given fireplaces, and their minimal size needed all the support it could get from draught excluders to keep the staircase warm. A cold staircase inhibits movement and makes for a house divided against itself, creating a sense of claustrophobia. The area immediately inside the front door is sometimes divided off from hall and stairs by glass-panelled double doors. Like so much else in the Victorian house, this arrangement worked

on three levels: the social, the aesthetic and the functional. A lobby or vestibule was a regular feature in grand houses, and thus lent status and dignity to a humbler dwelling. The vestibule doors are often an attractive feature in their own right, with fine carving and elegant bevelled, frosted or stained glass, and the division improves the proportions of a long, narrow hallway which might otherwise seem like an endless corridor. This second set of doors also served as a draught excluder, often supplemented by a heavy curtain, and the lobby provided a useful space for coat-hooks and umbrella-stands.

The living-hall revived by the Arts and Crafts Movement was a rather different kind of entrance. In essence a modest great hall, harking back to medieval origins, it was strictly more of a living-room than a hall. William Morris hated the precious clutter of the mid-century drawing-room; in a living-hall simplicity was the theme. The focus of the room was the inglenook with its welcoming, wide hearth, and broad low seats.

The decoration was plain, dominated by woodwork and heavily reliant on local brick or stone which served, undressed, for the hearth and inglenook. By the end of the century, the living-hall was frequently invaded by the clutter from which it originally provided an escape. Voysey complained that many a hall was full of 'vulgar glitter and display', a 'vast expanse of advertisement' that reminded him of a railway station.

A hybrid living-hall and great hall became part of the basic vocabulary of villas and smaller country houses from the 1880s onwards, lined with dark woods, filled with museum-like displays of trophies and decorated in a vaguely 'Jacobethan' manner, a revivalist mix of Elizabethan and Jacobean styles. The ceiling would be relatively low and might be elaborately plastered with strapwork detailing or left as open oak beams. A porch with a staircase leading off it fulfilled the strictly utilitarian functions of insulating the front-door area, with all its comings and goings, from the rest of the house.

Stairs were generally of wood in the south-east of England, and were often elaborately decorated, even in quite ordinary houses, with a mahogany handrail, turned balusters and prominent newel posts. Of the many different baluster designs, 'spindle' was the commonest, largely because it was easy to mass-produce on a lathe. Stone staircases were common north of Leeds and west of Ludlow. They are most often found in the kind of large Victorian house now converted into flats. Metal staircases as a rule occur only in the grandest Victorian houses and were normally reserved for external use, or hidden away for the servants.

The simplest way to deal with the stairs and landings of the terraced house is to run the same colours and carpet from top to bottom. This will supply a basic unity within which to arrange decorative features, built-in cupboards, pictures and furniture. Old-fashioned stair-runners with brass rods remain the most attractive way to treat wooden or stone staircases. However, narrow and more cheaply-made stairs may look better with

(continued on page 122)

Below: These attractive stone stairs at Cragside in Northumberland are enlivened by the thin band of tiles at the bottom of each riser.

Left: The blue tiles on this staircase at Leighton House in Holland Park, London, date from 1866 and combine beauty with resistance to wear.

Above: Pugin's staircase at the Speaker's House in the Palace of Westminster is a classic example of High Victorian style.

Opposite: First-floor landings were relatively large, as it was here that the hostess would greet her guests as they came up the stairs to the drawing-room.

Above: Stairwells can be more excitingly exploited for both storage and display than is achieved by the usual row of prints on the wall.

Right: Decorative schemes should give landings and staircases a warm and friendly aspect, so that they become extra living spaces for the family. In this country cottage with ledged and braced doors, fretwork motifs in the Victorian manner have been used successfully for both the balusters and boxed-in radiator.

(continued from page 118)

fitted carpet: the narrowness will make the rods seem awkward, and the wood may not be strong enough to hold the fasteners for the rods. Except when graining or marbling is used, skirting and the edges of the stairs are best painted the same colour; this will add to the sense of height.

On the top landing, where the balusters meet the floor above the last flight of stairs, it is often difficult to finish the carpet neatly. The best method is to abut the carpet against a strip of flat moulding cut to the width of the handrail and laid in front of the balusters.

If you need to build an additional flight of stairs, say to a newly converted loft, it is worth searching for balusters that match those in the original staircase. Alternatively, remove every other baluster in one of the lower flights, fill the gaps with square planed timber balusters and continue the design in the new flight of stairs, alternating plain and turned balusters in the same way. When you are building an entirely new staircase, the designs shown opposite may prove helpful in planning an attractive scheme.

Another feature that benefits from close attention to detail is the doormat inside the front door. The bigger the mat, the better it will look. The best treatment is to sink it into a mat-well. Suitable matting can be bought in rubber-backed rolls and cut to fit. In a wooden floor the well should be lined with wood, and in a tiled floor with tile. In carpeted floors, carpet can be turned over the edge of the well to form a lining. Where a hall is divided by vestibule doors, the entire lobby can be carpeted with matting.

Long, thin landings and halls pose special challenges. For many years, designers have been tackling the apparent endlessness of corridors in the larger hotels by incorporating arches, columns and alcoves. Some of these ideas can be applied in a domestic setting. Alternatively, if a long corridor leads to just one bedroom, it can be shortened and the space incorporated into the room, forming an inner entrance hall.

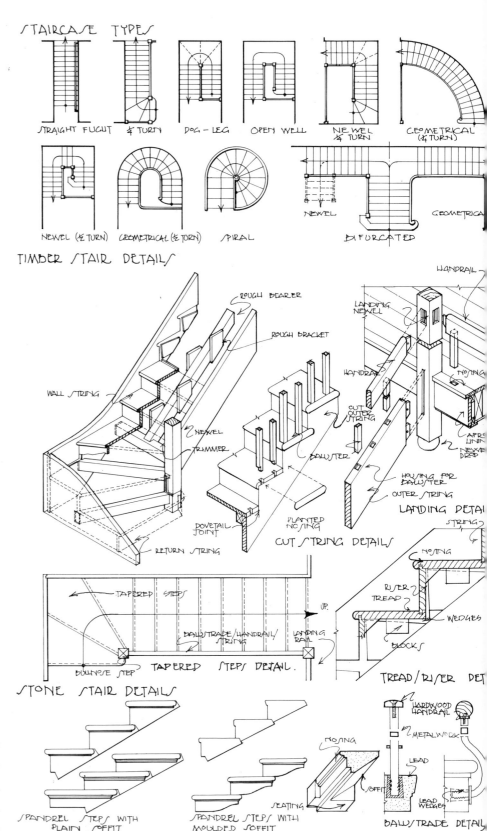

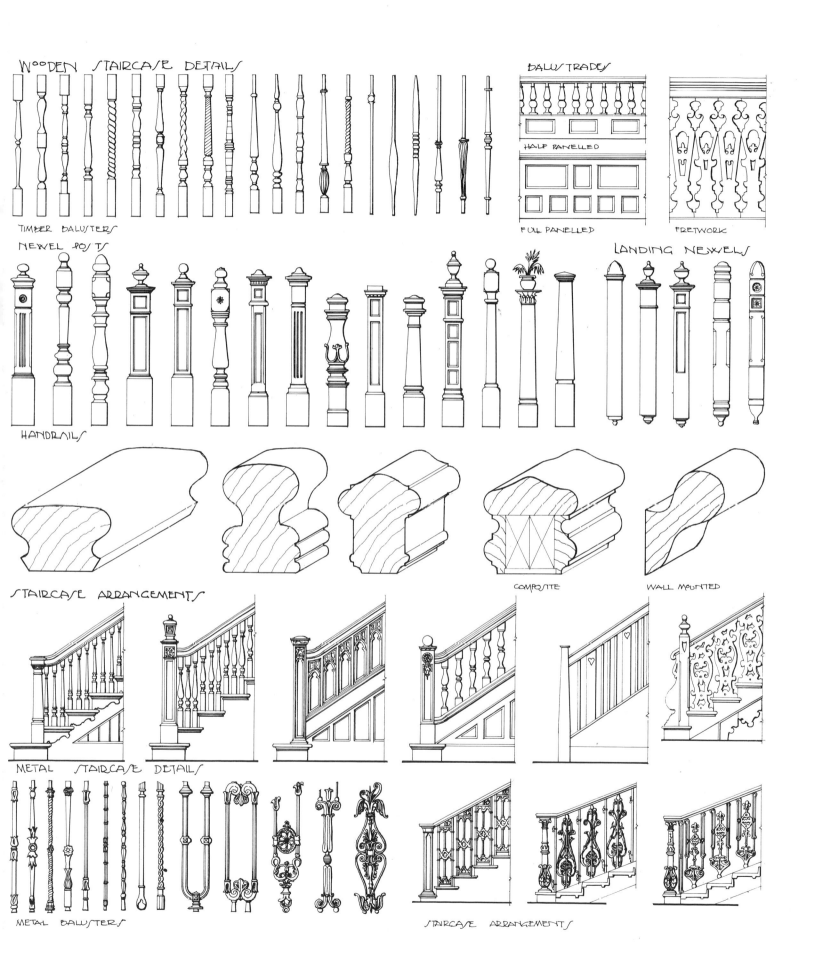

WOODEN STAIRCASE DETAILS

BALUSTRADES

HALF PANELLED

FULL PANELLED

FRETWORK

TIMBER BALUSTERS

NEWEL POSTS

LANDING NEWELS

HANDRAILS

COMPOSITE

WALL MOUNTED

STAIRCASE ARRANGEMENTS

METAL STAIRCASE DETAILS

METAL BALUSTERS

STAIRCASE ARRANGEMENTS

123

INTERIOR WALLS, CEILINGS AND THEIR DRESSINGS

Beginning at the skirting-board and moving upwards, a Victorian wall is made up of a dado and dado-rail; the filling or main body of the wall; a picture rail, or simply a horizontal band of paint or paper; above that the frieze, and finally the cornice which can be very simple or grandiloquent depending on the pretensions of the room.

Skirting was generally made of wood; its North American name, 'mop-board', keeps the utilitarian meaning of a surface which protects the wall when the floor is being washed or polished. Oak was for the top end of the market; painted, grained or marbled softwood or plaster was more usual.

The dado-rail had largely lost its function as a buffer between the wall and furniture by the Victorian era. It was retained as a decorative feature since it marked off a section of the wall that could take a different decoration from the

Opposite: The elaborate plaster-work on the cornice of this dining-room is a spirited pastiche of the fan- and pendant-vaults of the Perpendicular style. The cuspated ogee over the niche echoes the earlier Decorated style of Gothic; the way its leafy finial breaks into the cornice is a nice touch, bringing the niche forward and into the room.

Right: A ceiling-rose need not necessarily be the suspension point for a light fitting, but can look effective simply as an ornamental centrepiece. Whereas the Victorians often wished to be rid of the ubiquitous rose, most people today prefer to keep it as a valued period detail.

filling, reducing the monotony of the main wallpaper. The leather-paper or anaglypta generally used for this section of the wall was designed in imitation of the wooden dadoes of the Georgian period. Of course, wooden dadoes still continued, and in the 1890s the Aesthetic Movement introduced other alternatives, including matting and even Japanese fans. Walter Crane's designs for dado papers rejected the bland solidity of anaglypta and leather-paper, introducing more highly decorative patterns, but the excesses of the Aesthetic Movement gave the idea of an excitingly decorated dado a bad name, and tame 'Jacobethan' designs on leather-paper never had a serious rival.

Cornices are best considered as part of the wall and not the ceiling. In 18th-century houses, a cornice was often made of wood; by the Victorian era, plaster-work cornicing was mass-produced and arrived on site in standard lengths. These off-the-peg designs were made of solid or semi-solid plaster; simpler cornices, used in bedrooms, were 'run' on site. The plasterer mixed the plaster wet, and then ran a template with the chosen profile over it to form the finished moulding.

A Victorian cornice was often painted in several colours picking out different bands of motifs and relating to the colours used on the wall; the most elaborate designs had gilding applied. The multi-coloured cornice is the key to many Victorian rooms; surviving cornices, unfortunately, are almost always clogged with paint, leaving few details visible. Cleaning off the paint is a labour-intensive operation; with a very good cornice this may be a rewarding effort, but with a run-of-the-mill Victorian moulding, probably not. Painting with a single colour may then be the best solution. Above all, if you have a cornice, keep it. The very simplest moulding is valuable to soften the bleak right angle between wall and ceiling.

Even the most modest terrace house came complete with ceiling-roses. The rose gave a centre to the room; from it hung gas lighting or chandelier. As well as these roses, a 'builder's finish' might include subsidiary ceiling plaster-work. Ordinary wallpapers, or special ceiling-papers with a circular repeat, were taken right up to the edge of the rose; the rose itself was picked out in colours complementary to the wallpaper.

For the ceiling of a modest Victorian drawing-room, two colours are all that is necessary, as it rarely receives much scrutiny. Professional decorators of the late-19th century advised against a white ceiling: it tended to show off the inevitable cracks and had the distressing effect of making the rest of the room seem dirty. Victorian decorators either papered or painted it a lighter shade of the same colour as the walls.

Plaster ornaments were the cheapest form of decoration available to the builder, and once installed the landlord would not be keen for the householder to remove them. Much of Victorian decorating was finding ways to make a virtue of necessity. Today, we can suppress a ceiling-rose or moulding whereas a Victorian decorator had to spend effort rendering them inoffensive when a room was not to have a central suspended light, even going so far as putting up a second 'canvas plaster' ceiling to hide the original one.

Opposite, right: A florid coffered ceiling with applied decoration evokes the Rococo era. The pictures hang from brass picture rods.

Opposite, far right: The rich reds and gold of this ceiling, with its Tudor rose and scrolls, combine to produce a particularly lively piece of Victorian historical fantasy.

Opposite, right: Sometimes a relatively plain cornice was edged by an elaborate ceiling frieze; like the cornices, they were made from pre-cast panels, and are here left unpainted after laborious cleaning with a proprietary paint stripper.

Opposite, far right: An attractive sunflower motif lends a simple grace to this ceiling frieze.

Left: This typical Victorian hallway still has its original skirting, dado and richly painted cornice, as well as a small fireplace and gas wall lights.

THE ANATOMY OF WALLS & CEILINGS

PLASTER WALL & CEILING DRESSINGS

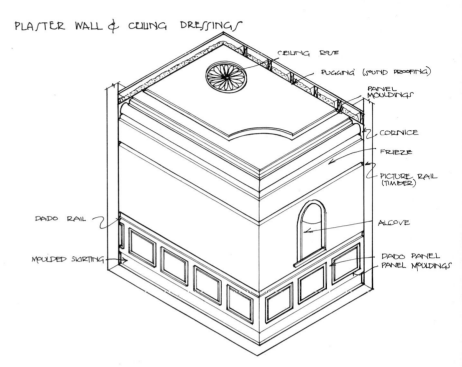

CEILING ROSE
PUGGING (SOUND PROOFING)
PANEL MOULDINGS
CORNICE
FRIEZE
PICTURE RAIL (TIMBER)
ALCOVE
DADO RAIL
MOULDED SKIRTING
DADO PANEL
PANEL MOULDINGS

TYPICAL FIXING DETAILS

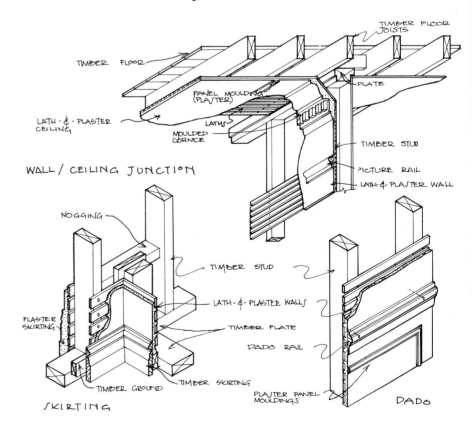

TIMBER FLOOR JOISTS
TIMBER FLOOR
PLATE
PANEL MOULDING (PLASTER)
LATH-&-PLASTER CEILING
LATHS
MOULDED CORNICE
TIMBER STUD
PICTURE RAIL
LATH-&-PLASTER WALL

WALL/CEILING JUNCTION

NOGGING
TIMBER STUD
LATH-&-PLASTER WALLS
PLASTER SKIRTING
TIMBER PLATE
DADO RAIL
TIMBER GROUND
TIMBER SKIRTING
PLASTER PANEL MOULDINGS

SKIRTING

DADO

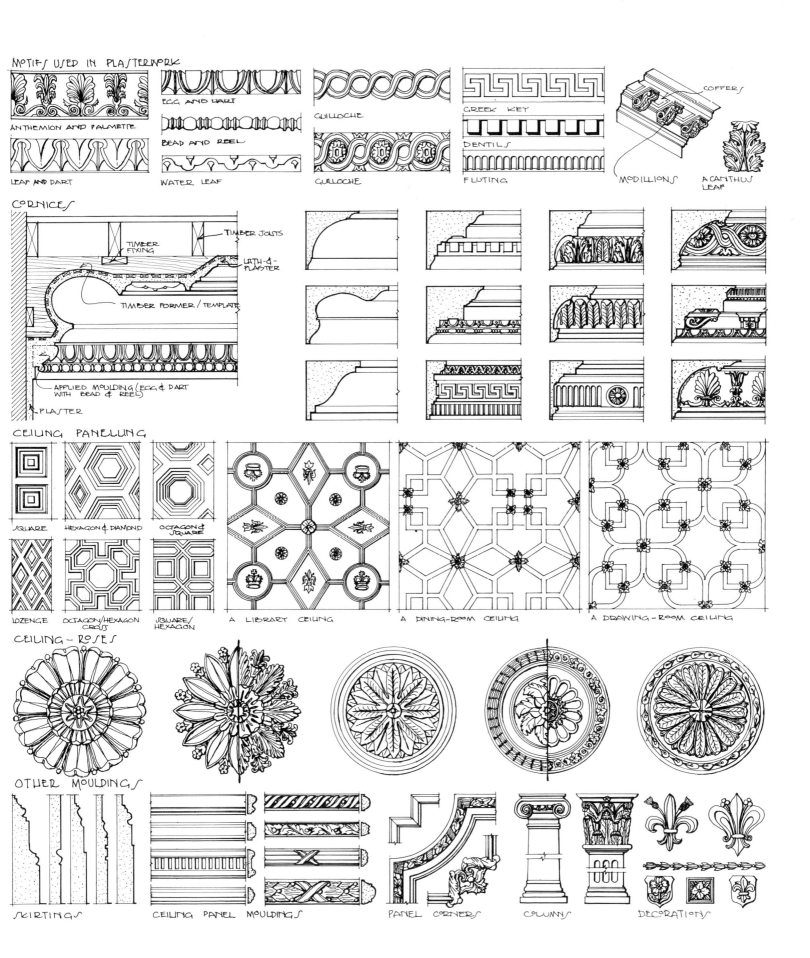

MOTIFS USED IN PLASTERWORK

ANTHEMION AND PALMETTE

LEAF AND DART

EGG AND DART

BEAD AND REEL

WATER LEAF

GUILLOCHE

GUILLOCHE

GREEK KEY

DENTILS

FLUTING

COFFERS

MODILLIONS

ACANTHUS LEAF

CORNICES

TIMBER JOISTS

TIMBER FIXING

LATH-&-PLASTER

TIMBER FORMER / TEMPLATE

APPLIED MOULDING (EGG & DART WITH BEAD & REEL)

PLASTER

CEILING PANELLING

SQUARE

HEXAGON & DIAMOND

OCTAGON & SQUARE

LOZENGE

OCTAGON/HEXAGON CROSS

SQUARE/ HEXAGON

A LIBRARY CEILING

A DINING-ROOM CEILING

A DRAWING-ROOM CEILING

CEILING-ROSES

OTHER MOULDINGS

SKIRTINGS

CEILING PANEL MOULDINGS

PANEL CORNERS

COLUMNS

DECORATIONS

JOINERY

At the back of the Victorian mind there was a nostalgia for oak-panelled rooms with oak doors. The ever-popular *Mansions of England in the Olden Time* by Joseph Nash (1845) carried illustrations of 16th- and 17th-century oak-lined halls, studies and dining-rooms. Originally, panelling was simply the most economical way of covering the walls; until well into the 18th century, plaster-work was expensive. By the 19th century, however, plaster had become the most cheap and reliable finish, and wooden panelling an expensive status symbol.

The Victorians developed various methods of simulating panelling at a lower cost. The anaglypta wallpaper used below the dado-rail, where the Georgians would have panelled, was often embossed with wood-grain patterns. By the 1880s thick veneers glued on to heavy cloth were available as ready-made panelled wainscoting.

Full-height panelling of the Gothic Revival or the Old English style was rare for most of the 19th century, partly because of the cost but no doubt also because large areas of dark wood made a room heavy and gloomy. Towards the end of the century, however, the new class of industrial barons, wishing to create estates that would compete with the stately homes of England, found the solidity of heavy wood panelling a congenial expression of their aspirations. The introduction of electric lighting meant that timber-lined rooms did not have to be gloomy, and panelled hallways, studies and dining-rooms enjoyed a revival. Oak, with its connotations of tradition and patriotism, was regarded as the most desirable wood. Similar considerations led some wealthy clients to commission linenfold panelling, an elaborate and costly Elizabethan pattern in which each panel was carved to resemble folded linen.

The Queen Anne revival introduced painted panel-work, usually finished in an off-white which complemented bright chintzes or William Morris wallpapers. The smallish, square panels ran three quarters of the way up the wall, and the top provided a superb shelf to display china ornaments. The light and airy aspect of Queen Anne rooms owes a lot to the large expanses of white woodwork.

Although panelling had attractive historical precedents, its practical advantages should not be forgotten. It provided extra sound-proofing and insulation, and in passageways its easy-to-clean paintwork was an asset. The introduction of machine-cut tongue-and-groove boarding made painted panels a cheap solution to architectural problems, in particular, the shuttering off of the space under the ground-floor stairs or in attics, where damp might need to be kept out.

Under the influence of the Arts and Crafts Movement, with its celebration of the skills of the carpenter and joiner, Edwardian woodwork became significantly more exciting than Victorian. Also the importation of cheaper hardwoods from Amazonia and Burma towards the end of the century encouraged more adventurous joinery, as did the change from leasehold to freehold tenure, which made serious home improvements worthwhile.

Rich and poor alike enjoyed what is to us the luxury of panelled or tongue-and-groove doors. Before the days of mass-produced plywood and building boards, these were the only practical ways of putting together a large enough piece of wood to cover a door opening. Even the humblest Victorian door was a complex piece of skilled joinery. The frame was mortised and tenoned together, and grooved on the inside to receive the panels. The vertical members on either side were called styles; the horizontals, rails; and the vertical pieces which ran up the middle between the rails were known as muntings. Most doors had four panels, although six was not unusual. The edges of the panels were often *(continued on page 134)*

Opposite: This door, in what the Victorians called a tack room, has tongue-and-groove boarding to fill the large panels, a style of joinery that was normally restricted to the more functional parts of a house, and to institutional buildings where large doors were necessary. Sometimes the boarding was placed diagonally inside the panels, producing a highly decorative effect.

Left: A ledged door hides the staircase in this Victorian cottage. The long iron hinges and thumb-latch are typical of 19th-century rustic building, as is the decorative carved bracket of the high mantelshelf.

Above: The arched doorways of a grand entrance hall, opening on to a magnificently panelled interior, reveal Victorian joinery at its most accomplished, with panelling inside the door frame and elaborate carving above.

(continued from page 130)
beaded. There were several types of tongue-and-groove boarding – also called match boarding or cleating – in use. The simplest consisted of plain matched boards with flush edges. The more decorative types had a V-shaped groove cut into the joint, or were beaded at the joint on one or both sides of the board.

The ideal Victorian door was oak; solid, soundproof, authoritative. The more common reality was painted softwood. Ordinary doors were therefore grained in imitation of hardwoods, and stencilling might also be applied to imitate marquetry. The upstairs doors would probably not have been grained, though lighter stencilled forms sometimes decorated the

panels. Doors in the kitchen or back-quarters might be the cheaper ledged doors, which were five tongue-and-groove boards held by two back bars and diagonal bracing and sometimes strengthened with a frame.

This type of door made in oak was the only proper door for the Arts and Crafts cottage. It had a thumb latch and hinges that stretched along both front and back. These hinges, in the hands of Voysey, for example, became highly elaborate decorative features.

In the last few decades many panelled doors have been removed and replaced by the characterless flush door. Reinstating a handsome panelled door acquired from an architectural salvage yard can quickly give some prestige back

Above left: In this charming example of Queen Anne revival panelling, the shelves and dressers have been left in natural wood to look like free-standing furniture. The skirting has been continued around each dresser to complete a most effective treatment.

Above: The entrance hall of Wightwick Manor illustrates the Victorian taste for 'Jacobethan' panelling.

to a room. From the same salvage yard, you may well be able to buy the odds and ends of panelling from which to rebuild rooms.

Panelling can be used to unify a difficult room. It can also be overpowering, though, and if not used carefully may overwhelm any authentic subtleties. The height and size of the panels is more an architectural question than one of furnishing, and relates to the proportions of the room rather than to anything in it. If plain, polished wood is to be used, then it should be old wood adapted to its new situation. If the panelling is less than first-rate it should be painted, as should new timber. If you are mixing old and new timber, it should be painted or stained to give it a consistent look.

Left: A light and vigorous sunflower motif designed by Pugin is one of the pleasant surprises to be found in the panelling at the Palace of Westminster.

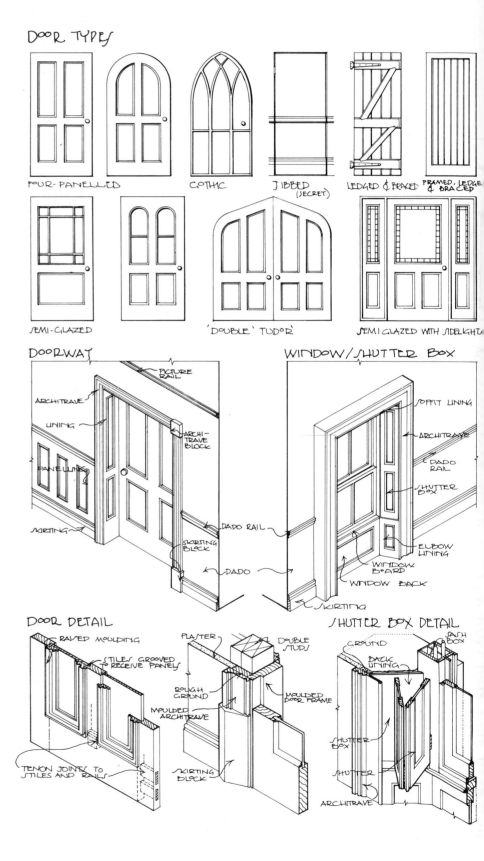

DOORS & OTHER WOODWORK DETAILS

DOOR TYPES

FOUR-PANELLED

GOTHIC

JIBBED (SECRET)

LEDGED & BRACED

FRAMED, LEDGE & BRACED

SEMI-GLAZED

'DOUBLE' TUDOR'

SEMI GLAZED WITH SIDELIGHTS

DOORWAY

PICTURE RAIL
ARCHITRAVE
LINING
ARCHITRAVE BLOCK
PANELLING
SKIRTING
SKIRTING BLOCK
DADO RAIL
DADO

WINDOW/SHUTTER BOX

SOFFIT LINING
ARCHITRAVE
DADO RAIL
SHUTTER BOX
ELBOW LINING
WINDOW BOARD
WINDOW BACK
SKIRTING

DOOR DETAIL

RAISED MOULDING
STILES GROOVED TO RECEIVE PANELS
PLASTER
DOUBLE STUDS
ROUGH GROUND
MOULDED DOOR FRAME
MOULDED ARCHITRAVE
TENON JOINTS TO STILES AND RAILS
SKIRTING BLOCK

SHUTTER BOX DETAIL

SASH BOX
GROUND
BACK LINING
SHUTTER BOX
SHUTTER
ARCHITRAVE

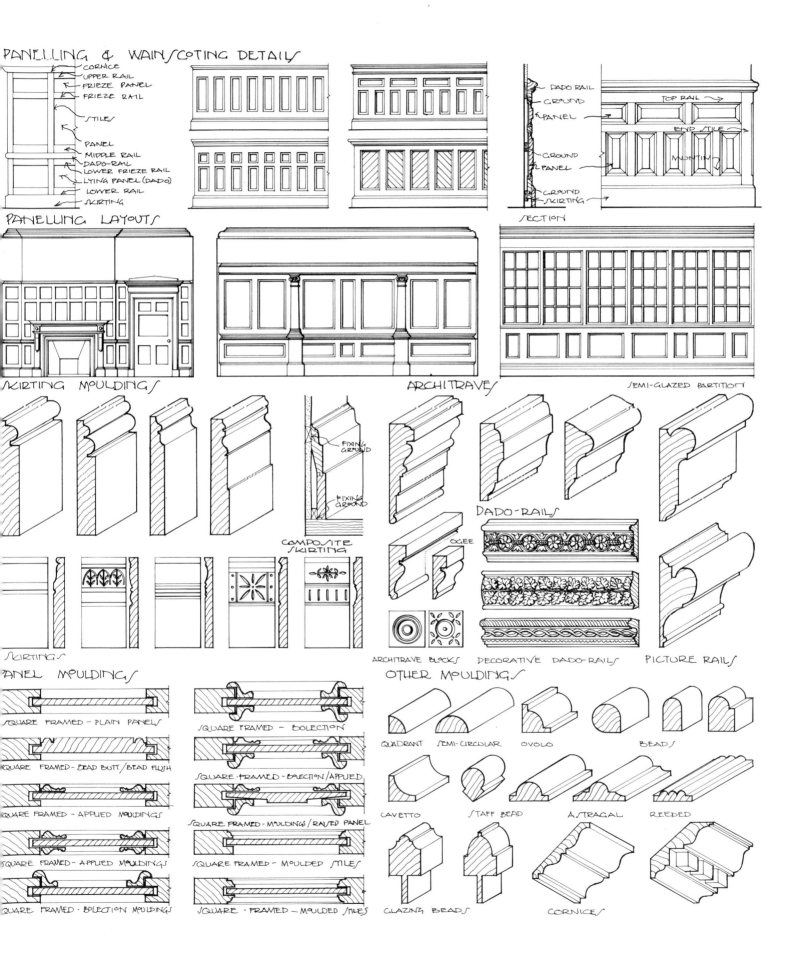

PANELLING & WAINSCOTING DETAILS

CORNICE
UPPER RAIL
FRIEZE PANEL
FRIEZE RAIL
STILES
PANEL
MIDDLE RAIL
DADO-RAIL
LOWER FRIEZE RAIL
LYING PANEL (DADO)
LOWER RAIL
SKIRTING

DADO RAIL
GROUND
PANEL
GROUND
PANEL
GROUND
SKIRTING

TOP RAIL
END STILE
MUNTIN

SECTION

PANELLING LAYOUTS

SKIRTING MOULDINGS

ARCHITRAVES

SEMI-GLAZED PARTITION

FIXING GROUND
FIXING GROUND
COMPOSITE SKIRTING

OGEE

DADO-RAILS

SKIRTINGS

ARCHITRAVE BLOCKS   DECORATIVE DADO-RAILS   PICTURE RAILS

PANEL MOULDINGS

OTHER MOULDINGS

SQUARE FRAMED - PLAIN PANELS

SQUARE FRAMED - BEAD BUTT/BEAD FLUSH

SQUARE FRAMED - APPLIED MOULDINGS

SQUARE FRAMED - APPLIED MOULDINGS

SQUARE FRAMED - BOLECTION MOULDINGS

SQUARE FRAMED - BOLECTION

SQUARE FRAMED - BOLECTION/APPLIED

SQUARE FRAMED - MOULDINGS/RAISED PANEL

SQUARE FRAMED - MOULDED STILES

SQUARE · FRAMED - MOULDED STILES

QUADRANT   SEMI-CIRCULAR   OVOLO   BEADS

CAVETTO   STAFF BEAD   ASTRAGAL   REEDED

GLAZING BEADS   CORNICES

137

BOOKSHELVES AND CUPBOARDS

Built-in cupboards did not enjoy the same prestige in Victorian times that they do today. The rich could afford elegant pieces of free-standing furniture; built-in fixtures were usually found in modest houses, or confined to the kitchen and servants' quarters. Made by a joiner rather than a cabinet-maker, they were simple structures with little ornament.

The one item of good fitted furniture that was found in many Victorian houses was the shelving for the library or study. This was very much a status symbol – books were still an expensive luxury – and would either have been designed by the architect or by the householder with the assistance of a pattern book and carpenter. Quite often an existing piece of furniture would be copied; a glass-fronted bookcase, for example, could be extended by constructing two matching wings.

Large cupboards were increasingly needed in the Victorian era as the ownership of clothes, particularly dresses, increased. Generous walk-in cupboards were provided in mansion flats and Scottish tenements where they offered an efficient way of using space cut off in the search for a well proportioned room, but the architecture of speculative terraced housing left no natural spaces for big cupboards. The larger terraced houses might have dressing rooms, and by the last decades of the century a fitted bedroom was a frequent feature in houses where space did not permit a separate room for storage. Arts and Crafts architects, who relished vernacular details, gave the built-in fixture a new status and made it the basis for many of their rurally-inspired interior decoration schemes.

In all houses, the traditional location for cupboards and bookshelves was in the recesses on either side of the chimney breast. The solidity of the chimney wall provided a firm support

Right: The recess beside the chimney breast is the natural place for built-in shelves. In this room the cupboard has been correctly designed so that it does not project in front of the chimney breast, and its height does not conflict with the line of the mantelshelf.

Far right: A plain, solid cupboard with traditional panel doors will stand the test of time and redecoration. In any built-in fitting, the shelves should be slightly thicker than habit or instinct suggest, say 1 in (2.5 cm) rather than 3/4 in (2 cm).

Left: In a small house, display shelving can be hung from the level of a picture rail, where it will be out of the reach of children. The simple mouldings along the leading edges of this attractive piece could easily be copied to give character to any set of newly built shelves.

Below: The fretwork surround of this niche in a child's room co-ordinates nicely with the bedstead.

for the woodwork. Equally widespread was a corner cabinet on landings which filled a space otherwise unexploited.

Built-in furniture suits the demands of modern living, and can be installed in a Victorian house without violating its character; indeed, a built-in cupboard can actually enhance the architecture by disguising an ugly conversion. It should be plain and sturdy; decoration and paint can hide many things but not bad proportions and flimsiness. Plainness, however, is relative. A cupboard will be more satisfying to live with if constructed from tongue-and-groove boarding rather than modern building board. If you can find simple panelling from architectural salvage yards or skips, a good carpenter and a coat of paint can unite them into a passable whole. When boxing-in electrical appliances, panelling or tongue-and-groove boarding will be less monotonous than hardboard, and easier to paint. Arts and Crafts architects might take woodwork the whole way along a wall embracing a bookcase with a bench underneath at one end, the fireplace in the centre and a fitted

Above: Natural wood is an attractive medium for built-in kitchen fittings, especially when constructed with good detailing, such as the beading round these recessed shelves.

141

wardrobe in the second recess. To have one wall painted white may bring welcome lightness to a room. Benches or seats set into a bow window recess may be the most effective way to make use of that space.

When installing fixtures which do not exploit recesses or cover awkward corners, it is important to pay attention to the proportions of the wall and of the room generally. The lower section of a cupboard or bookcase ought to be more solid, brought a little forward or made of slightly thicker wood. The top can be given a pediment and architrave, or Gothic mouldings. As a rule of thumb, such built-in furniture should reach to somewhere between the top of

the door and the picture rail. Wardrobes in bedrooms, where the cornice is not so dominant, can stretch to the ceiling. Half-height cupboards which serve as sideboards should line up with the height of the dado. Beware of having the top of a bookcase or cupboard too close to the level of the mantelpiece shelf; the horizontal effect will upset the balance of the room, making it seem bottom heavy.

If you are not employing an architect, the choice of the design of your cupboards or library is made easiest by copying from furniture illustrated in this book or in other houses. A number of designs are included on page 144. It may be helpful to have some element around

Basins in bedrooms, although useful, often detract from the appearance of a room. By fitting the basin inside a built-in cupboard, you can reduce its impact and use the area around and above the sink to good practical and decorative effect.

which to focus your thoughts, be it an elegant door you wish to incorporate, a piece of china you plan to display or the dimensions of the books you want to shelve.

At a more practical level, the back wall of a bookcase or display niche ought to be painted before the carpenter begins work, and any damage can be touched up afterwards. Lighting for display cabinets or sockets for stereos needs to be planned in advance. Make sure not only that the wires have been run in to the bookcase before it is finished, but also that the wiring can be altered later on. Modern electronic equipment changes with confusing speed, so it is probably best to err on the side of elaboration

and run some form of ducting into the shelving; new wires can then be drawn through without having to dismantle the whole arrangment.

Although it may be tempting to accommodate as many books as possible, do consider how easy the shelves will be to use. If they are over seven feet high, you will need steps. If they start less than one foot from the floor, you will have to stoop to reach them; the books will get dusty and may be damaged by furniture being stood against them. When installing cupboards in difficult places such as under stairs, put lights in them; all to often, cupboards are built with no thought for the fact that a torch will be necessary to see what is in them.

Boxing in a radiator avoids the difficulties of papering or painting around and behind it, and can provide an attractive decorative feature, especially in this case where the Victorian art of the fretsaw has been so successfully recaptured.

143

SHELF & CUPBOARD DESIGNS

BOOKSHELVES

PLAIN

WITH ARCHITRAVE

WITH COLUMNS

DIVIDED

CUPBOARD DESIGNS FOR RECEPTION ROOMS AND HALLS

GOTHIC DRESSER

GOTHIC LIBRARY CUPBOARD

END OF THE ERA

CURTAINED CORNER CUPBOARD

WINDOW SEATS

TIMBER BENCH

SOFA

TIMBER/CUSHION

CURTAINED

RADIATOR

RADIATOR DETAILS

SHELF

TIMBER FRAME

METAL PERFORATED PANEL

SHELVES & CUPBOARDS FOR CHIMNEY RECESSES

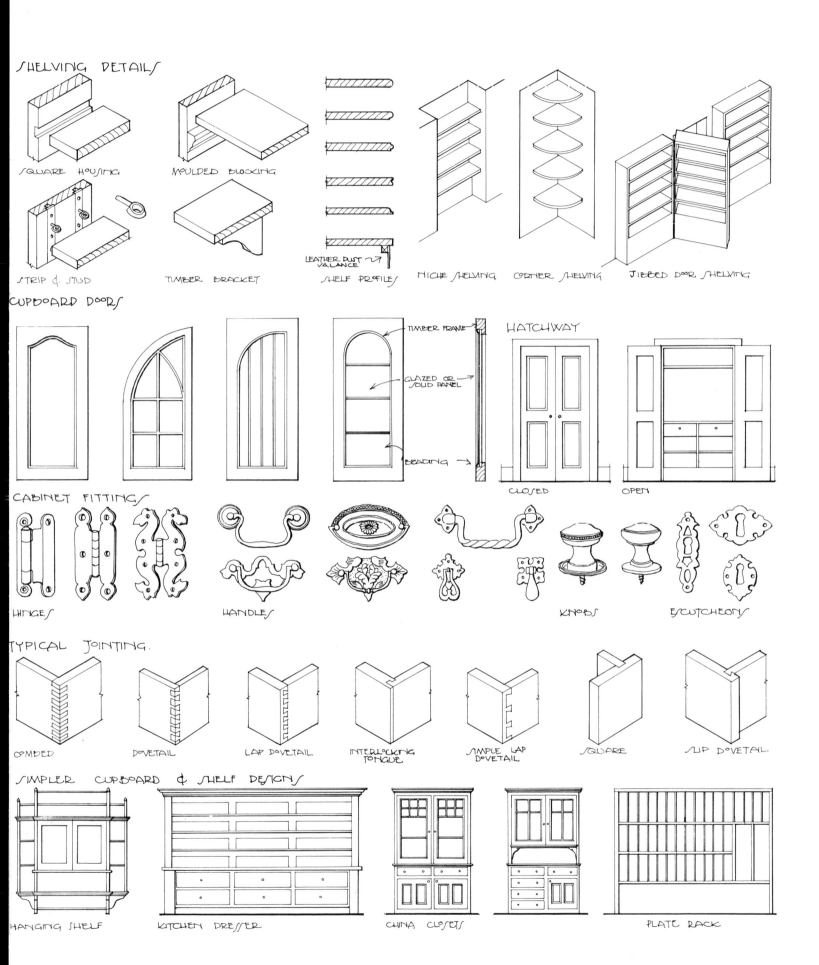

SHELVING DETAILS

SQUARE HOUSING   MOULDED BLOCKING

STRIP & STUD   TIMBER BRACKET   SHELF PROFILES   LEATHER DUST VALANCE

NICHE SHELVING   CORNER SHELVING   JIBBED DOOR SHELVING

CUPBOARD DOORS

TIMBER FRAME

GLAZED OR SOLID PANEL

BEADING

HATCHWAY

CLOSED   OPEN

CABINET FITTINGS

HINGES   HANDLES   KNOBS   ESCUTCHEONS

TYPICAL JOINTING.

COMBED   DOVETAIL   LAP DOVETAIL   INTERLOCKING TONGUE   SIMPLE LAP DOVETAIL   SQUARE   SLIP DOVETAIL

SIMPLER CUPBOARD & SHELF DESIGNS

HANGING SHELF   KITCHEN DRESSER   CHINA CLOSETS   PLATE RACK

FIREPLACES

The importance of the fireplace was one point on which William Morris and the average Victorian householder would have been in perfect agreement. For Morris, a blazing hearth was the soul of a room; for the average householder it was the cornerstone of domestic comfort. From being a minor decorative feature in a Regency room, fireplaces became increasingly prominent and central to interior design. This was partly due to the Gothic Revival, which brought back the big hearths and hooded fireplaces of the Middle Ages; it was also a result of the Arts and Crafts Movement which cherished the wide cottage-style fireplace with inglenook.

Most fireplaces were made up in two main parts: the fire-grate, which was manufactured in cast iron, and the chimneypiece or surround, for which marble, slate, timber or, less frequently, cast iron were used. Advances in grate design during the Victorian era created fires that threw a lot more heat out into the room. Early grates were mainly of the hob register type, an updated version of the 18th-century hob grate in which a narrow hob with three or four firebars stood high off the hearth, flanked by two integral side panels, or the late-18th century register grate variety, which combined the grate, fire-back and inner surround in one piece (see pages 152 – 53).

Opposite: A circular-headed register grate with tiled cheeks and elaborate cast-iron chimneypiece provides an eye-catching focus for a drawing-room. The summer decoration used here is preferable to the traditional embroidered firescreen, which would hide the good features of the fireplace.

Above: A simple register grate with a minimal surround was typical in bedrooms. Painting the whole fireplace white is quite appropriate in a room with simple furnishings and light decoration.

Right: This Gothic Revival fireplace retains the traditional hob grate; although the register grate was more heat-efficient, purists stuck to the historical form.

To improve the performance of the fire, manufacturers in the 1830s introduced the circular-headed register grate, with firebars lower down, and by the 1850s this type was fast superseding the earlier designs. However, the old register and hob register types continued in production right through to the end of the century, and simple hob grates were still installed in smaller bedrooms long after they had disappeared from the main rooms.

Grates, like everything else manufactured in the Victorian era, became very elaborate in design, and up to the 1860s detail proliferated in endless variety. At the same time architects devoted much attention to the design of the chimneypiece. At the beginning of Queen Victoria's reign, chimneypieces were mostly neo-classical in style, with simple brackets and plain pilasters. Good quality materials were used. Marble was the most common, especially the white and veined varieties. Among the cheaper alternatives was the slate chimneypiece, which

Above: Mantelpiece mirrors were sold in standard sizes to match mass-produced fireplaces. The correct size mirror will be 6 in (15 cm) shorter than the mantel-shelf at each end.

Right: In this magnificent French-style drawing-room, the high-relief, fully arched chimneypiece has ironwork shuttering to close off the grate in summer.

Above. The generous marble surround of this drawing-room fireplace, with its original marble fender, adds grandeur to a relatively commonplace tiled register grate.

Right: An Art Nouveau register grate has been attractively incorporated in an earlier dining-room fireplace which is somewhat large for the room it now occupies.

enjoyed great popularity in the 1880s. Many were cleverly painted to imitate inlaid marble panels on a black background with incised gold decoration. Timber lent itself to the older reeded designs with corner rosettes and other classical styles (see page 153), which continued to be used according to the taste of the builder. Later chimneypieces began to sport carved brackets and became heavier in appearance. Sometimes the cast-iron circular-headed grate determined the shape of the chimneypiece, which itself became semicircular where it enclosed the grate, instead of rectangular.

At the Great Exhibition of 1851 the firms of Carron and Coalbrookdale exhibited very ornate chimneypieces and one-piece register grates made entirely of cast iron, and by the late 1850s and early 1860s cast-iron chimneypieces were mass-produced. It was not until the 1870s, however, that all cast-iron designs began to rival traditional fireplace surrounds.

A subsidiary decorative feature in a register grate was a border of tiles in the jambs between the surround and the grate. Grates with tiled cheeks were used in the early 19th century in some of the larger houses, and by the 1860s and 1870s tiled register grates were being mass-produced with an endless variety of mostly naturalistic patterned tiles. Their popularity reached a peak in the last twenty years of the century.

A glance through a builder's or manufacturer's catalogue of the late 19th century is a

Above: Valances and draperies on the mantelshelf were popular in the mid-Victorian era, adding to the cosiness of the room.

Left: This cottage-style fireplace retains an open hob within a mantel of painted wood.

Far left: A German stove fits nicely into a traditional arched marble fireplace.

Left: The most basic form of register grate has been brightened up by a good set of patterned tiles.

151

fascinating exercise. Many of the designs of the 1840s were still available, while Art Nouveau and other influences combined to produce styles that were not only typically Edwardian but looked forward to the 1920s and 1930s. A selection is given on the right. Many builders continued to use the traditional marble, slate and cast-iron surrounds in the best rooms. Wood and cast iron were the norm in the bedrooms and servants' quarters. Grate designs followed much the same trends as those in the rest of the house. Manufacturers produced the same patterns in about four different sizes, although the very small ones found in servants' rooms rarely had tiles.

Today the owner of a Victorian house is likely to find that many of the original fireplaces have been covered over, partially destroyed or removed altogether. In bedrooms, their loss can be an advantage; in public rooms, a bare chimney breast will produce an incomplete and cheerless impression. When choosing a replacement, it is best to check on the size and design required by examining chimneypieces in neighbouring houses of the same date. However, exact sameness of design is less important than finding a fireplace that is the right size for the room. A full discussion of fireplace restoration is given in Chapter 8, on page 304.

Many Victorian fireplaces came complete with a matching fender or marble kerb. An 18th-century fireplace had a spacious hearth jutting out into the room to catch sparks and falling coals, but in Victorian times the hearths were smaller and the fenders correspondingly more important. Apart from the purely precautionary function of stopping a crinoline dress catching fire as you adjusted your bonnet in the overmantel mirror, and keeping small children out of harm, the fender was an integral part of the design. Finding the right one for your fireplace may be something of an odyssey, but a correctly restored chimneypiece and fire-grate will greatly enhance the character of a room, and deserves appropriate accessories.

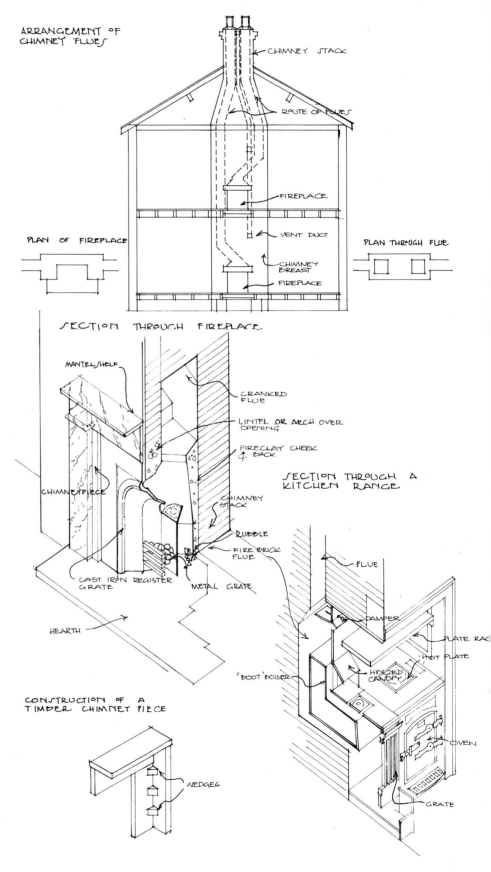

TYPES OF FIREPLACES & ACCESSORIES

ARRANGEMENT OF CHIMNEY FLUES

CHIMNEY STACK

ROUTE OF FLUES

FIREPLACE

VENT DUCT

CHIMNEY BREAST

FIREPLACE

PLAN OF FIREPLACE

PLAN THROUGH FLUE

SECTION THROUGH FIREPLACE.

MANTELSHELF

CRANKED FLUE

LINTEL OR ARCH OVER OPENING

FIRECLAY CHEEK & BACK

CHIMNEYPIECE

CHIMNEY STACK

SECTION THROUGH A KITCHEN RANGE

RUBBLE

FIRE BRICK FLUE

CAST IRON REGISTER GRATE

METAL GRATE

HEARTH

FLUE

DAMPER

PLATE RACK

HOT PLATE

'BOOT BOILER'

HINGED CANOPY

OVEN

GRATE

CONSTRUCTION OF A TIMBER CHIMNEY PIECE

WEDGES

TYPES OF GRATES

HOB GRATE

EARLY HOB REGISTER GRATE

1815 'COALBROOKDALE' HOB REGISTER GRATE

COMMON CIRCULAR-HEADED REGISTER GRATE (1830s-50s)

TILED REGISTER GRATE (1880s-90s)

TYPES OF CHIMNEYPIECE

EARLY CHIMNEYPIECES

EARLY TO MIDDLE CHIMNEYPIECES

CHIMNEYPIECE & ABBOTSFORD GRATE, 1885.

MIDDLE TO LATE CHIMNEYPIECES

COAL SCOOPS & BUCKETS

STOVE

COOKING RANGE & GRATE, 1910

FIREPLACE ACCESSORIES

VENTS

FIRE IRONS

THE 'BARNSLEY'

½ COVERED 'WELLINGTON'

THE 'WELLINGTON'

THE 'HEREFORD'

COPPER RANGE KETTLE

TYPES OF FENDERS

CAST IRON & BRASS

'BLANDFIELD' LIBRARY FENDER, 1878

BRASS FENDER, 1880

BRASS UPHOLSTERED FENDER, 1889

FLOORS AND FLOOR FINISHES

Most Victorians would have preferred oak floor-boards scattered with Oriental rugs. Oak, however, was expensive, and was only to be found in the grander houses. The average house-holder had to be content with softwoods. The parquet floor was popular in France, where great elaboration of design was practised. In Britain it was less universal, no doubt partly because par-quetry is sensitive to damp. Often a parquet border was laid around a room that had more modest flooring for the middle, and expensive houses and mansion flats might have parquet in hallways. Stone flagstones were traditional, but like marble or mosaics, they were relatively costly; linoleum, a Victorian invention, was used mostly in the kitchen and back-quarters.

In the standard terraced house pine and deal floor-boards were the norm. These would have been stained and varnished and then covered to a greater or lesser degree with carpets or rugs. In the public rooms, the fewer the carpets, the easier it was to keep the rooms clean; in the bedrooms and the family rooms where the traffic was less, rugs might cover the whole floor.

Varnish was easy to maintain. Staining and then applying oil or wax polish was labour intensive; only when the wood was of sufficient quality did a floor merit the effort polishing involved. When a single carpet was laid in a room, stencilled patterns (in imitation of parquetry borders) might be painted on the floorboards between the carpet and the skirting.

Today, vacuum cleaners mean that large carpets are no longer the same bother to keep clean. There remains, however, the problem of what is to be done with the uninteresting deal floorboards. My preference is to cover them entirely unless the wood is of particularly good quality, or the floorboards are nicely tongued-

and-grooved. The process of sanding and coating a floor with polyurethane varnish is unpleasant, and the result may not repay your labours. It is in the nature of pine to turn yellow when sanded and treated and the result is all too often a jaundiced-looking floor. Sometimes, by applying bleach after sanding, you can stop the floorboards yellowing after the final finish. Stain-ing, of course, is another answer. Before treating a whole floor you should test a small area to gauge the effects. The action of bleach and stain will roughen the grain of the wood and you will have to sand the floor again before sealing it with two coats of polyurethane. Beware, though, of bleaching parquet floors. Bleach attacks the black bitumen-like adhesive that is used to assemble the parquet, and may cause it to seep out and streak the surface of the floor irrevocably.

Above: In a detached suburban villa a patterned parquet floor has a simple border to delineate the edge of the room.

Right: Painting the floor-boards is a good alternative to sanding and sealing with polyurethane; here it is used to provide a light background for country oak furniture.

TILES

The Victorians used tiles more widely and in a greater variety of designs than in any other period. The encaustic floor tiles laid in entrance halls, and the glazed wall tiles used to decorate fireplaces, bathrooms, friezes, dadoes and skirtings remain one of the most distinctive features of 19th-century interiors.

The encaustic, or inlaid, tile was a medieval invention rediscovered by the Victorians and widely used in Gothic Revival churches. The tiles were made at first from red clay – sometimes with a coarser clay sandwiched in the middle – and fired in a mould with the pattern indented on the bottom. After firing, the pattern was inlaid

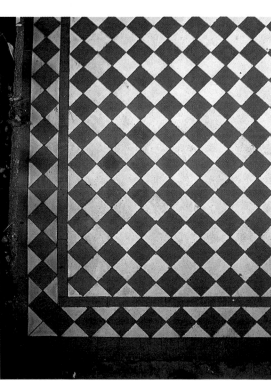

Right and opposite: Most geometrics took their colours from the natural tones of the clay: red, buff, black, white, grey and ochre, although brighter colours such as lilac were used occasionally.

with a lighter coloured clay or 'slip', and the tile was then fired a second time. Sometimes a lead glaze was added. Red- and buff-coloured encaustics gave way in the mid-1840s to greens with a blue inlay. Small, single-colour tiles or tesserae were known as geometrics and were the type normally used in hallways.

The glazed wall tile was developed by William Morris, following 18th-century Dutch traditions. There was some cross-fertilization with Islamic styles, especially in the designs of the potter William de Morgan, a friend and contemporary of Morris. In the late 1850s, Morris had been hand-painting Delft blanks; by the 1890s, commercial processes of design transfer had become so efficient that de Morgan could propose to re-facade most of London with his.

The hygienic advantages of pottery surfaces

Above: These four geometric pavements are designs for Minton tiles. The firm perfected the commercial production of encaustic and geometric tiles in the 1840s.

brought tiling into ubiquitous favour in late 19th-century Britain. Glazed wall tiles became so common in restaurants and shops, particularly butchers' and fishmongers', that there was some resistance to their presence in the public parts of the house. For the kitchen or basement passages, however, they were perfect, providing a washable, hard-wearing finish with a highly reflective surface that suggested an airy cleanliness. These qualities encouraged the use of tiles in masculine rooms and, by extension, public houses; the Arabic smoking-room with Islamic-style tiles was a frequent Victorian feature.

Traditional encaustic tiles are still made and architectural salvage yards may also have second-hand geometrics: both will be useful when you need to repair an original floor that has become loose and has lost some of its pieces. If the damage is extensive, the simplest solution may be to take up all the tesserae and redesign the floor. Relay the original tiles in a smaller, central area and use new or second-hand tiles to make a larger border. When redesigning passage or hall floors, the pattern should be kept simple; intricate designs will emphasize the narrowness of the space. A broad mass of a single colour in the centre with a simple border will be the most effective scheme, and is easiest to lay.

Good Victorian tiles, such as de Morgan's, were never cheap, and today they are sold at prices which class them as works of art. Tiles for hearths or fireplace surrounds provide a strong note of colour, and it may be worth paying for old tiles which match damaged or missing ones in fireplace jambs. Anyone put off by the cost, however, can take comfort from the fact that tile panels by artists such as de Morgan would only have been used in the best rooms. For passages, kitchens or bathrooms, the plain, single-colour tiles would have been used with decoration restricted to a border. Such middle-market tiles can be found in salvage yards, and there are several firms making reproductions that are not prohibitively expensive.

Above: Glazed wall tiles displayed a wide variety of styles and motifs.

Above: Earthenware panels such as this were frequently used to decorate hallways.

Right: This panel by de Morgan reflects the then-popular interest in Persian styles.

Top: A Kate Greenaway centrepiece is set off by an elegant *japonisme* surround.
Above centre: Minton produced designs in most of the fashionable styles of the century.

Above: The flowing plant forms of Art Nouveau enjoyed widespread popularity in tiles of the late- 19th century.

DECORATIVE GLASS

Sir John Soane credits himself with the introduction of stained glass for domestic decoration. Previously, the ever-popular heraldic panels of painted glass used by architects had been treated almost like pictures set into windows, and added no colour to a room. Soane's innovation was to use glass to impart picturesque tints to a room, adding variety as the sun moved round during the day.

The Gothic Revival brought a renewed interest in the manufacture of all kinds of coloured glass. Stained glass, which has its colour fused into the surface during manufacture, had been a lost technology since the Reformation. Chemical analysis undertaken in the 1840s led to its rediscovery, and large firms grew up between 1840 and 1860, initially making glass for churches. Stained glass enjoyed great vogue in Arts and Crafts circles; William Morris's firm Morris, Marshall, Faulkner & Co., founded in 1861, was noted for church windows as well as wallpapers.

By 1870 stained glass was being made increasingly for the ordinary domestic market, and numerous trade firms were producing not only stained glass but also flashed glass, which is painted on one side, as well as frosted, pebbled, sand-blasted and etched glass. For reasons of health, Victorians were eager to see more light in their houses, and coloured glass began to be utilized in surfaces that once would have been solid masonry or woodwork. Improvements in the manufacture of clear glass, which allowed larger panes to be used for every bar of light-reducing woodwork, also increased the liberty to install obscured glass in certain places. In the front entrance, coloured glass acted as a translucent wall that let in light but perpetuated the sense of security. In internal doors, borrowed lights of frosted or pebbled glass shed light from bathrooms or back-quarters on to dim passages or landings. Frosted, painted and stained glass in hall and stair windows served to block out the unsightly backs of neighbouring houses. This use of obscured glass to prevent a view out as well as guaranteeing privacy within gave builders licence to jam even first-rate houses together.

The designs of coloured glass available from the manufacturers' catalogues followed fashionable tastes with Ruskinian naturalistic motifs giving way to *japonisme* sunflowers in the 1880s and the sinuous forms of Art Nouveau by 1900. Under the influence of Art Nouveau the leaded joints of the glass came to play more of a role in the design than the colours, a trend that was particularly evident in the rectilinear style of C. R. Mackintosh and his Glasgow-school contemporaries, who produced designs of great virtuosity for domestic use well into the 1930s.

Stained glass is expensive, whether you obtain it from specialist glass-makers or from antique shops and salvage yards. Victorian house decorating manuals contain detailed instructions for embossing glass with acid, using a stencil, or gilding using gold leaf and isinglass. This is sport for the adventurous. Certainly pebbled or frosted glass will be cheaper. Ordinarily, flashed glass will be the best way to restore a colourful chiaroscuro to a hall. Pollution and footballs do not encourage the use of antique or good Victorian glass as the window proper, but if affixed inside the window frame, so that it is protected by the outer glass, it will still catch the sunlight and blot out neighbours and passers-by. Large expanses of stained glass can grow wearisome to look at, but in a work room coloured glass can be suitably placed to diminish the heat of summer light. W. H. Auden advised against working in a room with an interesting view; many offices seem to follow this advice. Coloured panels can fulfil the same function; at Savonarola's cell in the convent of San Marco in Florence, you can still see a glass picture of the Devil set into the window to discourage the idle from gazing out.

Opposite: A front door panel of obscured glass offers the waiting visitor a port-hole peep at a rustic scene, recalling the romantic idyll of the past so dear to the newly urbanized generations of the late-19th century.

Right: Obscured glass used as a translucent wall is given charm with the addition of a naturalistic bird.

Far right: A traditional diaper motif was adapted to glass patterns used in front doors from about 1870 onwards.

Below: Modern etched glass panels in a vestibule door show what can be done by present-day craft workers using traditional patterns and techniques.

Right: A roundel of decorative glass obscures a downstairs lavatory window.

Above: A cartoon for a Morris & Co. stained-glass window illustrates the high standard of design achieved by the leading studio workshops. Edward Burne-Jones, best known today for his pre-Raphaelite paintings, was Morris's chief glass designer.

Above left: Stained and obscured glass with Art Nouveau designs became widespread at the end of the 19th century.

Overleaf left: Botanical subjects were very popular in painted glass decoration until more stylized Art Nouveau designs took over in the 1890s.

Overleaf right: An Aesthetic Movement glass design has been fitted into a standard door of the 1880s, still in everyday use as the front door of a school of English.

Above: Painted and stained glass with a wild strawberry motif is an example of more naturalistic design.

Right: A traditional Greek motif has been adapted to a design for a hall or stair window.

LIGHTING

Right through the Victorian period, householders made do with lighting levels that would be unacceptably low today. Most Victorians relied exclusively on candles and oil lamps, which had innumerable disadvantages. Tallow candles smoked and smelled, and wax candles were expensive. Until the 1850s oil lamps burned Colza, or rape seed oil, and were manufactured to 18th-century designs. Their light output was poor, and it was only after the discovery of paraffin in 1847 that significant improvements were made. The duplex burner, invented in 1865, had two flat wicks set very close together which produced noticeably more light than two separate wicks. Between 1860 and 1880 about 2,000 patents for oil lamp designs were applied for. New styles came in: pendant lamps, table and floor lamps, student lamps with burners that

Above: A common type of gas bracket inspired this early electric light fitting; the continuity of style made the new fittings seem reassuringly familiar to their purchasers.

Right: Functional lighting works best when it is contemporary. This very Victorian assemblage of artefacts is given character by two downlighters directed across the corner.

could be moved up or down on a central column, all provided with globes and shades that were painted, stained, frosted or etched, finished with crimped or tinted edges and hung with silk and lace fringes.

Gas lighting was slow to compete with oil, though it had first been demonstrated as early as 1787. In 1807 the National Light and Heat Company was established to provide gas street lighting; by 1816 London had 26 miles (42km) of gas mains. Gaslight soon became common in large country houses – Sir Walter Scott installed it in his house at Abbotsford in Scotland in 1823 – but in ordinary domestic interiors it met resistance. The fishtail or batswing burners flickered and smoked, giving off sulphurous fumes which killed indoor plants, tarnished metal and discoloured paintwork and furnishings. Ceiling roses helped to hide the discolouration, and some had concealed grilles and pipes to carry away the

fumes. The standard of illumination was poor, and most people preferred wall brackets which were frequently designed to swivel from side to side, so that the light could be brought close to the task in hand. Gas brackets, like the earlier candle sconces of the Georgians, were often placed near wall mirrors to maximize the amount of light produced. Supply was uneven and at the discretion of the gas companies, who decreed the appropriate hour to turn it on and off.

The breakthrough in gas lighting came in 1886 when Carl Auer von Welsbach invented the incandescent gas mantle, or Welsbach mantle, a round or cylindrical net which, when placed over the jet, produced a light of exceptional brilliance. The flame itself was now hotter, thanks to improvements based on the newly invented bunsen burner. Soon afterwards came the inverted mantle, which directed the light down-

Below: A Gothic Revival bracket gas lamp has been adapted for electricity.

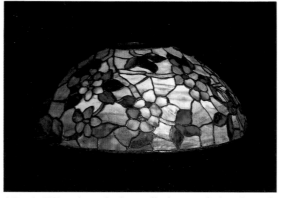

A Louis Tiffany lampshade recalls the popularity of mosaic glass in turn-of-the-century America.

This fitting was designed by Philip Webb.

Right: A 'Winfield' gas jet was one of many fittings designed for table-tops, complete with flexible gas pipes.

A pair of lamps shows distinction in metal and alabaster.

wards. By then gas was available in most towns and pre-payment meters were bringing it into more modest suburban houses. The new gas lights were instantly popular, and revolutionized the night-time character of the family parlour, making the whole room lighter and brighter.

Just when the suppliers of gas lights were enjoying a huge demand, they found themselves facing a powerful rival. In 1878 Joseph Swan invented an electric light bulb with a carbon filament, and in 1880 electric light was installed for the first time in a private house, at Cragside, home of Sir William Armstrong, in Northumberland. Early electric light bulbs produced much less light than modern versions and were made in clear glass only. At first they were left dangling naked on their cords, without shades – the style adopted by Armstrong. Later they were provided with simple conical shades, maybe with reflective white or silver interiors, to increase the light

output, and green exteriors, to be restful to the eye. Holophane shades came in around 1907; made of ribbed clear glass, they were a scientifically designed means of increasing light by prisms and grooves. Electroliers could often be lowered or raised on pendant cords, so that the light source could be brought close for reading, sewing or other tasks.

The big advantages of electricity were the lack of flame and the ability to switch it on or off at will. Initially the high cost of installation was a disincentive, but the invention of the tungsten filament in 1906 doubled the light output of the electric bulb and signalled the death knell of gaslight. Glare became a problem for the first time, and numerous designs of shade were produced to create indirect lighting, particularly the ceiling bowl, that archetypal central light so hated by later generations. When the frosted bulb became commercially practical in 1925, ac-

Mosaic glass, more popular now than at the turn of the century, survives in this modern 'Pyramid' shade.

A rise and fall lamp with blue madeleine shades is a type used over billiard tables.

A 'Beethoven' wall bracket has a shade typical of the oil and gas lamp era.

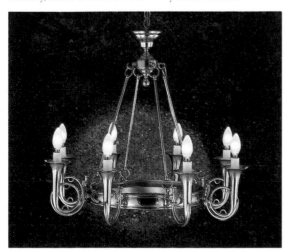
Above: A reproduction ceiling pendant with electric candle lights uses a hunting horn motif.

Above: A modern 'Beethoven'.
Left: An Art Nouveau light fitting.

companied by the first fuses, something approaching a modern lighting system was established.

The advent of electricity added to the already bizarre confusion of old and new fittings at a time when both oil and gas lighting were still undergoing improvement. A late-Victorian parlour might have as many as 20 different fittings running off oil and gas, including a central chandelier, alcove lights and table and floor lamps. Ceiling gasoliers made of copper or brass often had several burners shaded by etched glass or crystal globes designed after the oil-lamp style. From about 1910 the chandelier might be a combination fixture with upward-pointing gas mantles and downward-pointing electric lights, so that the householder always had gas available as a back-up if the electricity failed. In the hall a gas lamp or later an electric globe on the newel post might be held aloft by a bronze figurine. Some private houses may still have their original brass gas fittings, concealed under the grime of decades. Being non-magnetic, brass reveals its presence negatively by refusing to respond to magnets.

It is possible to echo Victorian styles in lighting in ways that are both practical and decorative. A number of quite satisfactory reproduction wall lights are available, along with matching ceiling pendants (see page 308 for suppliers). Some are manufactured in the original lamp factories using original dies and moulds, and may be obtained either wired for electricity or fitted with oil lamp burners.

PERIOD LIGHT FITTINGS

CANDLESTICKS AND CANDELABRA

C. 1820-40

C. 1800

SILVER CANDLESTAND, 1855

C. 1820

C. 1800

BRONZE GIRANDOLE, C. 1851

BRASS CANDLE LAMP, C. 1850s

STORK CANDELABRUM, C. 1851

OIL LAMPS AND SHADES

MODERATOR LAMP

PEAR SHADE

CRIMPED SHADE

DOME SHADE

TULIP SHADE

STUDENT LAMPS

SINGLE LAMP WITH INTEGRAL OIL RESERVOIR

OIL RESERVOIR

SINGLE LAMP WITH SEPARATE OIL RESERVOIR

DOUBLE LAMP

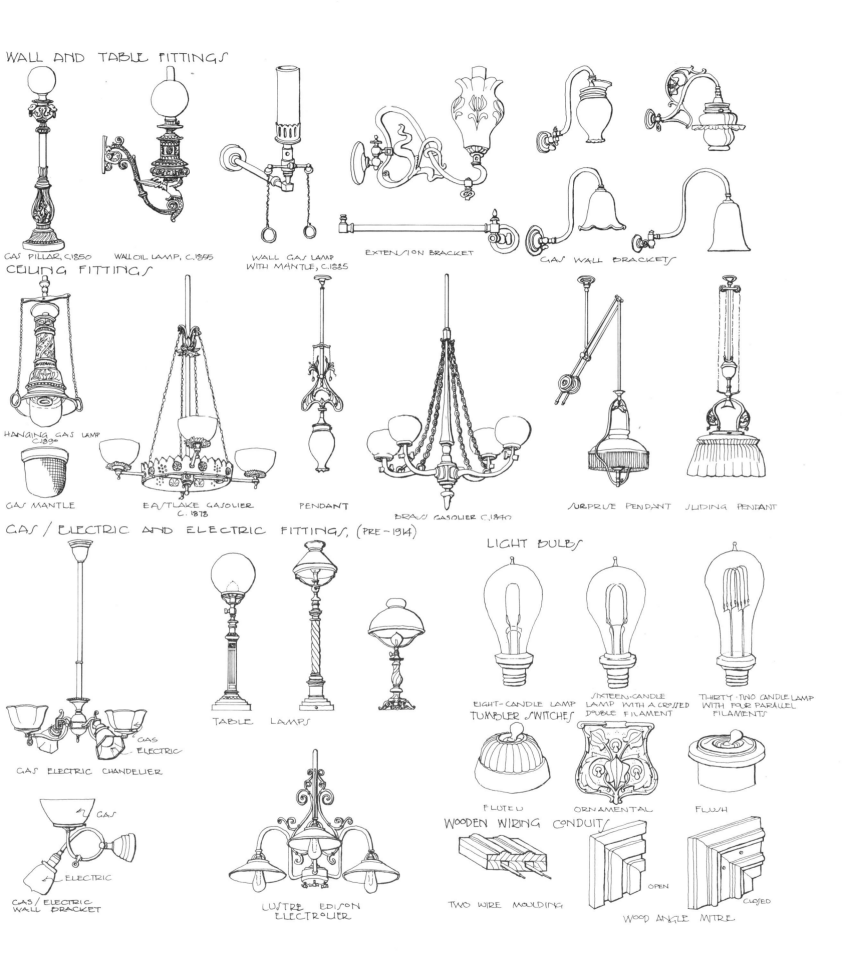

WALL AND TABLE FITTINGS

GAS PILLAR, C.1850 WALL OIL LAMP, C.1855 WALL GAS LAMP WITH MANTLE, C.1885 EXTENSION BRACKET GAS WALL BRACKETS

CEILING FITTINGS

HANGING GAS LAMP C.1890 GAS MANTLE EASTLAKE GASOLIER C.1878 PENDANT BRASS GASOLIER C.1840 SURPRISE PENDANT SLIDING PENDANT

GAS / ELECTRIC AND ELECTRIC FITTINGS, (PRE-1914)

GAS ELECTRIC CHANDELIER TABLE LAMPS

GAS
ELECTRIC

LIGHT BULBS

EIGHT-CANDLE LAMP SIXTEEN-CANDLE LAMP WITH A CROSSED DOUBLE FILAMENT THIRTY-TWO CANDLE LAMP WITH FOUR PARALLEL FILAMENTS

TUMBLER SWITCHES

GAS
ELECTRIC

GAS / ELECTRIC WALL BRACKET LUSTRE EDISON ELECTROLIER

FLUTED ORNAMENTAL FLUSH

WOODEN WIRING CONDUITS

TWO WIRE MOULDING WOOD ANGLE MITRE

OPEN CLOSED

BRASSWARE, IRONMONGERY AND PORCELAIN FITTINGS

Above: Bells to ring for the servants were usually positioned to one side of the fireplace.

The appearance of a house is greatly enhanced by the use of appropriate fittings for doors, windows and services. Changes in decoration and technology since the 19th century have, however, complicated the choice. Old styles of fitting have disappeared from the shops, and new ones have been introduced. Gloss paint and stripped wood have replaced the grained finishes and dark varnishes of the Victorian decorator.

In choosing door furniture – finger-plates, lock-plates, handles, hooks and hinges – you are limited by the fact that brass looks best against unpainted wood, and the standard oak or ebony handles of the Victorian era really only suit a grained door. Washable gloss paint has removed the need for the finger-plate.

Beware of over-loading a plain door with expensive brassware; door furniture should match the size and importance of the door. In general, brass and bronze door handles are right for public rooms, and need not match; old ones can often be found singly, and the patina of a century's use is far preferable to the anodized glitter of modern matching reproductions. White china handles are an acceptable alternative, and there are many good quality replicas on the market today. Private rooms may be given more modest fittings; back bedrooms often had finger-plates of stamped tin, while kitchen cupboards were finished with plain wooden knobs. Fitting elegant catches to windows may not be consistent with security, and the woodwork may be too weak to take any but the most functional catches.

Electrical fittings should suit the background. Unpainted wood deserves brass sockets and light switches; white skirtings or walls look best with plain white plastic fittings.

Right: The lock-plate was re-introduced by the Arts and Crafts Movement; the influence of this school of design made beaten metals an important feature of interior decoration in the 1890s.

Far right: A commercially-produced lock-plate combines both neo-classical and Art Nouveau motifs.

Opposite: This handsome Gothic Revival door furniture shows a perfect balance of function and form.

DECORATIVE METALWORK, CHINA & GLASSWARE

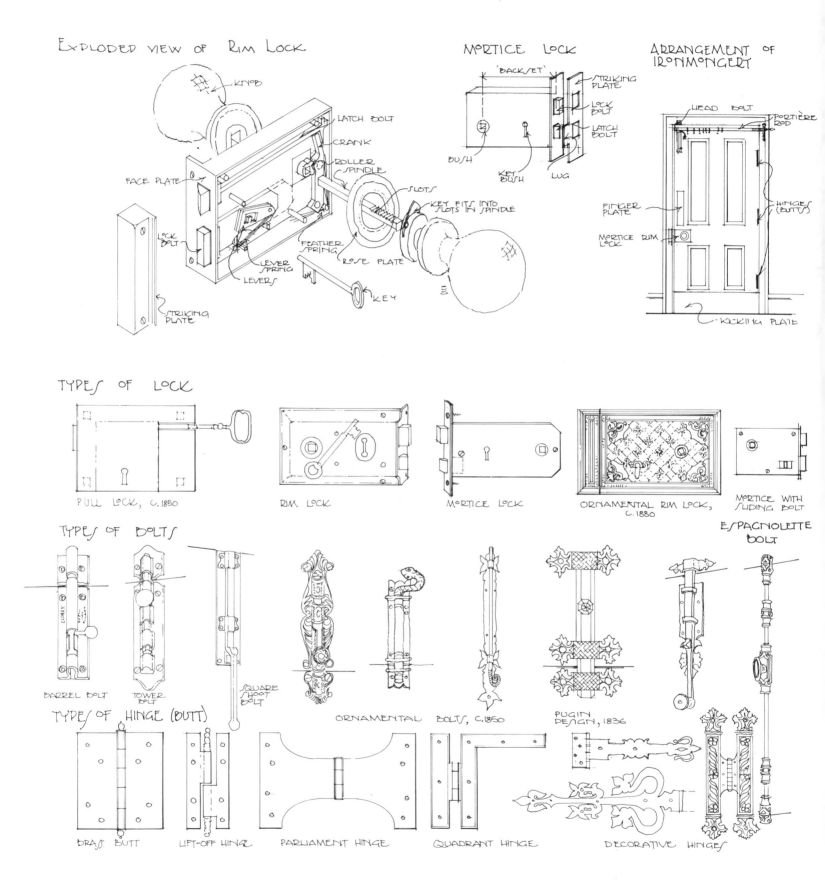

EXPLODED VIEW OF RIM LOCK

KNOB
LATCH BOLT
CRANK
ROLLER SPINDLE
FACE PLATE
SLOTS
KEY FITS INTO SLOTS IN SPINDLE
LOCK BOLT
FEATHER SPRING
ROSE PLATE
LEVER SPRING
LEVERS
KEY
STRIKING PLATE

MORTICE LOCK

'BACKSET'
STRIKING PLATE
LOCK BOLT
LATCH BOLT
BUSH
KEY BUSH
LUG

ARRANGEMENT OF IRONMONGERY

HEAD BOLT
PORTIÈRE ROD
FINGER PLATE
HINGES (BUTTS)
MORTICE RIM LOCK
KICKING PLATE

TYPES OF LOCK

PULL LOCK, C.1850
RIM LOCK
MORTICE LOCK
ORNAMENTAL RIM LOCK, C.1880
MORTICE WITH SLIDING BOLT

ESPAGNOLETTE BOLT

TYPES OF BOLTS

BARREL BOLT
TOWER BOLT
SQUARE SHOOT BOLT
ORNAMENTAL BOLTS, C.1850
PUGIN DESIGN, 1836

TYPES OF HINGE (BUTT)

BRASS BUTT
LIFT-OFF HINGE
PARLIAMENT HINGE
QUADRANT HINGE
DECORATIVE HINGES

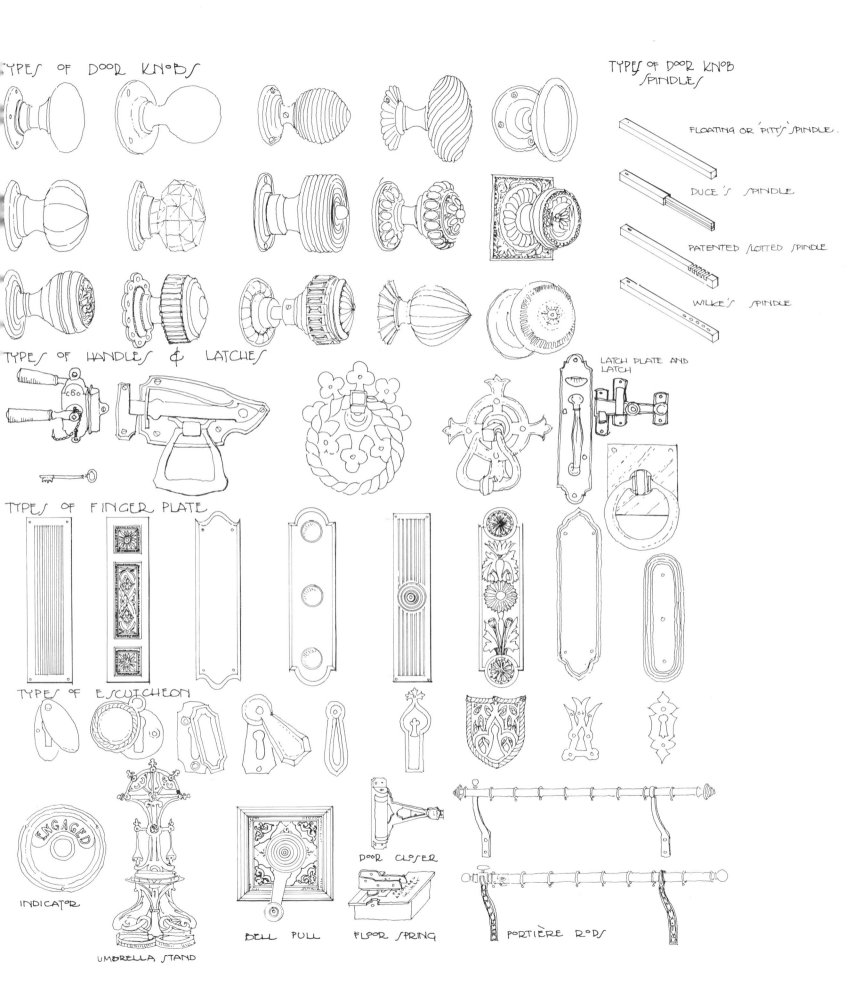

TYPES OF DOOR KNOBS

TYPES OF DOOR KNOB SPINDLES

FLOATING OR 'PITT'S' SPINDLE.

DUCE'S SPINDLE

PATENTED SLOTTED SPINDLE

WILKE'S SPINDLE

TYPES OF HANDLES & LATCHES

LATCH PLATE AND LATCH

TYPES OF FINGER PLATE

TYPES OF ESCUTCHEON

ENGAGED

INDICATOR

UMBRELLA STAND

BELL PULL

DOOR CLOSER

FLOOR SPRING

PORTIÈRE RODS

175

Chapter Four
DECORATING IN VICTORIAN STYLE

We can recognize a Victorian room by the aspect of comfortableness in its informal arrangements of furniture and its warm colouring. A cosy domesticity, exemplified by the Royal Family, was its hallmark, plenty its inspiration. The Industrial Revolution both created the wealth for the adornment of the home, and brought forth a profusion of new decorative materials in every conceivable style. Even if Victorian Britain did not produce one decorative style of its own that was not a revival of earlier styles, it was this ability to take a historical style and mechanically reproduce it in great quantity that instantly defines 'Victorian' to us and distinguishes that age from its predecessors. Before widespread mechanical manufacture, household items such as chairs and wallpapers were relatively dear. The facades of Regency terraces in Brighton, London or Bath might seem opulent, but their interiors would have been quite sparsely decorated. The elegant simplicity we so much admire in Regency styles was governed as much by cost as taste. When that constraint was removed, opulence and novelty took over.

The main influence on household taste in the first half of the 19th century was the pattern book. These publications carried illustrations of furniture and upholstery which were copied by local cabinet-makers, and they gave a degree of uniformity to British, European and American taste that had not existed before. In a thorough, Scottish way, John Claudius Loudon's *An Encyclopaedia of Cottage, Farm, and Villa Architecture and Furniture* (1833) lives up to its encyclopedic boast by illustrating and advising upon every detail of a house from curtains to drains. Loudon's informative and frankly improving book was seized upon by the newly rich who wanted their suburban villas decorated with practical comfort and with a knowing nod towards fashion.

The choice of styles and materials with which to adorn the house was extended throughout the 1840s and 1850s. The great international showcase exhibitions (London 1851, Paris 1855, Brussels 1860) displayed the manufactures of the big European firms to an eager public. The novelty of the decorative arts produced in Sheffield or Lyons, and their relative cheapness, meant that every middle-class home might become a Great Exhibition in miniature.

Although Pugin, Alfred Stevens and other great artists had

designed for Sheffield manufacturers and were represented by work shown at the London Exhibition of 1851, the majority of decorative arts on display there made it clear that good design and mechanical manufacture had yet to find a happy partnership. New techniques of production, notably the wider range of colours made available to manufacturers by aniline dyes and the increasing sophistication of weaving and printing – some wallpaper manufacturers used up to twenty colourways in their designs – fed the High Victorian appetite for novelty, with mixed results. This is most obviously expressed in the vogue for pictorialism in pattern design of the 1850s: naturalistic forms such as flowers were reproduced in profusion in carpets, fabrics and wallpaper; in an excess of illusionism, some even included shadows.

To Pugin, three-dimensional pictorialism that copied naturalistic forms did not qualify as art or design. The furniture of this period, with its heavily upholstered curves, was also condemned by architects and designers who saw no virtue in chairs with hidden metal frames, stuffed and padded. Charles Eastlake's *Hints on Household Taste* (1865) attacked the tawdriness of fashionable furnishings and proposed in its place a robust Gothic style. William Morris's reaction to High Victorian taste (or want of it) was the return to the hand-crafted artefact; his insistence on artisan craftmanship gave direction to the Arts and Crafts Movement and distinguished it from the styles of other designers working with commercial manufacturers, even those who sought out pre-industrial forms to find models for new furniture and textile designs.

Robert Edis's *Decoration and Furniture of Town Houses* (1881) capitalized on the middle-class vogue for the Artistic house. This is the frontispiece, showing his own drawing-room.

The word that came to describe the ideas of Eastlake and Morris was Art. Art furniture and Art wallpaper and Artistic houses became as much a social ideal as a decorative vocabulary from the mid-1860s onwards. Outside, the Artistic house was Queen Anne revival; in side there was a heterogeneous range of furniture and fabrics. The furniture would have been modelled on Old English, Ancient Greek or traditional Georgian forms; the fabrics were lighter in colour than those of popular taste, although during the 1870s the relatively intense effect of the tripartite wall – dado, filling and freize, each band with different colour or pattern – became fashionable. This self-consciously Artistic style of decoration was dubbed the Aesthetic Movement.

The Aesthetic Movement had its genesis in the tastes of a handful of working artists and architects who had a liking for Japanese prints and blue Chelsea china. The houses of these artists became the fashionable model for the Artistic middle-class home of the 1870s and 1880s. To surround yourself with the paraphernalia of artist-aesthete was not expensive: shops in the Tottenham Court Road sold cheaply made bamboo furnishings and 'genuine old Delft'. Later, Liberty's would sell all the arty knick-knacks for the Artistic interior.

Towards the end of the century, when a new generation had grown up with the ideas of the Arts and Crafts Movement, the William Morris-inspired cottage filled with simple, beautiful objects became the social ideal of the middle classes. These cottages with their low-ceilinged living-halls, oak settles and large hearths were more likely to have been suburban than rural, but it was the countryside which provided their inspiration, a way of life that became more attractive the closer it came to extinction. By the 1880s the tranquil isolation of rural communities was finally succumbing to the railways, which had brought much of Britain within easy reach of the great towns. A new wave of nostalgia for Merrie England, coloured with melancholy as that romantic vision receded further and further from reality, contributed greatly to the appetite for Arts and Crafts furniture and decoration.

By the turn of the century architects and designers who had learnt their profession within the Arts and Crafts ethos were beginning to see Arts and Crafts forms not as a social ideal but as a foundation for design. The radical pruning away of superfluous ornament since the 1860s had given designers a vocabulary of purer forms that they could refine and stylize.

A morning-room has been recreated with lavish enthusiasm in a style that evokes the clutter and comfort of the High Victorian family room.

Although pictorialism in patterns was frowned upon by designers as false art it still remained the dominant popular taste for most of the 1850s and 1860s.

P E R I O D   D E C O R A T I O N

LATE REGENCY

Town house, *c*.1837; first-floor drawing-room. Sofa and draperies are standards from an upholsterer's pattern book. Rosewood furniture. *Chaise longue* with buttoned upholstery. Cabinet and folding card table of common Regency type. Fireplace classical, surmounted by gilt mirror contributing to general lightness of the room.

HIGH VICTORIAN

Sitting-room, *c*.1857. Homely comfortableness: piano, family portraits, oil lamps and gas lights. Thick curtains, flock wallpaper, rich colours, glittery gold decoration. Velvet trimming on mantelshelf. Papier-mâché decorated chair. Furniture of no consistent style. Ornaments mainly factory-made.

AESTHETIC

Sitting-room, *c*.1877. Tripartite wall with dado, filling and frieze decorated in different ways. William Morris 'Fruit and Pomegranate' wallpaper. Art furniture: Edis-designed cabinet; vases designed by Christoper Dresser; dining-room chair by Norman Shaw. Japanese fans used as decoration. Bamboo occasional table. Strongly decorated frieze; hand-made china prominent.

ARTS AND CRAFTS

Living-hall, *c.*1897. A version of a Cotswolds cottage. Bare wooden floors, ornamental rugs. Ladderwork chair and settle designed by Ernest Gimson. Cabinet based on a design by Lewis F. Day. Walls pale; oak furniture. Antique fire-dogs and brassware.

END OF THE ERA

Drawing-room, *c.*1901. Style influenced by Voysey and Baillie Scott. Furniture has a stylized elegance; wall surfaces are light and have an easy-to-keep-clean simplicity. Arrangement of furniture a sparse neo-Georgian style.

COLOUR AND PAINT EFFECTS

The 19th-century painter and decorator was a true craftsman. He served a long apprenticeship, on average seven years of arduous and detailed work involving grinding and mixing of colours, colour harmony, the arts of stencilling, lettering, woodgraining, marbling and freehand line drawing as well as the principles of decorative art and elementary perspective. There were no ready-mixed paints so everything was specially mixed on site.

Walls and ceilings which were going to be left plain were painted in distemper, a water-based paint which was the Victorian equivalent of emulsion. Impractical in many ways, it stained easily and could not be washed without leaving a watermark. The Victorians had no effective way of dissolving colour or pigment in water-based paint. Instead they mixed it with glue size as a fixing agent. When distemper built up into a skin, it became unstable, and in unrestored Victorian houses white patches of flaking distemper can often be seen, peeling away particularly from ceilings and above picture rails.

If you find when trying to cover a wall or ceiling in emulsion paint that pieces of hardened paint crack off then you are sure to be painting on distemper. The only way to treat this problem successfully is to soak the wall or ceiling and scrape and wash the distemper off. On the positive side, distemper did have great clarity and purity of colour. It is still available in an oil-bound form which does not flake.

Above: The *trompe l'oeil* scarf hanging over the door adds a touch of humour to an otherwise slightly sombre room. The Pompeii Red of the walls was a popular colour, and the door has been boldly grained as a rich mahogany to match.

Right: A contemporary adaptation of Victorian techniques has created an elaborately marbled passageway, recalling the popularity of the marbled effect in entrance halls and corridors in the 1850s and the 1860s.

Left: The rag-rolled walls contribute to a simple, rustic quality which allows the window to speak for itself and dispenses with the need for curtains.

Above: The salient feature of this room is an elaborate *trompe l'oeil* frieze, carefully balanced by the black and 'gold' painted skirting-board and the typically Victorian colour scheme of walls and dado.

A solid oak door with a panelled doorcase exemplifies the effect emulated in paint and glaze by the trained masters of the woodgraining art.

All woodwork was painted in oil paint, as it is today, but in the 19th century its chief ingredient was white lead. Great care must therefore be taken when stripping or scraping old paint. If you are interested in finding out the original colours your house was painted in, then simply take a small sharp blade and scrape off the layers of paint one at a time.

Broadly speaking, until the middle of the 19th century, colours were not dark and sombre, as the modern imagination pictures them, but light, soft and used sparingly. To get a feel for early Victorian colour schemes it is best to think of the period as an extension of the Regency style, with Neo-Classical and Rococo accents, and pastel colours including pearl whites, delicate pinks and lavenders (see page 180).

In the mid-century colours became deeper and were employed in more complicated combinations. This turn of fashion was influenced by the scientific study of colour in the 1840s, undertaken by architects of the Gothic Revival, and by the work of Owen Jones who made the first systematic study of Moorish ornament at the Alhambra in Granada. These ideas on colour and design were taken up by commercial decorators and adapted for mass-production wallpapers. The basic idea was to use a complex pattern with one main colour and many subsidiary colours, often tonally the same, juxtaposed with some shades of the main colour. As a general rule no primary colour was used, unless it was tempered to make a deeper or softer shade by the juxtaposition of secondary colours. For example, a poppy red would not be used with a true yellow or a true blue, but with old gold, amber, hyacinth blue or grey blue. Some tertiary colours were employed, such as maroon, purple, olive green and ochre. These were mixed in among the Victorians' wide variety of deep neutral shades such as cream, slate, drab (a mixture of raw umber, ochre and Indian red), buff, sandstone and various greys.

Before starting work on a room the Victorian decorator would have taken considerable time deciding the best approach; in a new house a substantial delay was inevitable since freshly plastered walls might take up to two years to dry out. The first room to be decorated in the new dark and 'masculine' style was the dining-room, quickly followed by study, smoking-room and drawing-room. Bedrooms were thought more feminine and could take more convivial colours.

Great thought would go into getting the correct balance of both colour and texture for walls, cornice, ceiling and woodwork. This was especially true when a dado-filling-frieze combination was used, with a different decoration for each band. By the 1840s white was no longer fashionable as a colour for a ceiling; instead a tint of the main wall colour was used. To provide it with texture a lightly embossed paper was often put up. Stencilled borders and friezes became very popular in the houses of the rich. The decorator John Crace and the architect William Burges, among others, also used stencilling as an overall wall pattern. Stencilled motifs can be very simple or highly elaborate, copied from fabric patterns. Some wonderful examples can be found at Knightshayes Court in Devon, designed by Burges. Equally, *trompe l'oeil* effects were very much admired.

With these strongly decorated walls it was necessary to paint the woodwork with a deeply coloured woodgrain or to stain the natural wood in a dark colour. Staining wood in an ornamental fashion using stencils became very popular particularly for large doors and for floors around the edge of carpets. Door panels might also be decorated with a single motif such as a flower spray done either as a freehand painting or as a stencil design. Magazines like *The Studio* would carry stencil patterns on thin tissue paper ready to be traced on to stencil paper and cut out for painting with a stencil brush. Dado rails or architraves were often painted with small freehand decorations. Marbling, though less common than woodgraining, was also a popular finish.

Woodgraining reached its zenith at the end of the 19th century. The most popular woods to imitate were oak, mahogany, walnut and satinwood; bird's eye maple and other more exotic woods were copied to a lesser extent. Graining was done chiefly on internal doors and skirting-boards. The front doors of houses of the 1840s and 1850s were grained, usually in walnut or mahogany. The best graining was done using a water-colour glaze, diluted with vinegar and water, painted over an oil-bound distemper base; but this is a difficult technique, less often used.

Marbling found favour because real marble is a chilly presence in northern climates; also, real marble had to be imported, and was expensive, whereas marbling cost less and could easily be chosen and adapted to suit a particular scheme of decoration. The most popular finishes were verd antique, Sienna marble, Breche marble, white, black and gold marble, porphyry and malachite.

A number of special paint effects have recently become highly fashionable. On occasion the results are stunning, but nowadays graining and marbling require large amounts of time and money if they are to be done properly. Paint combinations are notoriously difficult to match at a later date, and damage is difficult to repair.

One of the curses of modern decorative schemes is the glaring white emulsion which rose to such popularity in the 1960s and 1970s. To obtain a more interesting effect, knock back any white paint using a little of the base colour of the room. The architectural detailing of a Victorian house will inevitably suggest a certain degree of complexity in decoration. You cannot have an elaborate fireplace and elaborate mouldings and hope to decorate the room successfully in a stark or simple style. Richness in one area demands richness in the others. Elaborate wall coverings lead on naturally to elaborate curtains and so on in a chain of necessary relationships.

A good starting point for a decorating plan may well be the fireplace. Curtain treatments, a fine period wallpaper or a beautifully copied stencil frieze are other features from which room plans often flow. A valuable piece of furniture or important pictures will tend to dictate their own background.

Right: The sky ceiling of a room designed in an Ionic manner recalls the Victorian fondness for painted ceilings modelled on those of Pompeii. Some householders incorporated sky ceilings inside four-poster beds.

Far right: A simple stencilled design has been used to enliven the walls of what would otherwise have been a somewhat cold room. The starting point for this bathroom scheme is an inexpensive translucent patterned paper stuck to the window.

GRAINING AND MARBLING

The basic technique for all graining and marbling is the same. First, a coloured eggshell or flat oil base is put down and allowed to dry. This coloured base varies according to the desired wood or marble effect. For woods, it is a light brown varying from creamy white to a deep dirty pink. For marbles, it is usually white, grey or black. Glaze, which is either a mixture of linseed oil and turpentine or a proprietary mixture, is then coloured and brushed over the base coat. Depending on the effect to be used a number of brushes, rags, combs and feathers can be used to allow the base coat to show through. Some of the more common graining and marbling techniques are described or illustrated on this page.

Marbling and graining must be protected with varnish. Over dark work a polyurethane varnish may be used, but it has a yellowness which will mar delicate effects. An emulsion varnish or a specialist oil varnish should be used on very pale work.

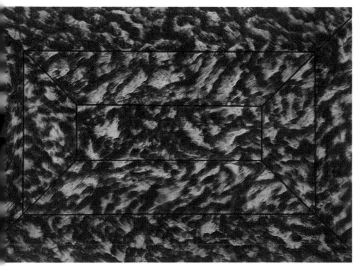

Above: Tortoiseshelling is achieved by laying paint over glaze and varnish. This was not a widespread technique during the Victorian period because the natural material was never in short supply.

SPECIAL PAINT TECHNIQUES

GRAINING

Mahogany Generally a pink base was used. When this was dry, a glaze containing a mixture of burnt sienna, crimson and burnt umber was painted over in a variety of designs. The 'flame' was a popular effect for door panels. Deeper colours were applied in the centre with perhaps a few flashes of deeper colour at the edges. A wide brush called a mottler was used rather in the manner of an italic pen to imitate the tapering shape of a flame. The design was blended in with a softening brush or overgrainer made either of hog hair or badger hair. The badger brush was initially used mainly for water-colour graining, but as it gives a very soft look it gained in popularity and was used on oil-bound glazes as well. Finally, a very thin coloured glaze was painted over the panel using both mottlers and overgrainers.

Oak A deep beige made up of white, burnt umber and yellow ochre forms the base colour. Over this a glaze of burnt umber and ochre is painted, giving darker and lighter streaks. A coarse, long-haired flogging brush and combs with variously

spaced teeth are pulled down over the work to show the base colour underneath. When the decorator is satisfied with the effect, the whole work is flogged by hitting the brush against the surface all the way up the panel. This process breaks the previously straight lines into short splinters.

Walnut The base is made up of white, raw sienna and a little raw umber. When a thin glaze of raw sienna and a little raw umber has been added, a folded rag is taken loosely in the hand and pulled down over the work with a waving but irregular motion. The areas which are not touched by the rag are stippled over with a fitch brush, made of polecat hair, and knots are put in using a number of different short-haired fitches so as to obtain different-sized knots. To obtain this effect, the brush is held in one position, perpendicular to the work, and twisted.

Satinwood An orangey red colour can be the base for this wood effect. It is made by adding burnt sienna and raw sienna to white eggshell paint. For a deeper colour burnt umber may be added. The glaze uses the same colours as the base coat save the white. When it

has been painted on, a ragging brush and combs are drawn down in long and slightly wavering movements in one direction, then back again in the opposite direction to soften the work.

MARBLING

Verd-antique A black base is used, then a glaze of chrome green mixed with a little oxide of chromium. The glaze is applied with several long-haired sable brushes held together in one hand and moved jerkily over the whole surface. The effect is softened, allowed to dry and overlaid with some thin whitish veins all running in one direction.

Black and gold marble The base colour is again black. Dark grey tints in a dryish mixture of paint without glaze are washed over the whole surface, leaving some black areas, and the work is softened. A mixture of ochre and red is made up and veins are run over the surface. Lastly very fine veins are run from the main veins to split the background into fragments.

Sienna marble The base colour is white or off-white. A thin glaze of white and yellow ochre is laid over the whole area and a little vermilion and white is added in parts, making sure there is not too much red. After dabbing the glaze with a small pad of decorator's cloth called stockingette, the whole effect can be softened. To break the monotony of this finish a short-haired fitch is dipped into white spirit and, when the excess has been removed, the spirit is flicked and splashed on to the surface. The wet patches are immediately softened. This process has the effect of revealing large and small spots of the base colour.

White marble Over a dry white base is laid a very light glaze with white colour in it. Some areas are made slightly darker with a little black and white, to make grey. This same colour is used to run in very soft veins. The surface is then padded over with stockingette and softened. A long-haired sable brush is dipped in white spirit, the excess is wiped off and veining marks are made over the surface in one direction. These strokes have the effect of taking off the surface colour and revealing the colour of the base. With a small sable brush some very fine veins in a light grey may be worked in in some areas.

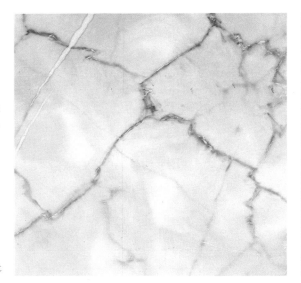

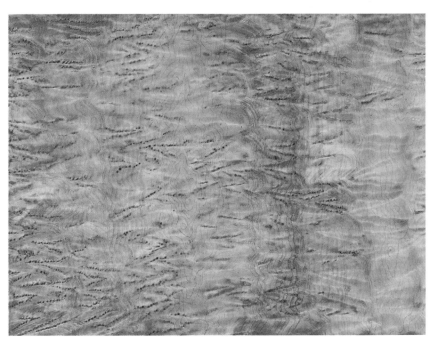

Shown on this page are four examples of sophisticated marbling and graining.

Above left: Sienna marble, see opposite.

Above: Rosa aurora marble, achieved by techniques similar to that of black and gold marble.

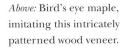

Above: Bird's eye maple, imitating this intricately patterned wood veneer.

Right: Samples of malachite finishes, achieved by combing a surface layer of light green applied on a darker base.

WALLPAPERS

'The father of modern wallpaper is Morris,' wrote Muthesius in *Das Englische Haus* (1904). Muthesius expressed unbounded admiration for William Morris's flat pattern design, and suggested that the wallpapers of the Arts and Crafts Movement had a 'light but sure touch' and had created a 'new kind of pattern that one can almost regard as the English national style'.

William Morris, however, was not alone among the great Victorian designers to devote considerable attention to wallpaper. Indeed, most leading Victorian architects designed wallpapers, sometimes on a commercial basis, often as a special design for an important commission. A.W.N. Pugin created wallpapers for the new Palace of Westminster, and also, in conjunction with the decorating firm of J. G. Crace and Co., put out commercial designs. Variations of the diaper (diamond) motif were the basis for much of his best work in this field.

Numerous wallpapers were produced by artists close to Henry Cole, who was superintendent of the Great Exhibition of 1851. After what he regarded as the major lapse of good taste that occurred at the Exhibition, Cole made a collection of historic textiles which were shown at the Museum of Manufacture, ancestor of today's Victoria and Albert Museum, in an attempt to point students towards 'the right principles of design'. The leading two artists in Cole's circle were Richard Redgrave and Owen Jones.

Jones enunciated the principle that wallpaper patterns should be flat; this was a sally against the fashionable decorative taste of the time with its pictorial patterns featuring three-dimensional reproductions of plants, flowers and animals. Such papers were wildly popular in the 1850s and 1860s. Among other representational designs, often brought over from France, were landscapes and panoramic views, with or without figures, and imitations of architectural features such as ashlar walls, cornices, friezes, mouldings and columns, statuary in niches, church windows, Gothic doors and pinnacles and wood carvings.

The 'impropriety' of pictorialism was criticized by men like Pugin and Jones on two counts: first, a wall is a flat surface and three-dimensional images falsely created an illusion of an uneven,

OWEN JONES AND THE GRAMMAR OF ORNAMENT

Owen Jones (1809-74) trained as an architect, but achieved his celebrity as a writer and theorist of colour and ornament. After an extended tour of the Continent and Near East, Jones published the beautifully illustrated *Plans, Details and Sections of the Alhambra* (1845) which introduced non-European design to a wide audience.

In 1850, Jones was appointed as joint architect to the Great Exhibition. He was primarily involved in designing the internal colour scheme for Paxton's Crystal Palace.

It was in *The Grammar of Ornament*, published in 1856, that Jones systematized all his ideas and concepts. The encyclopedic scope and the delicately drawn and coloured plates guaranteed *The Grammar of Ornament* wide currency as a handbook of design.

Prefaced to the illustration and examination of a wide range of ornament were 37 propositions of 'General Principles in the Arrangement of Form and Colour'. The most famous of these Propositions are: '5. Construction should be decorated. Decoration should never be purposely constructed'; and '6. Beauty of form is produced by lines growing out one from the other in gradual undulations: there are no excrescences; nothing could be removed and leave the design equally good or better.'

Jones's approach to ornament was that of a professional designer whose roots were in architecture, but whose interests increasingly lay in design for manufactures. In Jones's admirer and follower, Christopher Dresser, the 19th century had its first industrial designer.

Left: Examples of Greek art from Owen Jones's *The Grammar of Ornament* underline his theory that flat-pattern design reflects 'the laws which regulate the distribution of form in nature'.

Below: This dado paper by Walter Crane belongs to the 1880s, the heyday of the 'dado style'.

Bottom: The 'Daffodil' wallpaper was designed in 1891 by J.H. Dearle, chief designer of Morris & Co.

189

Right: This is a selection of wallpapers designed for the new Palace of Westminster by A.W.N. Pugin and reprinted from the original blocks during a recent redecoration of Speaker's House. The overall planning of the Houses of Parliament was in the hands of Charles Barry, but Pugin did the lion's share of the design and detailing, chiefly between 1844 and his death in 1852.

190

broken surface. Second, direct, almost photographic, copying of nature did not constitute a pattern. The three-dimensional cabbage rose, with or without shadows, violated principles of honesty and taste. Patterns should be formalized, stylized interpretations of nature.

During the 1840s and 1850s the predominant colours used were reds and greens. Henry Cole's *Journal of Design and Manufactures* (1849–50) advocated 'full tones in general' for wallpaper colourings, since rooms ought to be comfortable, and this was the impression full-bodied tones were most calculated to give. The same article went on to recommend flocked wallpapers since they added extra richness to the effect.

Although Morris was one among many trained architects who designed wallpapers, he developed a special genius for the discipline of pattern design which marks out his work. Whereas the designs of Pugin and Jones had been based on medieval motifs or heraldic devices with comparatively static repeats, Morris introduced patterns which were more rhythmical and also more representational. Ironically, Morris preferred to decorate his own houses with tapestry hangings, though it was from medieval and Gothic tapestries that he learnt the art of flat pattern and developed his talent for mixing strong colours to harmonious effect. In his writings, Morris said that patterns ought to have a 'mysterious' element and a narrative quality – ideas which tally with a thorough immersion in the art of medieval Europe when so much of its art and decoration was achieved to the greater glory of God. In Morris's case it was achieved in the hope of betterment for the common man.

There is another irony associated with Morris & Co. wallpapers: because they were produced by hand, many of the designs remained current for decades. Machine-printing became the dominant mode of production after about the 1840s, but most of these papers disappeared from the market after a few years, since the cost of setting up the machines made small runs prohibitively expensive. Thus many of the designs by E.W. Godwin and other architects who worked for commercial manufacturers drifted into history, leaving Morris & Co. a continuing presence.

Just as Morris & Co. have come to stand for Arts and Crafts textile design, C.F.A. Voysey represents late Victorian design that stood on the cusp of Art Nouveau and modernism. Voysey himself rejected both Art Nouveau and modernism as an act of temperament and belief. In the same moral way he repudiated Morris's patterns as too 'sensuous'. Voysey's textile designs fall into two categories. The first were produced in the late 1880s and early 1890s, when he was a young and struggling architect; they tend to be rather formal, urban patterns which show his debt to the Aesthetic Movement. In the mid-1890s, when Voysey had become a fashionable architect, his textile designs took on a lighter and more individual tone. The colours are paler and the design sparser, leaving the lightness of the background to predominate.

A wallpapering scheme for a Victorian room was typically far more complicated than is usual today. Between skirting-board and ceiling, a room could have several different patterns of papers. The dado was traditionally covered in 'leather-paper', a thick embossed paper more

Right: A William Woollams wallpaper of *c.*1870 betrays French influence in the pictorialism of its design.

Below left: One of Voysey's earlier papers includes the flowers, foliage and birds characteristic of his style.

Below right: The Bower design is one of the 41 wallpapers created by William Morris from 1862 to 1896. He was also responsible for five ceiling papers.

Left: The Acanthus wallpaper produced by Morris & Co. in 1875 was one of the firm's most popular lines.

Left: This design for a flocked wallpaper is by A.W.N. Pugin, *c.*1850.

The five wallpapers below are *(from left to right):* a Sunflower design from Watts & Co. of Westminster; a Rose and Coronet design, also from Watts & Co.; a stylized flower design produced for Jeffrey & Co. by Owen Jones; a pink bird design by Watts & Co.; and a modern anaglypta paper.

HAND-PRINTED WALLPAPERS

Hand-printing was and is expensive, but it is a process that keeps alive some of the best Victorian designs.

To transfer a design to the wooden printing block, which is generally veneered with a layer of fine-grained pear wood, those parts that are not intended to be printed are cut away.

The printer inks the resulting relief pattern by placing it face down on to a colour blanket. With the wallpaper unrolled over his work bench, he registers, or 'pitches', the colour-laden block over the paper by means of pitch pins at each corner, and lowers it, applying pressure through a foot pedal which operates a system of levers. The amount of pressure varies from one design to another.

Many blocks may be needed to print the whole of the pattern and colour range in a single design, and the paper must be allowed to dry between each application. The method is slow and cumbersome, but the modern results are often quite as good as the originals. The re-created Pugin papers in the Palace of Westminster (see page 190) are a fine example of what can be achieved.

commonly called anaglypta today. Anaglypta was originally one of several similar patent relief papers; others were Lyncrusta and Tynecastle Tapestry. These papers were a new invention and became very popular as they were produced in a wide variety of patterns and widths, and were tough and durable and could be coloured to suit a room. They were at first made in imitation of the stamped Spanish leather which had been used as wall coverings in the 17th century. Ana-glypta papers were similarly coloured by painting them a dull brown and laying on a darker brown glaze which was then stippled. They were often stamped with Jacobethan strap-work motifs. Gradually the connection with leather was lost and anaglypta was painted in a variety of colours. Later on, papers were produced that looked like plaster friezes. They were usually painted in a tint of the main colour of the room.

Embossed papers were very useful because not only were they practical and resistant to damage at the level where scrapes and knocks inevitably occurred, but they created areas of texture and pattern which could be plainly coloured to provide a suitable background for furniture. They were frequently used on ceilings and friezes as well as dadoes. These areas could then be counter-balanced by richly patterned wallpapers, woodgrained doors and marbled skirtings. Anyone trying to remove anaglypta today will see just how robust it is: old paper can be extremely difficult to strip off as the embossed pattern will have filled up from behind with the glue which was used to fasten the paper to the wall. The most effective way to remove anaglypta is to scrape and soak the paper with methylated spirits and water.

By the 1870s it had become fashionable for the dado to reach a fair way up the wall, and the frieze a good way down, leaving the filling quite narrow. Many artists, such as E. W. Godwin and Walter Crane, designed all-in-one dado-filling-frieze papers. In the 1890s the dado was increasingly dropped, leaving the two divisions of wall

and frieze in sole possession of a room. However, there might also be ceiling papers with circular repeats which could cover an entire ceiling or be set inside plaster frames, and usually a decorative border which ran just below the cornice mouldings or above the picture rail.

It is the dominance of a decorated frieze band that most obviously sets a Victorian room apart from rooms of today. Special frieze papers, supplied as strips, were often supplemented by a stencilled frieze. R.W. Edis, in *Decoration and Furniture of Town Houses* (1890), recommended mural paintings for the frieze. This fashion for installing numerous different patterns within one room alarmed Muthesius, who warned his German readership that it was 'easy to decorate and patternize to excess'.

The first thing on which to make up your mind when hanging wallpaper is whether you want to make it to be merely background or to form anything like decoration. That will depend, to some extent, upon whether the walls are to be furnished with pictures or not. A simple wallpaper might be used for the walls, as a background for pictures, while a more exciting frieze paper might be hung above. Richard Redgrave produced a design in the 1840s specially for showing off pictures. A rich crimson flock also provided a neutral background, as did some of the denser patterned Morris papers.

Although many of the best Victorian papers are still produced (Arther Sanderson and Sons Ltd took over the printing of Morris & Co. wallpapers in 1930, and has continued to sell them since Morris & Co. went into liquidation in 1940), it is difficult to find the frieze papers that would have accompanied them. Maybe a doctored wallpaper with stencilled additions could provide the necessary excitement. Many frieze papers were designed to have stencilling applied as highlighting, and you could choose a vertical or horizontal emphasis depending on whether you needed to raise the apparent height of a room or lower it.

The Cray design by Morris & Co. Most of the firm's designs were for textiles and wallpaper.

'Lenoble', a painstaking modern reproduction of a mid-19th century design by Charles Hammond Ltd.

This page: The range and vitality of Victorian pattern design can be seen in these samples. Such designs were often used for both fabrics and wallpapers.

Peacock feather design, from the Silver Studio (Arthur Silver), *c.*1890.

'Palmyra', a design originally produced in about 1850, reproduced by Charles Hammond Ltd.

Morris's 'Artichoke' design, *c.*1875.

The design for the Morris & Co. 'Avon' chintz, *c.*1886.

'Botanica', a modern reproduction by Osborne & Little.

Another 'Botanica'.

CARPETS AND FLOOR COVERINGS

By the middle of the 19th century house-holders could obtain a wide variety of floor coverings, ranging from inexpensive matting and oil-cloths to the best Wilton and tapestry carpets, machine-woven in many colours and designs. Factory-produced oil-cloth was made in pieces up to 27 feet (8.2m) wide and 70 feet (21.3m) long and provided a seamless covering suitable for halls and parlours; it was frequently used in kitchens. Made from canvas, smoothed and sized and covered with three or four coats of stiff oil paint, and sometimes a top coat of varnish, these cloths were extremely hard-wearing and practical, and could be wiped clean with a damp cloth. Oil-cloths were produced with printed designs imitating tiles, flagstones or wooden floors, or motifs from Persian or Turkish carpets. Some householders made their own floor-cloths and decorated them with stencilled patterns or hand-painted designs.

Matting was recommended for almost any room in the house. Imported from India and the Far East, it came in strips up to 3 feet (0.9m) wide which could be seamed to make a fitted covering for cheap floorboards. In modest homes matting was popular in rooms where the wear was light, such as front parlours and bedrooms. Carpets or rugs were often placed over it, especially to create a warm sitting area in front of a fire; conversely, in summer, matting laid over carpet made a room cooler. When cushioned by the matting, carpeting wore better than when laid directly on wood.

Carpets were a major item of household expenditure; they were expected to last a long time and were looked after with care. Many people laid drugget, an inexpensive cloth of wool, or wool and flax, over the top of better carpets. In dining-rooms, drugget was often

Above: In this hall designed by C.R. Ashbee small rugs liberally strewn about the floor create an informal room. This was an advantage from the point of view of cleanliness since smaller carpets could be beaten out daily.

spread under the table and chairs as a crumb-cloth. In less well-off homes, drugget would be the sole floor covering.

Carpeting in the early Victorian period was mainly flat-woven body carpet manufactured in strips between 9 and 54 inches (0.2 and 1.4m) wide. It was similar in appearance to a modern cord, and was reversible. That fact that it could be turned and given a second lease of life made it popular in most middle-class homes.

Pile carpets of various kinds became more readily available after about 1850, and increasingly replaced the flat-woven types in the best rooms. Brussels carpet had a level-looped pile, Wilton a cut pile. Tapestry carpet, woven with pre-printed threads, could contain an almost limitless number of colours. Designers pounced on this new-won freedom to indulge the contemporary taste for three-dimensional naturalism. Hermann Muthesius, in his *Das Englische Haus*,

Right: The Hammersmith rug was produced by Morris & Co. in the 1880s. Morris followed Pugin's example and finished the rug with a fringe, since knotting the edges was the traditional way of securing the fabric against fraying.

was not alone in expressing distaste for their 'strident flower patterns, their naturalistic animals and landscapes, their imitations of Rococo gilt borders and other monstrosities'.

By the mid-1870s the fashion for covering the floors of the main rooms with a fitted carpet was disappearing among the wealthy. In *Housewife's Treasury*, Mrs Isabella Beeton wrote, 'At the present day in very many houses where tasteful effects are studied, carpets are tabooed to a considerable extent. The old style is now giving place to the far more healthy and cleanly mode of laying down a square of carpet in the centre of the room.' Stained or polished wooden floors or parquet flooring became popular, with the addition of an oriental rug or two for comfort, or later a carpet to the design of William Morris, C.F.A. Voysey or Walter Crane.

Fitted carpets today come in two forms: in addition to the body carpet which was standard

throughout Victorian times, we now also have broadloom carpet. Body carpet is generally sold in 27 or 36 inch (67 or 90cm) widths. Special care is required when laying this: if the seams come in the wrong place the effect can be unpleasant; seams should run the length of the room and not sideways across it. Broadloom carpet is usually 12 or 15 feet (3.7 or 4.6m) wide and only presents such problems if the

Above: An English rug of the 1860s sums up the popular taste of the time. Eastlake in his *Hints on Household Taste* ridiculed this kind of English naturalism as an example of 'the thousand and one pictorial monstrosities which you see displayed in the windows of Oxford Street and Ludgate Hill', then the two main areas of carpet showrooms in London.

room to be fitted is wider than the roll.

Fitted carpets in Victorian houses are prone to 'tramlines' which develop with the regular use of a vacuum cleaner. Even if a felt or underlay is put down, gaps between floorboards allow dust and dirt to be sucked up from underneath the floor. It is best to lay down hardboard if the carpets are light in colour. The sequence to be followed is: hardboard, then felt paper, then underlay and finally the carpet.

Another option open to the modern householder, and now back in fashion, is to adopt the Victorian custom of laying rugs over matting or directly on wooden floors. Even the traditional oil-cloth is experiencing a modest revival; some interior designers have created elaborate hand-painted oil-cloths for the present-day Victorian sitting-room.

Below: Standen in Sussex is one of the few surviving houses designed by Philip Webb. Webb worked closely with Morris & Co., and Standen represents the best existing Morris interior. The carpet was specially made for the house, and designed by J.H. Dearle.

CURTAINS
AND BLINDS

The Victorians, though keen to get more light into their houses, took care to control the impact of sunlight. Sun rots fabrics; sunlight, and strong light in general, was considered not kind to complexions. With swagged and curvaceous curtains and deep valances, the effect of large 19th-century windows was often cancelled out and the amount of light admitted to a heavily draped room was less than in the preceding century.

Male and female commentators agreed that curtains, in Loudon's phrase, gave 'an air of comfort to a room'. Grand rooms decorated in the perennially fashionable Louis Quatorze style would have had elaborate curtains in keeping with the opulence of the furnishings. The component parts (from ceiling down) were the pelmet (or cornice), the valance, the curtains themselves and the accompanying fringes and ties. The pelmet, a boxed-in area which blended into the cornice of the room, carried the valance, which hid the rod or pole from which the curtain was hung. Valances could also be entwined around the pole with swags and tails, hence dispensing with the pelmet. The curtains had fringes in contrasting colours and there were ties to loop back the curtains in the daytime. The screening function of curtains would have been performed by blinds or secondary curtains of a translucent material such as lace or muslin, and in the evenings the shutters would be closed.

Loudon deprecated the imported French fashions for their 'enormous folds of stuff over poles', which he considered 'abominable in taste'. His encyclopedia gave designs for window

The windows in this room are covered by Holland-blinds – a simple treatment, but perfectly adequate in a richly decorated setting.

draperies of some extravagance, but on the whole he considered the elaborate confections of hangings to be unnecessary and a taste only encouraged by upholsterers who sought a steady income from arranging ever more complex designs. Loudon admitted, all the same, that 'window curtains give the mistress of the house an excellent opportunity for exercising her taste in their arrangement'. In the 1890s, *The Lady* (a magazine for the 'gentlewoman') suggested that one of the marks of being a lady was the graceful arrangement of curtains and draperies.

Eastlake, in his *Hints on Household Taste*, called for simpler treatments, advocating curtains that hung straight down, attached by brass rings to a stout metal rod. In order to stop the draught from the gap between the top of the curtain and the window frame, he proposed a 'boxing in of wood', or pelmet, and a plain valance.

Curtain material and the style of treatment was chosen to complement the colour and status of the room, but in any arrangement the fabric had to fall into attractive folds. The Misses Garrett, in their *Suggestions for House Decoration* (1879), insist that the 'chief beauty of any drapery should be looked for in the folds into which it naturally falls'. Damask, silk and lightly glazed chintzes all found ready buyers, but by the mid-century, repp, a ribbed or corded weave, dominated the market. Writers emphasized that curtain material need not be costly so long as it had the right plastic qualities; the humbler fabrics, such as cotton, repp or cretonne, were also easier to keep clean, as well as being less prone to retaining smells than richer, denser materials.

Secondary curtains served much as modern net curtains. Where there was leaded glass in the top half of windows, half curtains suspended by a rod were ample protection from sun and rude passers-by. Sun blinds, which protected furniture and fabrics from fading, were usually full length. The two standard blinds used were the Venetian and the Holland (or roller) blinds. Victorian Venetian blinds were often very solidly made

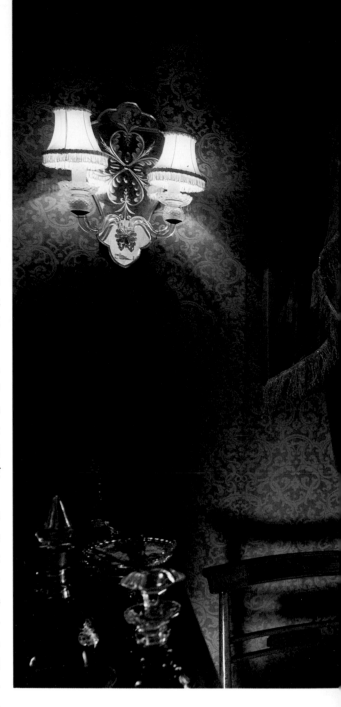

Above: This modest-sized room has been given full-blown curtains with cornice, valance, swags and tails. The actual work of screening the room is done by Holland blinds. Though it can be dangerous to overload a window with grand drapery, in this case a *recherché* window treatment has pulled the room up with it to add an importance belied by its size.

Opposite: In this illustration from J.G. Sowerby's and T. Crane's *At Home Again,* there is a curtain which is half a *portière* and half an ordinary window curtain. The curtain displays a simplicity modelled after Ancient Greek forms which had been one of the *points de départ* of the Aesthetic Movement.

Top: These curtains in the House of Commons were designed by Pugin. Pugin's thesis was that the fringe should be the same colour as the curtain, in contrast to the French taste which depended for effect on the use of a variety of fabrics and colours.

Above: Victorian Venetian blinds were wooden and tended to be a trifle heavy and sombre. Metal blinds, though lighter in construction, too often have an office-like soullessness, though such a style is the intention in this room.

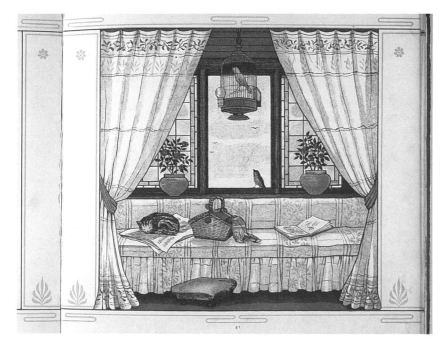

with wooden slats; dark green was the recommended colour, and although the green was intended to face into the street to give a unified aspect to the exterior, the effect could be rather dark indoors. Holland blinds were frequently treated as transparencies, and painted with landscape scenes or arabesque patterns.

The more showy festoon blinds, made of ruched-up fabric, could be used as the only window covering, though it was more usual to hang them in conjunction with curtains. As today, they had their admirers and detractors: an architect of the 1890s described them with their 'baggy flounces' as 'dressy-looking but very cradles for cherishing dust and dirt'.

Choosing a style of curtain today will depend on the size and importance of a room. The more ornate, layered French treatments presuppose quite a grand room, or else the curtains will overawe the rest of the decoration. The simpler treatments, such as Eastlake favoured, are best seen as background decoration as their impact in a room will be small. Bearing in mind the relative costs of good fabrics, it is as well to choose your curtains before making too many firm commitments about decorating the rest of a room.

Where Eastlake's stout metal rod fails us today is in dealing with bay windows. Victorian ironmongers sold knuckle joints which allowed a pole to turn the corners of a bay window. The proportion of window to wall in a bay window rarely allows a pole to sit along each face of the window with any elegance. Unless you can find a brass-founder to create a 'U' shaped curtain pole, the best solution is probably to use modern plastic fittings and a valance to disguise them. The more extreme solution is to suspend a pole right across the bay window opening and accept that you lose that space for the evening: in a room that has to be safe and tidy for guests as well as serve as a family play- or work-room, having a place to hide away toys and papers may be a distinct advantage.

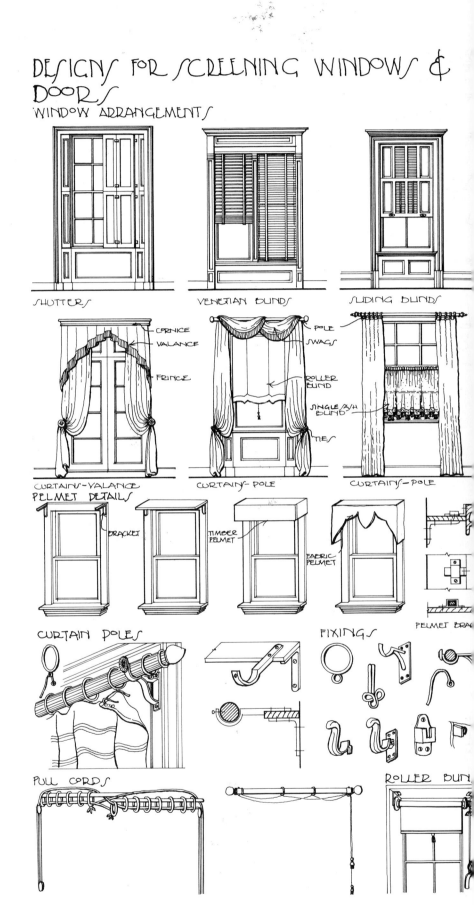

DESIGNS FOR SCREENING WINDOWS & DOORS

WINDOW ARRANGEMENTS

SHUTTERS   VENETIAN BLINDS   SLIDING BLINDS

CORNICE
VALANCE
FRINGE

POLE
SWAGS
ROLLER BLIND
SINGLE/3/4 BLIND
TIES

CURTAINS - VALANCE   CURTAINS - POLE   CURTAINS - POLE

PELMET DETAILS

BRACKET   TIMBER PELMET   FABRIC PELMET   PELMET BRAC

CURTAIN POLES   FIXINGS

PULL CORDS   ROLLER BLIN

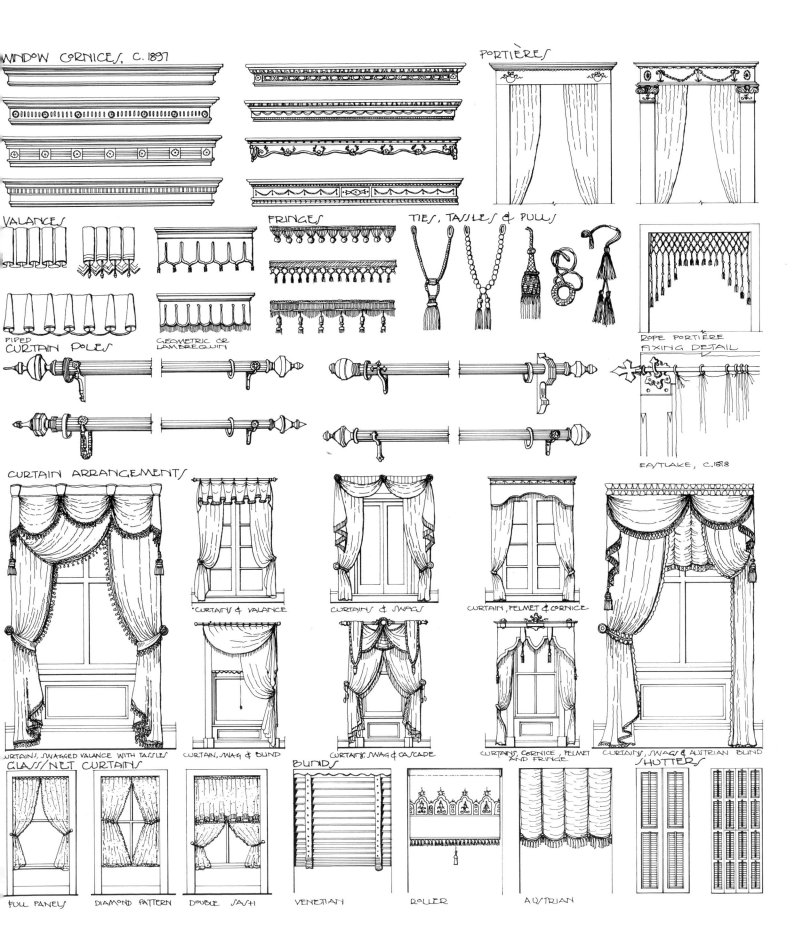

WINDOW CORNICES, C. 1897

PORTIÈRES

VALANCES

FRINGES

TIES, TASSLES & PULLS

PIPED

GEOMETRIC OR LAMBREQUIN

ROPE PORTIÈRE

CURTAIN POLES

FIXING DETAIL

EASTLAKE, C. 1818

CURTAIN ARRANGEMENTS

CURTAINS & VALANCE

CURTAINS & SWAGS

CURTAIN, PELMET & CORNICE

CURTAINS, SWAGGED VALANCE WITH TASSLES

CURTAIN, SWAG & BLIND

CURTAINS, SWAG & CASCADE

CURTAINS, CORNICE, PELMET AND FRINGE

CURTAINS, SWAGS & AUSTRIAN BLIND

GLASS/NET CURTAINS

BLINDS

SHUTTERS

FULL PANELS

DIAMOND PATTERN

DOUBLE SASH

VENETIAN

ROLLER

AUSTRIAN

203

FURNITURE AND UPHOLSTERY

Even more than heavily carved mahogany and walnut, it is the richly padded curves and deeply sprung chairs and sofas of the mid-century that seem to epitomize Victorian furniture. Upholstery changed dramatically with the invention of the coil spring, which made it possible for the upholsterer to produce the deep-buttoned forms which were at the heart of Victorian notions of comfort.

The new furnishings, their construction hidden under at least two layers of stuffing, demanded much skill and labour on the part of the upholsterer. Underlying all the coverings were the springs, stitched to webbing. Horsehair was used throughout the 19th century for both the first and second layers of stuffing in all good-class work. Other cheaper materials were hay, seaweed and woodshavings, in fact anything which when placed under hessian or scrim gave the desired shape. Scrim is a loosely woven but tightly spun linen which was used to enclose the first stuffing. A second stuffing of horsehair was covered with calico, which stopped the hairs working through the layer of soft cotton wadding placed under the top covering. To complete the effect, a wide range of fabrics was available with new colour combinations and patterns, matched by ever more elaborate trimmings, buttons, ruching, cords, tassels and fringes.

Button-back chairs, sofas and *chaises longues* were much in evidence at the Great Exhibition, but such feats of High Victorian upholstery never eclipsed earlier styles. In fact, Victorian furniture design is mainly a story of revivals:

Right: For winter, a cosy look may be created by draping a sofa with paisley shawls and a selection of cushions.

Victorians would have used repp and printed cottons as the standard material for upholstery. Today a linen union is popular for curtains and chair covers. These are examples of modern fabrics based on 19th-century patterns, produced by Bernard Thorp, London.

Top: Chester; a glazed cotton or chintz.

Above: Rainbow Shell; a Bargello style of design in a cotton-polyester tapestry-weave.

Right: Vine Leaves; hand-screen-printed cotton in two variations.

every historical style was copied and developed. There was an appetite for antiques, and a thriving industry existed in Wardour Street in London cannibalizing pieces imported from northern Europe and re-making them into Jacobean and Tudor designs. Many pieces, such as the 18th-century wing chair, remained current right through the century, and the white and gold painted furniture of the Louis XIV period was ever popular as the *nouveau riche* style.

The Regency period favoured a Grecian style of furniture which was upholstered in rich silk velvets, damasks and satins or, for dining-room and library, in morocco leather. Nearly all upholstery was 'French stuffed', with an extra roll of stuffing wrapped in scrim and stitched in place round the front edge of the piece, which gave a fine shaped elegance to Regency furnishings. The better pieces were of solid rosewood or mahogany; the lesser pieces were more often made from soft wood, and veneered. These agreeable designs stayed current and then became part of the Regency revival of the 1890s.

The best of mid-century Gothic furniture was designed by architects who had learnt their art while designing church furnishings; this led to the tendency for Gothic Revival furniture to be relatively massive. The Gothic Revival and the Arts and Crafts Movement overlap in the figure of Philip Webb who was the chief furniture designer for the firm of Morris & Co.

Later upholstery can be seen as a reaction to the tastes of mid-century. Designers of the 1860s and 1870s, working within hand-crafted Arts and Crafts ideals or with commercial manufacturers, began to produce lighter pieces using English hardwoods, sometimes influenced by Japanese forms but generally under the banner of Art furniture. Art furniture's significant trait was its antipathy to deep upholstery. In the 1880s there was a change towards neo-Georgian and simpler vernacular-based furniture which was less dependent on springs and stuffing to give it its shape.

STYLES OF VICTORIAN FURNITURE
THE RULING TASTE

The furniture of the Ruling Taste was dominated by the new upholstery and techniques of mechanical manufacture. This usually meant that the structure was hidden under layers of stuffing and heavy padding further loaded with ruching, cords and trimmings. The design of these deep-cushioned pieces varied little, but their ornamentation was adapted to new fashions which were largely Paris-led. Foreign hardwoods, such as mahogany and walnut, were commonly used for the frame; these were French polished to render the surface hard and bright.

LADIES EASY CHAIR   CHESTERFIELD

EASY ARM CHAIR OR 'FAUTEUIL'

PEDESTAL SIDEBOARD

BALLOON-BACK CHAIR

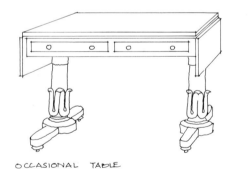

OCCASIONAL TABLE

BALLOON-BACK CHAIR

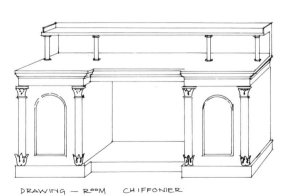

DRAWING — ROOM CHIFFONIER

LOUIS XIV-STYLE CHAIR

ADVANCED AND ARTISTIC TASTE

Victorian architect-designed furniture begins with Pugin, whose motto 'form follows function' became the *leitmotif* of furniture designers who came after him. The sham of French upholstery, where structure had no relation to shape, drove designers into the kitchen to find furniture untainted by what was seen as the dishonest upholstery of the Ruling Taste. As well as the kitchen vernacular, architects adapted Gothic, Jacobean and Georgian forms which had an elegance and simplicity in contrast to the curved, soggy comforts of the average Victorian drawing-room.

LIBRARY BOOKCASE BY C.L. EASTLAKE, 1878

PUGIN TABLE

LOUNGING CHAIR BY E. GODWIN, 1878

MORRIS & Cº ADJUSTABLE CHAIR, 1866

BUFFET - MORRIS & Cº 1880

MORRIS & Cº SUSSEX CHAIR

MORRIS & Cº TABLE

CENTURY GUILD SETTEE, 1888

VIOLLET-LE-DUC CHAIR

VOYSEY CHAIR.

QUEEN ANNE SOFA

MACKINTOSH CHAIR.

DRAWING-ROOMS

T he Victorian drawing-room was an essentially feminine room; it was supposed to be
pleasant and cheerful; most of all it was to be
comfortable. A drawing-room was the main
public room of the house: here guests were
received and, it was hoped, impressed by the
wealth, culture and taste of the household.

The twin aims of comfortable hospitality
and social showing-off did not always make for a
happy effect. Mid-Victorian rooms were notori-
ous for their 'showy discomfort'. The generation
which had been brought up in such rooms
rebelled against the contorted and over-stuffed
furniture, and created for themselves the lighter
and more relaxed Artistic rooms of the 1870s
and 1880s. These were modelled on the amusing
and individualistic rooms of architects and
professional artists, who had become a socially
acceptable class by the late 1860s.

Of course, even the Artistic room soon filled
up with clutter. The Victorian drawing-room
resembles an abstract painting which could be
endlessly added to. As new fads and crazes came
on to the market, it became a repository for the
stream of manufactured products, curios from all
corners of the Empire, as well as new art forms
such as photography, all available at relatively
modest prices. And then there were decorative
trimmings galore: stencil work in the panels of
doors, draperies on mantelshelves, on tables and
over chairs. The furniture came in every possible
revived historical style, as well as in oriental lac-
quered bamboo or Indian brasswork.

The Victorians' employment of colour is the
aspect of their decoration most often overlooked
today. There were more colours and there were
stronger colours, but they all related to one
dominant effect. Colours were applied in gradu-
ated tints of the colour used for the filling, the
main part of the wall above the dado and below

This drawing-room is in
many ways an exemplary
recreation of a Victorian
room: the quaint and jokey
clutter is successfully
controlled by the all-
embracing dark reds of the
walls and fabric. The effect
is deceptively simple, but
much skill has been
invested to achieve it. The
scale and colour of each
object has been carefully
thought out.

the frieze. The cornice and ceiling would be in lighter tones of the main wall colour. The woodwork too was taken in with a colour that harmonized with the wall treatments. This practice of harmonious decoration had the effect of uniting the room into a visual entity within which all other items of decoration could blend.

There was disagreement about dadoes in drawing-rooms; since many Victorian drawing-rooms were too high for their size, an extra wall division was often useful to reduce the impression of height. Eastlake felt that a room with a single wallpaper running from skirting to ceiling was the 'most dreary method' of decoration. It

Above: The attraction of this living-room, decorated in late-Regency style, is the way in which the garden has been effectively brought indoors, as was recommended by Humphry Repton and also by his admirer, Loudon.

Right: A country house decorated in a loosely Loudonesque way employs the intermediate styles of the 1840s. The walls are covered in green damask, and the curtain or *portière* hangs down from a pelmet which has been taken in as part of the Gothick cornice of the room.

Above: In a cottage sitting-room a screen makes a homely family corner, blocking off the sofa from the doorway and its traffic. In large rooms, especially, screens can make a virtue of intimacy while also hiding unfortunate eyesores or stopping draughts.

has the attendant problem that such a room will require a fairly consistent scale and style of furniture. Eastlake recommended a plain dado; later, the dado received every kind of Artistic treatment; stamped anaglypta, however, was always the safe option.

Dealing with a drawing-room in a Victorian house today, experimentation with colour is required on a little more daring scale than has been customary since the last war. The Modern Movement and the Neo-Georgian fashion rejected the dense colour arrangements of the Victorians and have left a legacy of conservative pastels and whites. The varying of colours and textures in a more Victorian style can accommodate a far more heterogeneous accumulation of furniture and objects than the average modern room scheme. Even modernist furniture, if good, can well hold its own in Victorian

Left: This terraced cottage parlour has an ordered informality and simplicity emphasized by the white walls and ceilings. Cottages in pre-industrial times would have had white-washed interior walls. This bareness was updated and stylized by many Arts and Crafts architects.

Below: The large amount of daylight entering this converted chapel allows flowering plants to become the principal decorative feature. A virtue is made of the woodwork to compensate for the difficult spaces inherent in such an extensive living area.

Right: This room is dominated by a French ceramic Art Nouveau fireplace whose colours have been used to create the decorative scheme. The walls are painted and stencilled to give a faded finish, echoed in the upholstery.

Below: The small scale and simple features of this sitting-room have been enhanced by an elaborate curtain pole and decorative wall panels created with Victorian frieze papers. Curtains that are looped back during the day will 'puddle' when drawn. Here the effect is used to soften the bareness of parquet flooring.

surroundings. The also-rans of modern furniture can at a pinch be softened with drapery, or re-painted to blend into the wall. Pictures, however, can pose insuperable problems. Continental modern art in particular, is deliberately antagonistic to Victorian rooms and their bourgeois pretensions, and will not harmonize with an elaborate treatment. The re-instatement of a Victorian drawing-room is made less difficult since the wallpapers of the Arts and Crafts Movement are still manufactured, as are many Morris & Co. chintzes. These will be pricey, but they do represent examples of the finest pattern designs. The white ceiling is now part of the national psyche, but if wallpapered or densely coloured ceilings are not to your taste, a complementary off-white may suffice to harmonize with the walls.

Above: Converted from a malthouse, this cottage has preserved the openness of the original industrial space. The open plan, although creating problems with heating and services, allows the architecture and the character of the malthouse's interior to be retained.

Left: This converted mews has had the ceilings taken away and a large French chimneypiece added to create a witty pastiche of a baronial hall. The fireplace, walls, and galvanized sliding window shutters have all been given a faded, old look so that they work together.

Above: A minimal background has been created by using grey tiles and carpet, with one yellow wall acting as the animating spirit of the room. The danger of hi-tech within the Victorian house is that it can look more like 1950s revival than contemporary.

DINING – ROOMS

In a Victorian house the dining-room was on the ground floor: in larger houses it was the front room, while the back room was a morning-room or back parlour. In smaller houses, the drawing-room was the front room, and the dining-room, separated by double doors, was at the back. It had to be on the ground floor to be close to the kitchen quarters which were in the basement or ground-floor back extension. In better-preserved 19th-century houses you will find flap tables in the hall outside the dining-room for the maid to put down the tray before opening the door.

The masculine tone of the Victorian dining-room was set by the heavy fireplace, the dark family portraits and the sideboard which was an

Right: The dining-room at Flintham, Nottingham-shire, built in 1854, combines echoes of the banqueting hall with a high degree of comfort. The Victorian dining-room was traditionally the stage upon which a family's largesse could be displayed.

Opposite: The dining-room at the Linley Sambournes' home in Kensington is an example of the softer artistic decoration of rooms which appeared in the 1870s and 1880s. The black marble fireplace, which tended to dominate most dining-rooms, has been obliterated by being taken in with the same colour as the woodwork.

ornate and bulky object in dark stained wood. Then there was crimson flock wallpaper (if a north-facing room), or green (if south-facing). Grand houses would have panelling. The colour of the walls was decided by the fact that warm browns and reds were best to hang pictures against. In the absence of a picture gallery, a north-facing dining-room was a good place to have works of art and at night the glass in the picture frames added sparkle to candelight.

Today the dining-room is the first room to be sacrificed: a nursery is more immediately useful, and it is no longer regarded as 'interesting' or unusual to eat in the kitchen. It must be said that not eating in the kitchen allows for a certain theatricality which makes for a more exciting event (as well as making work easier for the cook). Modern metropolitan taste is for a softer, more intimate ambience than the traditional Victorian formality. In the country and suburbs, however, where neighbours come to dinner more often than friends, formality and its conventions may be an advantage, especially when dealing with unknown quantities.

Above: The boxed-in radiator acts as a sideboard in a room that leaves little space for other furniture. Inexpensive folding chairs and simple table dressings provide a sense of lightness in what was originally a rather dark hallway.

Right: Open-plan living presents excellent opportunities for creating a theatrical dining-room setting.

STUDIES, LIBRARIES AND BILLIARD ROOMS

Portraits of Victorian Man in his study reveal a dark room with solid furniture which stands in contrast to the female equivalent of the boudoir. A study was the place of daily business, with a desk for answering letters and paying bills. It could also be a working office and was fitted out with appropriate symbols: dark oak panelling, pictures with civic and patriotic subject matter, professional certificates, sporting trophies, a coat of arms, perhaps, and other evocative mementoes.

In most middle-class homes, the line between study and library was never firmly drawn. A study might contain the bulk of a household's books just as a library had a writing desk as well as the standard central library table.

In the 18th century, books had been expensive and a library was a status symbol. In the 19th century, books and journals multiplied, as did

readership. Humphry Repton popularized the idea of the library as a family room and suggested that it should give on to the conservatory, thus making for a more airy and agreeable space than the chilly antiquarian parlour of the previous century. This more sociable library remained popular, especially in the new suburban villas.

The traditional library remained a *sine qua non* of the large country house. There would have been built-in bookcases of some architectural pretension: pedimented and pilastered in classical style, or suitably Gothicized. Free-standing bookcases had obvious advantages in leasehold town houses, and their glazed doors also protected the books from city pollution. One Victorian architect advocated using roller blinds fastened to the tops of bookcases to protect the contents, and it was standard practice to suspend a tooled or embossed leather valance from each shelf to reduce the dust gathering on the tops of the books.

A room devoted to books becomes expensive when all the bookcases are made to match. Two free-standing bookcases and a wall of built-in shelving will serve the purpose, but will lack the charm of a unified style. To gain that atavistic authority of a library, the architecture of the bookcases really does need to be prominent.

If you devote a room today to a study, you will have two main options. With funds, you can create the womb of leather and woodwork favoured by Victorians. This is fine for effect, but unless you feel happy working in such dim surroundings, it may be best to produce something closer to a modern office. It will probably be a functional room – private and secure, where mess can remain unmolested until 9 o'clock the next morning. In planning such a room, the starting point is a series of questions: how many books, what kind of shelving, how many filing

Opposite, above: This 1890 room in the home of B.B. Comegys, President of the Philadelphia National Bank, shows the study as a masculine retreat filled with a display of cultural and historical artefacts. Part museum, part office-at-home, the effect is obviously meant to impress the visitor and signal the occupant's wide range of interest and learning.

Opposite below: In this writing-room the wallpaper is hardly conducive to serious thought, which suggests that it was not intended for everyday use. Country houses generally had such a room where guests could write their letters.

Left: The library of Horstead Place, Sussex, was fitted up in the mid-19th century by a local carpenter. Bookcases were always carefully sited away from external walls to prevent damp penetrating from outside, and placed where they would offer the best sound-proofing.

cabinets, what machinery – computer, telex, fax machine and so on – in short, what must the room accommodate? For the office-cum-study purpose-built shelves, counters and cupboards will probably serve best. These fixtures can be incorporated into the style of the room by painting or graining, as can the filing cabinets.

When siting your bookcases you should pay attention to sound-proofing, not simply to blot out television and record-player noise from outside, but also to muffle the reverberations of your typewriter or printer from inside. A built-in bookcase will help cut down noise passing through a wall, and heavy carpets and underfelt have a useful deadening effect.

In the late-19th century many libraries housed a billiard table, a pertinent indicator of the intellectual ambitions of the middle and upper classes. In country houses, first-rate town houses and middle-class villas, a separate billiard room was an essential feature. It was usually a ground-floor room at the back of the house where a strong floor could be provided to take the weight of the table. The grander type of billard room had high wood panelling on the walls and was decorated in a masculine style, with some concession to women in a large inglenook or raised platform with comfortable upholstered leather seats. The wooden floor was left bare except for wide runners round the table. Silk-shaded ceiling lights hung above the table.

Traces of billiard rooms sometimes survive in the form of tell-tale relics such as cue fittings on the walls. Today, a billiard room (where you will play snooker) may have limited appeal. To house a full-size billiard table you need a large room 18 feet by 24 feet (5.5m x 7.3m), giving a minimum of 6 feet (1.8m) round the table. The bulk and weight of the table limits which floors will accommodate it. Although the room loses most of its floor space, it will double perfectly as a picture gallery – or indeed a library.

Open-plan living of the 1960s had obvious antecedents in the 1950s office, with its rejection of private space. If this plan is used for a private house which is to incorporate a work space, as here, it will only be satisfactory if the household and the vicinity of the desk have low noise levels.

Left: This example of the late-Victorian country house billiard room was designed by Webb for Standen in Sussex. Billiards was the big, male social pursuit of the late-19th century, and billiard rooms were usually given a clubland feel. Most middle-class villas and town houses had them, not only to entertain the males of the household but also to attract potential husbands to the house.

Above: A newly built library has been designed with traditional features such as tailor-made bookcases, glass-frontcd cupboards and fully panelled walls, and some modern facilities as well, including concealed lighting. The grilles of the lower cupboards are screened with fabric that matches the curtains over the Gothic arched windows of the room.

KITCHENS AND BATHROOMS

The greatest changes in the use of the Victorian house have occurred in the kitchen and bathroom, and in everything to do with washing and sanitary arrangements; few Victorian homes had anything we would recognize as a bathroom.

Compared with advances in transport, engineering and manufacturing, progress in kitchen and bathroom design in the 19th century seems surprisingly sluggish. 'A New Design for a Kitchen Range', first patented by Thomas Robinson in 1780, remained the basic pattern for cookers for over a century: a cast-iron, coal-burning hearth, with the fire becoming increasingly enclosed as improvements were introduced. Gas stoves were shown at the Great Exhibition of 1851, but they were not in general use until the end of the century. The reason for this lack of progress is probably social: the availability of servants meant that the housewife could keep out of the kitchen, which remained the jealously guarded sanctuary of the cook.

The kitchen in most early 19th-century houses was in the basement; by the 1860s, however, new health acts and byelaws were discouraging the use of basements as habitable rooms and so increasingly kitchens were housed in an extension at the back. In larger houses the necessity of keeping this part of the house away from the owners and their guests was more important than providing easy access to the dining-room. In poorer households the kitchen was not separated; as in many cottages and farmhouses today, the kitchen formed the principal living-room, any other ground-floor room being reserved as a parlour for entertaining visitors.

Kitchens were bare and functional rooms, such cosiness as they possessed deriving from the range, and from the simple china-lined dresser and wall shelving for utensils. Otherwise the furniture was serviceable rather than comfortable, with perhaps a rush-seated Windsor chair for Cook to sit on after working hours. The sink would have been in fireclay, probably manufactured by Doulton & Co., with teak drainers and a wooden plate rack hung above. There was no working countertop as understood today, all preparation being carried out on a central deal table, scrubbed daily, which contained the working cutlery underneath in drawers. Hot water was obtained either from kettles or pans suspended above the open range or from a cast-iron boiler situated on one side of the fire-basket. On the other

The great kitchen at Lanhydrock in Cornwall, fitted out in the 1880s, contains all the elements one associates with a Victorian kitchen: the low scrubbed table in the middle, the dresser with its open shelves, and ranks of copper pans and jelly moulds. Although not built for elegance, it has its own beauty in its utilitarian simplicity.

A modern kitchen/dining-room combines the traditional look of the Victorian kitchen with the eating requirements of the present day. No money has been spent on upper cupboards. Instead, there are open shelves where everything can be seen, and the white stove does not look out of place next to the pine cabinet because the room is primarily functional.

side of the grate was the oven, which was used for baking only, as the heat was too uneven and variable for roasting. Roasting was carried out on spits in front of the fire, the melting fat being collected below in trays. Ranges with flat hotplates on top, as on modern stoves, worked by means of a system of flues and dampers which passed hot air under the plates and around the oven. The more advanced the range – or 'kitchener' as it became known – the more enclosed the fire, but regardless of improvements, this central piece of equipment was the bane of every cook's life, going out in winter, insufferably hot in summer.

The scullery, which in large houses was exclusively set aside for washing-up, became in late-Victorian times attached to smaller suburban houses as well, where it was always positioned next to the kitchen. Larders frequently led off from the scullery rather than the kitchen, to be free from the heat and smells of cooking.

Bathrooms as we understand them now were not widely installed until the end of the century. The famous Red House, built for William Morris in 1859, did not possess one. For most of the century bathing was carried out in large portable tubs, preferably in front of an open fire. They varied from a shallow tray to stand in while sponging oneself down, to the hip bath with a high sloping back. The bather lay half in, half out, with knees inevitably protruding. There were also full-size reclining baths, though these were rarer. Needless to say, servants provided the hot water in buckets, and removed the waste afterwards in the same way.

All washing took place in bedrooms in middle-class homes, or in tubs placed before the kitchen range in poorer homes. The familiar marble wash-stand, with its china bowls and ewers, gave good service for decades.

A significant advance came about with the provision by water companies of water under sufficient pressure to drive the supply

The exuberance of this decorated porcelain basin, with its blue transfer motifs, is matched by the ornate paper, mirror and fittings in a rich, High Victorian style, providing a good example of the use of pattern on pattern.

In one of the bathrooms at Castle Drogo, built by Edwin Lutyens from 1910 onwards, the basin is a plumbed-in version of the traditional marble wash-stand set upon an oak plinth, a satisfying marriage of end-of-the-period elegance and hygiene.

into the roof space of private homes, where it could be stored in cisterns. Water could now be piped throughout the house, and with the introduction of the first, formidable-looking geysers, the fixed bath with its own supply of hot water made its appearance.

Piped running water also inspired the rapid improvement of the 'water closet' after 1875; previously, most households had depended on earth closets and privies in an outbuilding or at the bottom of the garden, and chamber pots.

Now rooms began to be set aside for bathrooms, often converted dressing-rooms adjoining a bedroom, which were usually provided with a fireplace and furnished with chairs and other comfortable accessories. Thus they were sometimes pleasantly large by modern standards. Conversely, when purpose-built bathrooms were installed in new houses from the 1880s onwards, they were comparatively small, reflecting the low priority given to the activities performed in them.

Right: The comfortable, rustic feel of this kitchen comes from a subtle use of Victorian elements. The Aga occupies the same space as the original kitchen range; the sea green of the stove has been picked up in the newly made dresser.

Below: In a kitchen of the 1890s, pride of place goes to the black-leaded, cast-iron range with its two ovens, semi-enclosed fire-grate, hot plates and warming compartment. Such ranges required a constant and very hot fire, and are estimated to have consumed more than a dozen scuttles of coal a day.

KITCHENS

It is almost impossible to create anything like a faithful replica of a Victorian kitchen without compromising modern standards of convenience and comfort. One of the options is not to take this path at all but to go for a highly modern treatment; very often, the kitchen is in a part of the house not provided with elaborate mouldings or architectural details, so modern fittings will not look out of place. The other option is to evoke the Victorian past through fittings and decoration, but we must remember that whatever we do in this direction will be largely pastiche rather than anything approaching faithful reproduction.

Today, of course, we have the modern cooker in place of the range, the fridge instead of the larder and meat-safe, and perhaps a dishwasher to replace the work of the scullery. This means that if we do wish to include a Victorian

element, it will have to revolve around such features as mouldings, panelling and tiles, fittings such as old-fashioned taps, and – most atmospheric of all – a Victorian dresser.

If the kitchen is to be used for eating in, the traditional table (particularly one with drawers) may be too low for comfort, but a new wooden table need not look out of place, and its working surface will probably be at a better height. Open shelves and simple wooden floor units will also be in keeping. A work top in wood or quarry tiles supported on a wooden framework with open shelves below will look rather better than many of the modern 'antique' or 'country' units now advertised, which are fitted with elaborately panelled doors, and are correspondingly expensive.

Many excellent modern kitchens have been assembled out of assorted Victorian pieces of more or less junk furniture. If the woods do not match, then the whole assembly can be painted, perhaps in the traditional colours of chocolate or apple green.

In a new kitchen it is important to choose your appliances first, decide where they should

be placed, and ensure that they are all adequately supplied with power and plumbing. Then build the storage units and work surfaces around them. The kitchen will be one of the most complex rooms in the house in terms of pipework and electrical supply: any lack of forethought in the planning of these services is bound to prove costly and painful to rectify at a later stage.

There is rarely much of a role in the kitchen for the avid restorer: the changing social function of this room since the Victorian period has seen to the removal of most authentic features. Few ranges survive, except in some rural buildings, but where they do they are well worth retaining, if only for occasional use.

Below: A modern hob has been built into the chimney breast, and is given a traditional look by the copper hood and a simple white tiled surround.

Right: The fitted cupboards of this kitchen have been designed to match the Gothic windows, themselves replacements for a single ugly picture window which had been knocked through the facade before the house was restored.

Two matching dressers
show what can be done
with a very simple design,
using tongue-and-groove
boarding, a finely detailed
architrave at the top and
open shelves at the bottom.

The kitchen of an
unmodernized tenement
flat in Glasgow provides an
excellent reference for a
modest, turn-of-the-century
family kitchen, down to the
built-in coal box behind the
table. Dun colours
predominate, and *trompe
l'oeil* wallpaper
masquerades as wood
panelling and tiles.

This splendidly robust display of china, heaped upon a fine kitchen dresser, convincingly revives the Victorian fondness for clutter.

In the kitchen of Cragside, built in 1870, ornament has been reduced to a minimum, resulting in an impression of austere efficiency.

DRESSERS

In the Victorian kitchen, apart from the obligatory range, the only item of fitted furniture would probably have been the dresser. Though very often stripped today, it would have been painted in Victorian times, with cup hooks along the shelves and narrow grooves or strips of wood along each shelf to hold the plates displayed there in an upright position. The bottom part of the dresser would hold drawers and deep cupboards or large open shelves for a breadbin and other bulky objects.

In today's nostalgic kitchen, it is often a good idea to leave out a wall of fitted cupboards and have one very large dresser, either found or purpose-built, with china and other objects displayed in the original way. A simple dresser can be made from an old double cupboard with new shelves of the same length fitted above, held in position by a frame of plain vertical planks. Suitable mouldings to decorate the top of the dresser can be obtained from most timber merchants.

If the kitchen is small and modernistic, do not be tempted to put in a dresser just to soften the starkness of it. If you really cannot live with a hi-tech kitchen, do not have one. You will not soften it up: you will mess it up.

CUPBOARDS AND SHELVES

Above: The traditional glass-fronted cabinet of the butler's pantry provides the inspiration for a simple kitchen design with no expensive fripperies and a dark paint colour which really works.

Opposite: A thoroughly practical and elegant kitchen has been created under a pitched glass roof in this modern extension. The traditional touches in the foreground provide the link with the elaborate period treatment of the other rooms of the house.

Right: A modern fitted kitchen unit plays upon Victorian themes and has been painted to give some semblance of age, but the blue and white crockery looks as though it is hardly ever used.

Far right: A stylish window treatment with a fretwork pelmet provides a wonderful example of how to draw on the past and simplify, but still achieve a very Victorian feeling.

Many people today want built-in cupboards, yet the Victorians, like hard-working chefs in modern restaurants, almost always went for more easily accessible open shelving, where utensils in daily use could be kept within easy reach.

If authentic Victorian kitchen furniture is beyond your means – or not to your taste – you may be able to adapt other pieces of furniture, such as shop-fittings, to achieve the desired effect. Old-looking lower cupboards are easier to find than upper. I sometimes wonder why we need upper cupboards at all. I much prefer open shelves around the kitchen, stocked with uniform and handsome storage jars and interesting bottles. Everything is on display in a neat, attractive and accessible fashion. But for those who still will not give in, perhaps there is something to be said for the 'pantry look', based on the traditional butler's pantry, with glass-fronted cabinets at eye level and simple panelled cupboards below.

An alternative is to build cupboards to your own design, achieving some degree of Victorian atmosphere by copying architectural details from elsewhere in the house. Then it will look as if the cupboards were made at the same time. If you live in a Victorian Gothic house, for instance, you can put a Gothic arch moulding on the front of the kitchen cupboards or echo the

mouldings on the doors of the house. This is what I mean when I say that the modern Victorian kitchen must contain a large element of pastiche. But it can be a pastiche that is effective and enjoyable.

If the house you have bought has fitted kitchen units which you dislike, a simple way to change them is to remove the doors and get a carpenter to make up panelled or boarded wooden doors to the same size. The replacements can then be attached with the same hinges as the old doors, while the carcase and shelving of the cupboards can remain in place, totally obscured by the new cladding.

On the other hand, if you are going to install a modern fitted kitchen the task is relatively easy and needs little comment from me. But one important caveat: don't be tempted to fit the kitchen in such a way that the feeling of the Victorian architecture or the proportion and scale of the rooms are lost. It is not necessary to lower ceilings and remove cornices. I think it better to place a minimal hi-tech kitchen around the walls of a Victorian room rather than try to streamline every nook and cranny. Or, as some designers propose, you can take this idea one step further by placing all your modern kitchen equipment in a carefully designed island in the middle of the room.

Above: The tongue-and-groove back to these shelves is entirely in keeping with the period, although their use as a backdrop to a kitchen sink certainly is not. None the less, this is a delightful and inventive solution.

Above right: This is modern living with a Victorian veneer. The hob and sink unit have been set into an old sideboard, bringing the kitchen into the dining-room rather than the more customary converse.

Right: The open style of this sink area follows in the Victorian tradition, while a miscellaneous collection of Victorian tiles helps to bring interest to what would otherwise be an insignificant corner.

S I N K S   A N D   S U R R O U N D S

Other than using the traditional deep butler sink – generally found in the scullery and usually made of a heavy and unforgiving china called fireclay – there is little you can do to introduce a proper sense of authenticity to the sink in the modern kitchen. Modern stainless steel sinks are probably a necessary compromise, but you might like to consider those that are finished in colours rather than shiny metal.

There is no need to put the kitchen sink underneath a window. This is a throw-back to a former age when the washing-up would take half the day, and can entirely spoil a kitchen plan.

A lot of modern kitchens do not have full-sized draining boards on the assumption that a dishwasher will be used for most kitchen and dining ware, but in practice this often proves to be a mistake. Draining boards still have their uses; teak draining boards may be the most sympathetic.

Old-fashioned taps, or at least taps that look old-fashioned, are available in brass. Public health regulations may in some cases require the supply of cold drinking water to be kept totally separate from the supply of hot water in the kitchen and you should find out how these regulations will affect you before deciding to install mixer taps.

Tiles – used in the splash-back to the sink and elsewhere – are particularly effective in giving a Victorian look to a kitchen. But a complete set is one of the hardest things to find. There are reproduction Victorian tiles on the market, but most of them look reproduction. One trick is to buy various old tiles and not attempt to match them. When arranging the electrical power points at work-top level, try to take the tiling grid into consideration. There is nothing more irritating than to find, after buying some old Victorian tiles, that there is a socket which cuts into the corners of four of them. It is worth laying them out on a template and giving the drawing to the electrician before he starts wiring.

Above: The kitchen of Cragside is splendid in its austerity. Modern purists would have to go this far to be authentic.

Right: The elements of this modern kitchen are similar to the above, and the same era is evoked, yet this design manages to marry practicality with affection and warmth.

SURFACES AND LIGHTING

Opposite: The hand-painted motifs on the doors bring a note of individuality to an otherwise stark room, and are authentic, but they have worn badly and will be difficult to restore. The sink is well lit, and the idea of mounting plate racks above it is both traditional and efficient, provided that the supporting framework is left open at the bottom to let the drips through.

Below: The units in this kitchen are built into surrounds inspired by a traditional hearth and the surfaces and shelves of a dairy or wine cellar. The fluorescent lighting works well under the chimney breast, but is harsh and uninviting when used unshaded above the window.

Apart from the central deal table, Victorian kitchens had no work surfaces. We definitely require them; and to my mind a hardwood finish, such as teak or any of its close cousins, unquestionably looks best. Tiled work surfaces look good when new but are difficult to keep clean: the grouting and edging soon begins to look unhygienic. Slate is a fine looking alternative, and not too expensive if it does not require awkward cutting.

Vertical wooden surfaces in a kitchen, including doors, cupboards, hatches and panelling, are the most used of any in a house and need hard-wearing finishes. Stripped wooden furniture and bare wooden surfaces may achieve a nostalgic effect, but they are quite unhistorical as well as impractical. The Victorians themselves were great enthusiasts for paint and varnish, but beware of special paint finishes. Graining, stippling and other such effects do not last well, and I tend to avoid using them in kitchens. For a nostalgic look, I would recommend tongue-and-groove boarding, all painted in one colour. Proper recessed panelling is more expensive to do, but looks good, especially if it matches the style of the original doors of the house.

For kitchen floors I have no hesitation in using tiles, provided that there is a sound concrete base on which to lay them. They could be old-fashioned Victorian tessellated tiles, or ordinary quarry tiles. But putting tiles on top of a wooden floor can be risky. Wooden boards move, and then tiles crack. A tiled floor is only likely to be successful if you remove the floor-boards, infill between the joists with wire mesh, put a concrete bed into that, and finally tile on top. But even then, the method is not perfect. There may still be movement in the floor because of the flexing of the joists.

After tiles I favour cork floors; they have the advantage of being less hard on the feet. The Victorians, however, preferred linoleum above all other floorings in their kitchens and traditional linos still have their place. But they are becoming increasingly hard to find.

As we have already noted, lighting must be either functional or decorative. By all means have a wrought-iron white-painted lamp in the middle of the room as a decoration, but that is all it should be – you will also need more efficient lighting to carry out kitchen jobs. Use shadow-free task lighting, either in the form of track lighting or strip lighting fixed underneath the cupboards and shining down on work surfaces. There is much to be said for low voltage spot lighting. But if you are using recessed down-lighters, do not forget that by cutting into the ceiling to position them you will have removed one layer of insulation protecting the rooms upstairs from the smells and noises of the kitchen. Additional insulation must be provided.

Preparation of food will require bright task lighting, but when the family come home and want to eat in the kitchen a far lower level will be appropriate. This makes it convenient to have two separate lighting circuits, each of which is controlled by its own switch. This is also useful if your kitchen opens on to another room, so you do not always face the glare of task lighting.

Far left: The use of roughly hewn stone and decorative lighting makes this walk-in larder very inviting – both practical and a delight to the eye.

Left: Victorian panelled doors have been adapted to slide open and provide a wide entrance to a modern utility room.

BATHROOMS

To create a modern version of the Victorian bathroom we have to dream a little: the image that comes before the mind's eye is one of space, warmth, the luxury of enjoying a bath surrounded by pictures, carpets and elegant furnishings.

It is not a complete lie: this is the bathroom of the transitional period when the first fitted and plumbed baths were housed in dressing-rooms and spare bedrooms and still recalled the days of the hip bath before the open fire.

Even the later, hygienic bathrooms of the turn of the century, all tiles and functionalism, provide a valid model for an attractive modern scheme, reminiscent perhaps of the spa town hotel or the gentleman's club.

Above: The purpose-built furniture of the Cragside bathhouse combines a forward looking stylishness with the late-19th-century concern for a functional and hygienic environment in the bathroom.

Right: This very thorough – and lavish – evocation of the early Victorian bathroom has entirely modern plumbing. Such a bath, full of water, is extremely heavy, so it is essential to check that the floor is adequately supported.

242

BASINS AND LAVATORIES

A design with white tiles offset by a green band demonstrates the merits of using a simple setting to highlight fittings of good quality.

This richly decorated modern bathroom recalls a High Victorian ornamentation more readily associated with libraries or churches than with the plumbing.

For most Victorians, the place of ablution was the wash-stand which, until the introduction of internal piping, belonged in the bedroom or dressing-room. Wash-stands usually took the form of a wooden dresser with a polished marble top, upon which was placed a variety of china basins and ewers, dishes for soap, shaving equipment, tooth brushes, and perhaps a brass can, filled by hand, to supply hot water. When piped water arrived the same style of wash-stand was, quite simply, plumbed with taps, but this hybrid form was soon superseded by the all-ceramic pedestal basin – familiar to us today – which was considered easier to clean and thus more hygienic.

The word lavatory would, in the Victorian period, have indicated a wash basin. It only developed as a euphemism for the water closet after the 1880s when the water closet began to feature more and more as an internal fixture, usually placed in the same room as a wash basin. Prior to this, indoor water closets had suffered from the poor state of the sewerage system outside and were prone to foul air. Since the 1848 Public Health Act demanded that all households had a fixed sanitary arrangement of some kind – be it an earth closet, an ash pit, a primitive

water closet, or just a seat over a cesspit – it seemed more agreeable to keep it out of doors.

The turning point came in around 1875, the year that marked the arrival of the first commercially successful 'wash-out' water closet, manufactured by Daniel Bostel Bros. It represented a significant advance on the design which had held sway, with only minor improvements, since the 1770s, when Alexander Cummings and Joseph Bramah produced and patented versions using levers which operated a flap in the bottom of the pan. The new water closets dispensed with the flap and depended on the rush of water from an overhead cistern to flush waste matter through the S-bend. Further improvements in the last quarter of the 19th century – by such familiar names as Twyford, Jennings and Shanks – took advantage of piped water to feed overhead cisterns, as well as improvements in the public sewers, and quickly brought the technology of the WC to a level which was wholly acceptable indoors, and is still current today.

Many late-19th-century water closets were elaborately decorated on the outside with raised scrollwork, and coloured both inside and out with transfer-printed foliage or landscapes. The seat was invariably made of wood and usually suspended over the bowl on two cast-iron wall brackets. Boxes for paper were sold as part of the suite: rolls of lavatory paper were available from the 1880s. A high cast-iron cistern was operated by a chain with a porcelain handle, sometimes inscribed with the word 'pull' for those unsure of the technique. Low-level cisterns, which reduced the disagreeable noise of rushing water, became possible after the 1880s through the introduction of the 'syphonic' system from the USA, which improved the effectiveness of the flush by creating a temporary difference in pressure in the S-bend. But even this improvement was not sufficiently persuasive to all: many Victorian houses remained without an inside lavatory until the 1950s.

Left: The quality of this vanity unit is well matched by the William Morris-style wallpaper. Spot the lavatory!

Below: Simple white and blue ceramics give prominence to the elegant brass cross-topped tap.

Above: A traditional design owes its strength to the bold use of the horizontal line along the tiled dado.

Right: This transfer-printed Victorian lavatory might look more in keeping on a wooden floor.

245

BATHS AND SHOWERS

Below: Completed within a comparatively modest budget, this arrangement well evokes the interregnum of Victorian bathrooms, when dressing-rooms or bedrooms were converted to house fixed baths supplied by piped water.

To most Victorians, having a bath meant immersing the middle of the body in a hip bath. Hip baths had to be filled – and emptied – by hand, so when mains water under pressure enabled householders to pipe water through the house, a genuine labour-saving improvement could be celebrated. The fixed bath as we know it today – with its plumbed-in taps and the plughole leading to the drains outside – had arrived.

This arrangement only made sense, however, if the water could be heated. Various precarious solutions were tried, including primitive circulatory systems emanating from the kitchen range, boilers fitted into the bedroom fireplace, and burners which applied gas flames directly to the base of the bath. The breakthrough was the introduction of the gas geyser in the late 1860s. The pace of development was none the less slow

and it was only at the end of the era that the great Victorian bath – the vitreous enamelled, cast-iron roll-top with its ball-and-claw feet – became at all widespread.

The heyday of the Victorian shower arrived with the fixed bath. Showers had always had a following, even when they were little more than a tank of water suspended over a tin bath, enclosed by a tent-like curtain; the tank was filled by hand or by a pressure pump, and spilled its contents like a watering can at the pull of a chain. Now one end of the fixed bath could be given over to a fixed shower stand, served by water under pressure from a head of water in a tank in the roof. Designers often also included horizontal jets of water, with a rank of taps labelled 'shower', 'jet', 'spray' and 'plunge', as well as 'hot' and 'cold'. But these were the playthings of the well-to-do; the majority continued to make do with the hip bath.

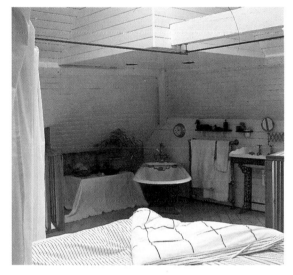

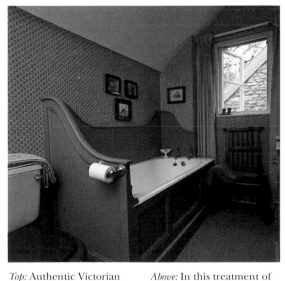

Top: The shower-cum-bath is a classic child of Victorian invention. Water for the shower came from the rose overhead and from holes in the horizontal bands in the side of the shower stand.

Top: Authentic Victorian bathroom fittings have been set in an uncompromisingly modern context, which serves to highlight their solid good quality.

Above: In this treatment of a Victorian bath the panels are extended to form an elegant partition. The boxing-in of sanitary arrangements was the subject of controversy; many believed free-standing fixtures to be more hygienic.

Above: What this shower at Cragside lacks in pressure, it makes up for in volume. A chain operates a simple valve to produce a stream of cold water.

247

VICTORIAN AND MODERN

'A well equipped bathroom will contain a bath, shower bath, wash-basin, hip bath, bidet, heated towel rail, mirror, clothes hooks, a shelf for towels and a receptacle for used towels.' This is the assessment of the German commentator Hermann Muthesius, the author of *Das Englische Haus*, at the turn of the century, demonstrating that although the bathroom was late in coming, when it did come, it came virtually complete.

If we are to try to reproduce the Victorian bathroom today, it should be based on a late 19th-century model, if we do not wish to compromise our demands for modern hygiene and comfort.

Most of the elements of the Victorian bathroom are now available in reproduction (see page 308 for suppliers), particularly taps, wash basins and lavatories. Genuine antique fittings are often cheaper than their counterparts in reproduction, but they may be tiresomely inefficient, and the dimensions of the pipework and washers are likely to be non-standard. If you want a very large cast-iron roll-top bath, you will probably have to buy an antique one, which, if properly re-enamelled, will cost a great deal. Reproduction cast-iron baths are made to standard length only, but are considerably cheaper by to buy.

There is no reason why a new bathroom, using inexpensive modern fittings, cannot be dressed to fit comfortably into a Victorian house. The bath, for example, could be boxed in by simple panelling with the skirting detail of the rest of the bathroom running along the bottom. Furnishings and decoration can be used to supply the keynotes: the Victorian bathroom contained much more free-standing furniture than ours, and chairs, wooden towel rail, pictures and photographs on the walls, matched by a varnished wooden lavatory seat, will create a convincing result.

The Victorians were much troubled by condensation, which became an issue after the introduction of very hot water supplied from a geyser. In order to avoid the damage to decorations caused by dampness, they often covered both the floor and walls with tiles – but of course the cold tiles only made matters worse. Anaglypta or Lyncrusta wallpaper, heavily encased in an oil-based paint, provided a cheaper and more effective solution. For the floor, linoleum was popular, with cork mats to stand on. The solution to condensation, however, lay in reducing the amount of hot water exposed to the air, and this was not really achieved until the invention of the mixer tap at the end of the era.

Today, with mixer taps, extractor fans and central heating to raise the ambient air temperature, we can concern ourselves less with condensation and turn our attention to decorative effect. Tiles provide a long-lasting surface for areas exposed to splashing, but modern water-resistant wallpapers can be used elsewhere. Painted anaglypta beneath a dado rail provides a true note of authenticity.

Tiled bathroom floors seem more attractive in warmer climates and have long slipped out of fashion in Britain. A Victorian effect can be achieved by covering the floor-boards with hardboard and laying dark cork tiles on the surface. Polished wood or simple flooring materials like jute matting can also be effective. I tend to avoid fitted carpets in the bathroom. Rag rugs were used by the Victorians – as convenient and washable then as they are today.

For bathroom lighting a combination of the traditional and the modern is probably the happy medium: recessed low voltage spots and pelmet lighting, for example, so that you can see properly in the mirror, and decorative lighting for effect.

Of course a bathroom in a Victorian house does not necessarily have to have a Victorian look. A modern bathroom can be both efficient and pleasing, and may match all your requirements rather more effectively.

Left: The clean, uncluttered lines of a modern bathroom may be the most appropriate solution in a very restricted space, leaving decorative touches to evoke the period of the rest of the house. Here the basin has been fitted into the space that would normally have been taken up by the window sill.

Above: The references to the Victorian world here are subtly implied: a round-topped window set in an asymmetric configuration, with frosted glass bordered by tinted glass and patterned by lead tracery.

BATHROOMS, BATHROOM FIXTURES & FITTINGS

TYPES OF BATHS

FREE STANDING

MARBLED

LIONS CLAW

PANELLED

PATTERNED ENAMEL

TYPES OF WASH-BASIN

TRADITIONAL WASHSTAND

PLUMBED IN LAVATORY

BASIN ON CAST-IRON SUPPORTS

CORNER BASIN

PEDESTAL BASIN

CABRIOLE LAVATORY

TYPES OF WATERCLOSETS

PEDESTAL WASH-DOWN CLOSET

PEDESTAL WASH-OUT

THE LAMBETH 1895

SWING LAVATORY

RAISED ACANTHUS 1895

PEDESTAL LION CLOSET

PULL CHAIN

LOW-DOWN SUITE, 1895

ART NOUVEAU, 1907

TYPES OF SHOWERS

TYPES OF TAPS

ACCESSORIES

TOWEL ROLLER

PAPER HOLDERS

JUG & BOWL

TOWEL RACK

Chapter Six

THE PRIVATE ROOMS

Beyond the first-floor drawing-room, the Victorian house was an intensely private place, hidden from public view and rarely entered by visitors. If we lack a vivid mental picture of this intimate world of bedroom and boudoir, dressing-room and nursery, this is perhaps due to the reticence of Victorian novelists and illustrators on this subject; not for them the bedroom romps of a Fielding or a Hogarth. Fortunately, the stalwart domestic economists of the day were more forthcoming, and such books as Lady Barker's *Bedroom and Boudoir* (1878) and Robert Edis's *Decoration and Furniture of Town Houses* (1881) have left us with an excellent record of Victorian taste in the private rooms.

When trying to imagine what everyday life was like in a family house of the time, the most obvious thing to bear in mind is the large number of people occupying even the smallest houses. Families were huge by present standards, with six to nine children quite the norm. As the children grew up and left home, space became free for ageing grandparents, bachelor uncles, spinster aunts, cousins on hard times and a host of other relatives in need of sanctuary. In houses where the kitchen was still located in a basement, the family lived in the privileged centre of a sandwich, with the servants living and sleeping above and below them. In poorer homes, spare rooms might be let out to lodgers and basic board provided. There was clearly far less room for personal privacy than today; indeed, privacy was then a luxury enjoyed only by the very rich. From comfortable detached houses down to the meanest terraces, bedrooms were shared and most rooms were in use for much of the day.

Away from the public rooms, the ostentation we associate with the period was minimal, becoming virtually non-existent in the servants' sleeping quarters. The simplicity that informed such fixtures as cornices, mouldings, architraves, skirting-boards and fireplaces was echoed in the decorative scheme; the rich paintwork and wallpapers favoured in the main rooms gave way to pretty pastel shades and a general air of cheerful cleanliness.

In larger houses, a husband and wife had separate bedrooms with a connecting door. Each room might have had its own dressing-room, and adjoining the lady's bedroom would have been her private sitting-room or boudoir. This was the feminine equivalent of the study, a private retreat where she could read, write letters or

Opposite: In country houses and the grander town houses, the opulence of the public areas extended to the bedrooms. Sumptuous red drapes are here combined with chinoiserie panelling to create an air of refined exoticism. Where space was no object, a sofa and occasional table were often placed at the foot of the bed.

a journal, and practise music. In France, the boudoir was one of the most ornate rooms in the house; English taste inclined towards a more sober and businesslike room. Lady Barker, an adventurous, much-travelled woman with a taste for the Arts and Crafts Movement and the Queen Anne revival, thought of such rooms as 'one's own little private den' where a woman could be 'busy and comfortable'. The dado, where present, could be covered in leather-paper or deal panelling painted light blue or pink; for the upper part of the wall, a William Morris wallpaper might be used. The furnishings could include a desk, an armchair, a piano, shelves for a small collection of favourite books and a few treasured ornaments.

In the bedrooms, walls were covered with pale shades of distemper or light, delicately patterned wallpaper, both of which could be renewed frequently. Robert Edis expressed a widely prevailing distaste for strong patterns in bedrooms, believing that they 'might be likely to fix themselves upon the tired brain, suggesting all kinds of weird forms'. Rhoda and Agnes Garrett, in *Suggestions for House Decoration* (1879), considered soft olive or sage greens suitably restful, while Lady Barker preferred 'a pearly gray' or 'tender seashell pink'. Bright greens were avoided since the pigments used to produce them contained arsenic. Walls could also be covered in a pastel-coloured chintz, stretched tightly over panels which could be easily removed for cleaning.

Hygiene was a major concern. Webster and Parkes, writing in 1844, believed that bedrooms should be 'neat and plain, and every thing capable of collecting dust should be avoided as much as possible,' and this advice was echoed by almost every subsequent writer on the topic. Furniture was supposed to be simple, easy to clean and kept to a minimum. Plain varnished boards with a few scattered rugs were preferred for the floor; carpets were permissible provided they were not fitted, and could be taken up and cleaned frequently. Window blinds were considered more hygienic than curtains, although festoons of chintz or cretonne, which could be removed and washed easily, were also recommended.

The Victorians believed that frequent air changes were necessary for refreshing sleep; good ventilation was considered very important. The practice of making bedrooms low-ceilinged to allow for a grandly-proportioned drawing-room below was widely deplored. It was frequently stressed that every bedroom should have a fireplace to encourage a through draught; windows should be left open when the weather and the health of the occupant permitted; alternatively, patent ventilators might be installed.

The growing taste for fresh air and horror of dust traps had a great effect on the type of beds in use. When Queen Victoria came to the throne, those who could afford it still had a bed that could be curtained off completely, either a four-poster (or 'full tester'), a French bedstead with a central support for the drapes, or a tent

Left: This 1883 illustration shows a typical nursery of the period, equipped with a simple half-register grate – modern safety precautions would certainly preclude the boiling kettle – and a little hanging bookshelf on the wall. The floor is covered with linoleum or matting.

Right: A cosy but dignified interior has been created through a stylish combination of decoration and furnishings: lightly patterned wallpaper; a lace counterpane on the bed; a folding screen covering the door; and the desk in a pleasant, sunny window.

bed with an arched frame (see pages 266 – 67). A hangover from the days when houses were built without corridors, and people had to pass through one room to reach the next, such beds provided some warmth and privacy. By the middle of the century, however, Webster and Parkes were already recommending partial curtaining of the bed as a healthier alternative. The 'half tester' – with hangings around the head only – gained in popularity. By the last quarter of the century, critics such as Eastlake were recommending simple wood or iron bedsteads with no hangings at all.

If this preoccupation with bedroom hygiene strikes a modern reader as somewhat excessive, it must be remembered that there were pressing reasons for it. Victorians gave birth to their children at home, so the bedroom frequently had to act as a maternity ward. In an age when infectious diseases such as typhoid and cholera were widespread, it also had to function as a sick-room. Moreover, since fitted bathrooms did not become standard until the end of the century, most washing went on here too, with maids bringing up hot water and emptying the waste in slop buckets. The fact that so many home economists felt the need to stress – in terms often bordering on stridency – that bedrooms should be light, cheerful and clean suggests that the reality was often very different.

Despite these strictures, there was more flexibility in the way bedrooms were arranged and used than is generally recognized today. For the sons and daughters of the house, and those living in smaller properties, the bedroom often had to double up as a private sitting-room. This may have a surprisingly modern ring to anyone brought up on the idea that a Victorian bedroom was a desolate, fusty place containing only a bedstead, a washstand, a chest of drawers and a looming, ugly wardrobe. Many young people used sofa beds and closed washstands to disguise the fact that anyone ever slept there, and plain wooden bookshelves, Japanese chests, South American ceramics, palm plants and gipsy tables were all pressed into service under the influence of the Arts and Crafts Movement. The cheerful bohemianism of this late-Victorian approach may well seem appealing today, particularly in houses and flats where space is limited.

Although many Victorian householders liked to dignify their home by setting aside as many rooms as possible for specific purposes, in practice they had to be more flexible. A dressing-room next to the main bedroom might be allocated to a child for a few years, reverting to its original function later on. Children of both sexes shared nursery rooms in infancy, but soon moved into segregated bedrooms reserved for either boys or girls.

In the bigger houses, there would be a night nursery for the children to sleep in as well as a day nursery for play. The decoration of the nursery followed much the same principles as it does today: bright, cheerful wallpapers and hardwearing, washable sur-

A low-ceilinged cottage room has become an attractive and comfortable bedroom with a genuine period feel. The small register grate and the fitted cupboard with its tonguc-and-groove ledge door have been treated with respect; the iron and brass bedstead is of a type that became popular in the last quarter of the 19th century.

faces. Purpose-built nurseries sometimes occupied the attic space, where swings could be hung from the exposed rafters.

As the last of one generation grew out of the nursery, the children of the older brothers and sisters would move straight in, providing a comfortable sense of continuity. There was almost always an adjacent room for the nanny, who enjoyed a special status in Victorian families, below a governess or tutor in big houses, but above the cook and the other servants. She would always have a room of her own, even if small, and would not socialize with the other staff. A general reform in the treatment of servants, who earlier in the century had often slept in miserable unventilated recesses, led to their being better accommodated as time passed. Their quarters were plain but decent and had simple washing facilities. 'Maids' furniture', although cheap and crude, was an improvement on what their predecessors had been allowed.

B E D R O O M S   A N D   N U R S E R I E S

Below: Although the four-poster bed became less popular in the late 19th century, it was occasionally revived for its medievalist effect. Here, in the Acanthus Room at Wightwick Manor, embroidered linen drapes in the Arts and Crafts style are set against the William Morris wallpaper that gives the room its name.

The furnishing of bedrooms is an intensely personal matter, today just as in Victorian times, and tastes have changed less in this part of the house than in any other. Bedrooms were always the most simply furnished rooms, and Victorian papers, fabrics and curtain treatments can still be most attractive to us today. Modern householders may well prefer the cheerful sobriety of early and late Victorian styles, and will probably want less furniture than mid-Victorians,

but with careful selection even some High Victorian pieces can make a suitable starting point round which to build a decorative scheme.

Apart from the bed, the largest piece of furniture was the wardrobe. For mid-Victorians, the most popular design was a massive double wardrobe with a central mirror. Big heavy wardrobes have long been unfashionable, and can be picked up cheaply. Stripped of dirty, blistered

(continued on page 262)

Left: A charming attic bedroom with a simple register grate and overmantel has been given a touch of period elegance by the gilt-framed portrait.

Above: The dark varnished furniture of this High Victorian bedroom draws on Renaissance and classical styles. The sombre gravity of the bedstead and the double-fronted wardrobe would be oppressive were it not for the light walls of the room.

Left: The simplicity of the late-Victorian bedroom lent itself to warm climates. The pink gauze drapery of this Australian bedroom is actually a mosquito net.

Below: High Victorian taste finds its full expression in this bedroom at the Speaker's House, Westminster. The half tester bed, the rich drapes and the oak panelling and doors all betray a strong Tudor influence.

Left: The false bookcase concealing the door of this London bedroom, and the corona of drapes over the bed, evoke the French *Deuxième Empire*.

Above: The Victorian taste for matching drapes in light cotton fabrics lends itself to modern reinterpretations, such as this airy bedroom.

varnish, they can look surprisingly good in the right setting. For those who find wardrobes un-appealing, a Victorian alternative can be found in Cassell's *Household Guide*, which recommends hanging one's clothes from a brass pole across the chimney recess, with pretty chintz curtains across the front. This idea could work well in an old-fashioned cottage with deep recesses either side of the fireplace.

The washstand was an essential part of the Victorian bedroom, the top often made of marble and the splashback tiled; pitchers, soap dishes and wash bowls were usually decorated with flower motifs; the free-standing furniture could also include the dressing-table, on which

Above: Draperies can provide useful sound-proofing for bedrooms, as well as creating an atmosphere of warmth and comfort.

Right: In Victorian country houses, it was quite common for the lady of the house to spend the morning in bed, reading or writing letters. These ivory lace pillows, counterpane and bed drapes would have represented considerable luxury in Victorian times, as today.

combs and brushes were displayed along with candlesticks, bowls and bottles and tiny trays; an easy chair or two around the fireplace and, if there was room, a sofa at the foot of the bed. As drapes around the bed went out of fashion, screens were used to exclude draughts and ensure privacy. The wide variety of finishes included Dutch leather, floral paper and Indian and Japanese designs. There might also be a small table for books and papers.

Many of these pieces find a natural place in the modern bedroom. Bedside tables do not have to match; an antique table or reproduction military chest on one side of the bed can be paired quite easily with a simpler table on the other side, covered with a cloth and skirt. Before buying bedside tables, measure the height of the bed from the floor. It will probably be much lower than you imagine. Screens are not much used today, but they have great potential for altering the contours of a room or hiding an ugly but necessary piece of furniture. It is not difficult to find them in markets, and they can easily be re-covered with an attractive period paper.

Many traditional ideas may also be used in nurseries, which can be among the most attractive rooms in a house. In a nursery, however, safety comes before everything else. The windows should be child-proofed, even if it means using bars or grilles. The next essential is cleanliness and comfort. The floor should be both easy to mop and easy on the knees. In less well-off Victorian households, linoleum was often laid in upstairs rooms. Cork or thermo-plastic tiles are good modern alternatives, and may be covered with big, easily washed cotton rugs. Hearth rugs in Victorian times were designed with special patterns for children; Voysey produced several with scenes from fairy tales. Most artists who designed wallpapers did special ones

The best nursery cupboards are deep and wide, allowing big plastic baskets or toy hampers to be stored easily.

for children, and Walter Crane's nursery-rhyme wallpapers were popular from the 1870s. Children's book illustrators such as Cecil Aldin and John Hassall designed friezes. These pleasant traditions are now experiencing a revival. A sink will always be useful in a nursery, and also a work surface where a kettle can be boiled. A comfortable armchair for adults adds an aspect of the parlour or sitting-room.

The built-in cupboards that came into vogue in the 1880s were promoted as being less liable to harbour dust than free-standing furniture. Fitted cupboards, however, are expensive to build and do not offer the best way to see your clothes. They often have small cupboards at the top which can be reached only by standing on a chair. If I must use fitted cupboards, I put in big sliding doors that can be decorated to match the walls of the room. I generally start a fitted cupboard with what is called a potboard – a shelf just off the floor – and build the cupboards up from there. The space between the potboard and the floor is then finished with skirting. This follows my principle of running Victorian-style details round almost all new fixtures, so that they become an integral part of the room.

But wherever possible, I avoid fitted cupboards and adopt the American type of walk-in cupboards, the modern equivalent of the dressing-room. Having found or created a suitable space the size of a very small room, I start my design at the bottom with a potboard, trimmed with skirting. Then I allow space for two clothes rails, one above the other, for hanging ordinary-length dresses, skirts, suits and jackets; coats and long dresses will have to go elsewhere. Above the upper rail is a shelf, open to the ceiling, where suitcases, hat boxes and other tall items can be stored within reach. The hanging space may be divided vertically to provide deep drawers and shelves along some of its length. To conceal the clothes, I use a method that closely follows the Cassell's *Household Guide*, and run a simple cotton curtain all round.

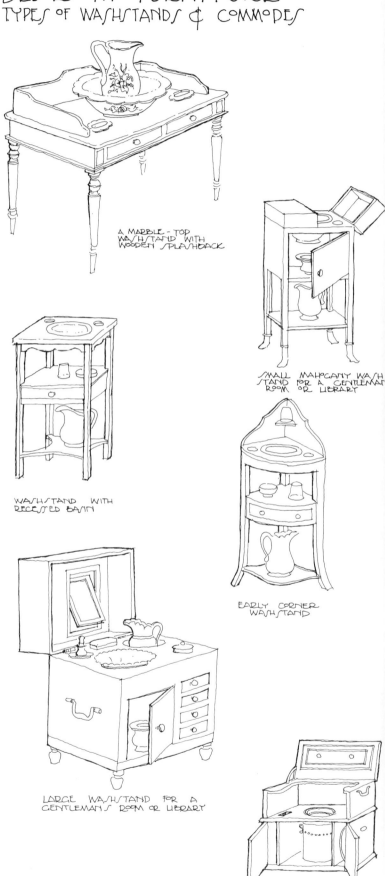

BED ROOM FURNITURE
TYPES OF WASHSTANDS & COMMODES

A MARBLE-TOP WASHSTAND WITH WOODEN SPLASHBACK

SMALL MAHOGANY WASHSTAND FOR A GENTLEMAN'S ROOM OR LIBRARY

WASHSTAND WITH RECESSED BASIN

EARLY CORNER WASHSTAND

LARGE WASHSTAND FOR A GENTLEMAN'S ROOM OR LIBRARY

AN EARLY COMMODE.

TYPES OF BEDS

TYPES OF WARDROBES

WINGED WARDROBE

FULL TESTER

FRENCH BEDSTEAD

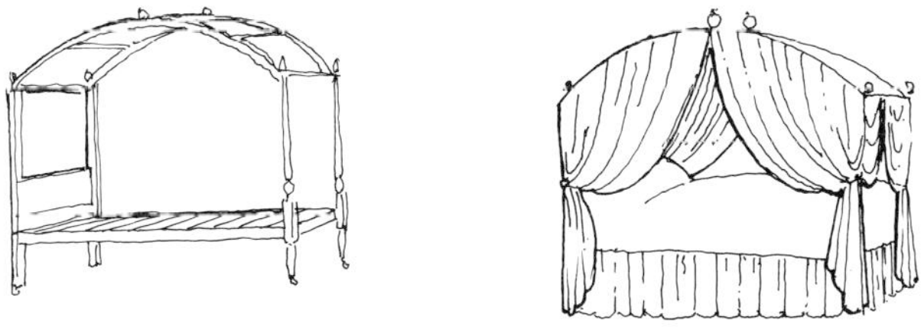

DWARF WARDROBES

TENT BEDSTEAD

SIMPLE PRESSES

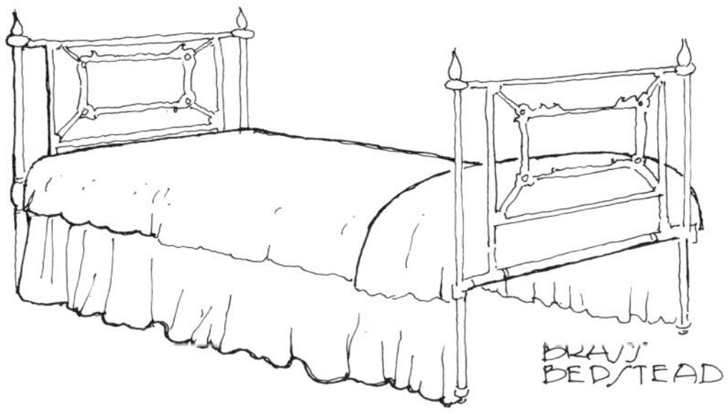

BRASS BEDSTEAD

HALF TESTER

LATE WOODEN BEDSTEAD FROM HEAL & SONS

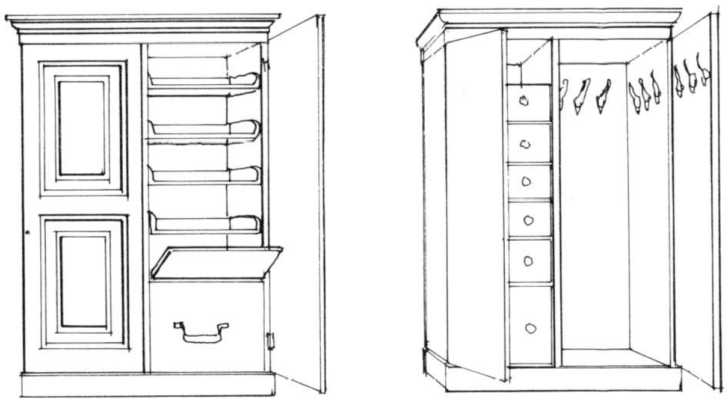

IRON COT

FULL LENGTH DRESSING MIRROR

267

Chapter Seven

GARDENS

If the fabric of a house is at the mercy of architectural fashion and the corner-cutting owner, the survival of the garden in anything like its original form is even more precarious. Where a Victorian house may have endured through a century and then been spoiled by the addition of an inappropriate dormer, it is at least possible to make out the intentions of the original. In the case of gardens, a few months of vigorous reshaping and replanting – to say nothing of a year or two of neglect – will obliterate almost all evidence of what was there before. Conservatories, summer houses, pavilions, pergolas and garden seats are also more at risk than houses, exposed to weather, forgotten and abandoned during the winter. Were it not for these processes of decay, we would have far more evidence today of the changes that gardening underwent in the Victorian period.

Gardening ceased to be an occupation pursued only by the rich for their pleasure and the poor for their survival, becoming instead a pastime for almost anyone with a little plot of land to cultivate. This popularity reflected not just changes in Britain's social composition and the distribution of wealth, but also the imperial and international status which allowed it to ransack the world for plants. The interest among the general public led to the foundation of the Horticultural Society in 1804.

It is difficult today, with our immense catalogue of readily available species, to realize how restricted was the range of plants in the British garden right up to the beginning of the 19th century. Many of the everyday plants we are inclined to take for granted as long-established if not actually indigenous varieties were in fact newly introduced from abroad. Dahlias came in 1788, followed over the next few decades by tea roses, hydrangeas, salvias, camellias, hybrid rhododendrons, gardenias, chrysanthemums and fuchsias, among countless others. The aspidistra, an indoor plant which was to make steady headway under the Victorians and then entrench itself as an essential adjunct to suburban Edwardian living, first arrived from the East in 1824. So-called 'old roses' were propagated about this time, mainly by the French, and were in turn overtaken by coarser varieties bred for longer flowering at the expense of colour and scent.

Kew Gardens in London played a vital role in this process and foreshadowed developments in many other horticultural institutes. When Victoria came to the throne in 1837, Kew already had a reputation as a centre for scientific botanical study. In 1838 John

Opposite: The late Victorian garden was a balance between romantic informality on the one hand and the regimented geometry of bedding designs on the other. This two-acre garden at Peckover House in Cambridgeshire, with its geraniums, rose pergola, sundial, classical urn and palm tree shows a harmonious combination of eclectic interests typical of the era.

The garden of a house in Mayborough, Queensland, shows the same use of lawn and borders that typified the Victorian garden all over the globe. The invention of the lawn mower put the tidy management of lawn within reach of householders of all levels.

Lindley compiled a report on its future, recommending that it be maintained as the Royal Botanic Gardens. So in the 1840s it was given a new lease of life; thousands of horticultural specimens, gathered all over the world by botanists and travellers, were sent home for classification and cultivation.

Through the work of the growing ranks of commercial nurserymen a huge new range of plants became known, popularized by new gardening magazines cheaply printed on steam-powered presses. In this way, the new middle classes in their new villas were kept abreast of fashion. The most important of the early garden magazine editors was John Claudius Loudon. Before writing *An Encyclopaedia of Cottage, Farm, and Villa Architecture and Furniture* (see page 176), he set up a school of agriculture in Oxfordshire and, in 1822, produced *An Encyclopaedia of Gardening.* This was followed by *The Gardener's Magazine,* published from 1826 and carried on for many years after Loudon's death by his talented and industrious wife Jane. The greatest difference between Loudon and the majority of his predecessors lay in his recognition of the social changes which were taking place in Britain. He addressed himself not merely to aristocratic and landed patrons, as had been the previous practice, but also to the new villa owners.

During the 18th century, Capability Brown had created the 'English Park' look, still familiar today in the grounds of great country houses. Brown's successor Humphry Repton (1752–1818), working mainly for country landowners with smaller estates, did much to reinstate the flowerbed and formal parterre in the immediate vicinity of the house. Loudon admired Capability Brown but in his own work developed themes mainly associated with Repton. The word 'gardenesque' was coined to describe Loudon's approach, suggesting a combination of the small layout with the picturesque style promoted by the 18th-century gardeners. Brown showed off the beauty of landscape; the new gardens showed off the skill of the gardener.

Loudon's suggestions, published in his magazines, represent an attempt to combine both the formal and the romantic. He recommended an enormous number and variety of plants, yet these were to be contained in formal French-style parterres which he thought would suit even the smaller garden, with *allées* flanked by statuary and stopped with classical features such as urns or closed arches.

The intricate layouts commended by Loudon were made possible by the availability of labour. Large estates had always had their own specialist gardeners just as they do today. During the Victorian period and well into the present century almost all middle-

Horticultural techniques advanced swiftly in the 19th century with the aid of industrial technology. Here glass panes fixed into a cast-iron frame form a very rigid cloche to force plants and protect them from the frost.

class detached houses also had gardeners, so that the householder could command according to his wishes.

The Victorians were ever on the lookout for new devices. One of the most notable of these was the lawn mower, patented in 1832. Up to this time, cutting the grass called for intensive hand-labour, using scythes, sickles and shears, or cropping by domestic animals. Now every villa could have its smooth greensward and, as a bonus, the new machine was advertised as providing beneficial exercise for the country gentleman. No doubt, too, the possession of such a contraption would have provided one of the earliest suburban status symbols. The hard work such as weeding, digging and clipping hedges, however, would have remained the province of the garden staff.

'In the Garden' by George Bernard O'Neill (1828–1917) displays a fashionable sentimentality, but also demonstrates the way in which a natural, informal garden design of lawn, trees and shrubs could be reined in by formal touches in topiary and brickwork.

The relationship between exuberance and control provided the main theme for debate among those who concerned themselves with garden design. W. A. Nesfield, an ex-army engineer, carried out vast 'Italian' layouts at Witley Court, Harewood House, Holkham and many more. His former profession seemed to be reflected in layouts that were obsessively correct and regimentally precise. Yet his parterres depended on extravagant use of colour. Nesfield was one of several specialist gardeners who helped to promote 'bedding out', a fashion whose lasting popularity, even today, can be seen in municipal gardens all over the world. Nesfield was criticized by other 'bedders out' for the narrow scope for bedding which he provided in his layouts, but his effects were achieved on a prodigious scale. Contemporary accounts show that sometimes the plants of an entire parterre would be changed overnight by an army of gardeners, the last one fleeing just before dawn in order to spare the sensibilities of any early-rising guest who might chance to glance out of his bedroom window. After breakfast gardeners would generally remain out of sight, confining themselves to the kitchen garden and potting sheds and so on.

But other forces were at work apart from Nesfield's mixture of military precision and superabundant, swiftly changing colour. Eclecticism became fashionable in gardening as in architecture. In contrast to Nesfield a strange and beautiful garden was created in 1842 by James Bateman and his talented designer Edward Cooke at Biddulph in Derbyshire. The proposal appears to have been twofold; first to provide for a vast collection of imported species and also to create a private and romantic garden for Bateman's personal use and pleasure. Even so a nod in the direction of Nesfield is displayed by the small parterre in front of the rather undistinguished Italianate house itself. The genius of the gardens lies in their surprises; the visitor never knows what to expect around the next corner yet the whole ingenious itinerary is confined to a park of a mere twenty acres.

During the 1870s and 1880s there was a strong movement associated with the Queen Anne style of architecture that sought an 'old-fashioned' look to the garden. Instead of the brash, newly introduced plants used by the parterre designers, Queen Anne gardeners favoured romantic, informal drifts of tall flowering plants – sunflowers, hollyhocks, tiger lilies and abundant climbing plants such as convolvulus and passion flower – many of which were the sort of plants considered by William Morris and his followers to evoke the medieval garden. A balancing element of formality would still be provided by low hedges of clipped box and topiary.

The contention of formality versus informality, old versus new, found its mediator in the most important garden journalist of the middle Victorian years, William Robinson, an Irishman who came to work in the gardens of Regent's Park in 1861, where he was put

The cramped and shaded spaces created by back extensions – a typical feature of Victorian houses after the kitchen was raised from the basement – pose a challenge for the gardener. The use of dark-leaved plants (which have higher chlorophyll content and so need less light) provides an effective solution here, brightened by the summer display of busy lizzie, pelargoniums and fuchsias.

This modern piece of eclecticism brings life to a blank brick wall with a moulded concrete plaque and a Victorian firegrate used as a plant holder – touches that successfully evoke the era.

in charge of the herbaceous section. For Robinson the purpose of gardening was not so much to create a formal composition in which flowers played their part as to create a layout which would show off plants to their best advantage. Developing a passion for native wild flowers, he sought to incorporate them into traditional flower borders, mixed in with such foreign introductions as he thought would not destroy their essentially English character. Robinson found, in the traditional cottage garden, a perfect synthesis of the practical and charming and he went further, advocating 'wild gardens' where exotic plants could be cultivated as if in the wild. In 1871, Robinson published a magazine called *The Garden*, and later *Garden Illustrated*, for the owners of smaller gardens. Both publications were highly influential. One of Robinson's contributors was Gertrude Jekyll, an embroiderer turned gardener, who created gardens of great delicacy of colour and arrangement. Her designs were carried out mostly in the Home Counties, and particularly in her ten-acre garden at Munstead Wood in Surrey.

Robinson and Jekyll set shapes and colours against one another with sensitivity. Jekyll in particular, in her wild gardens and herbaceous borders, was extremely subtle in her use of the related tones of a single dominant colour. In the closing years of Victoria's reign she moved towards a synthesis of gardening and architecture, collaborating with the young architect Edwin Lutyens (see pages 40 – 41) in layouts which recall traditional Italian gardens but were transformed by a newly minted English formalism.

The best evidence of how the small garden was laid out and planted a hundred years ago lies in the illustrations of gardening journals, in photographs (though these are only in black and white) and in the backgrounds of paintings of the period. It seems clear there was much scaling down of grander gardens to suit the town or suburb. Just as today the influence of Sissinghurst or popular gardening magazines or the current television expert can be followed, so the various 19th-century fashions were reflected in the smaller gardens of the time. Parterres shrank to a mere terrace of brick or crazy paving, and bedding out was confined to a semi-formal border separating the terrace from the lawn beyond, with a pair of miniature mass-produced urns to mark the centre. Perhaps the winding path, a feature so readily associated with the romantic garden, survived further down the plot, leading to a wild garden in the form of a shrubbery.

In these respects, the smaller Victorian garden may justly be accused of confusions of scale. Old-fashioned cottage gardens look right because they relate so perfectly in every way to the cottage, just as wide lawns and ample parkland are perfect for the great house. But the average suburban plot can take only so much design and many Victorian gardens must have presented a confusing array of ornament, shape and colour.

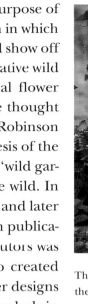

The classical sculpture and the conservatory recall two major themes of the Victorian attitude to gardens and garden design. The conjunction of the two here displays the marble in exceptionally sympathetic light.

The cottage-garden effect in front of this late 19th-century house is brought about by a mixed planting using a broad and vibrant palette. The straight path indicates a workmanlike attitude to the garden: tall borders such as these would provide a decorative screen in front of the less presentable vegetable patch.

RAILINGS AND GARDEN WALLS

Opposite: Any danger of monotony in this wall is relieved by the polychromatic brickwork and the sculpture.

Below: Brick walls provide a sympathetic backdrop to a garden, as well as warmth and protection for plants. Here the effect is embellished by the unusual shapes of a 'crinkle-crankle' wall.

Bottom: An old majolica water caddy offers the pleasurable surprise of the 'found object', set against a weathered brick wall.

The concept of privacy was central to the Victorian ethos, and strict limitations were imposed to control who entered where. New owners of small gardens wanted to create boundaries to mark out their territory, in just the same way that the landed gentry in the previous century had erected walls around their estates.

Whilst the front entrance provided a justifiable focus for elaborate walls or railings (see pages 56 – 57), the borders around the garden itself normally received more modest treatment. Back garden walls of brick were rarely above 3 to 4 feet (1 to 1.25m) high in south-east England, but in places north of Derby walls 6 to 8 feet (2 to 2.5m) high were not uncommon.

Brick walls, however, were expensive; the alternative was fencing. Most of this was of a kind familiar today: overlapping boards in panels supported on intermediate posts. But lighter, more open styles – such as criss-crossed split larch, or comb-like palisade fencing – were more widespread than now.

In smaller gardens the cult of the earlier 'picturesque' style found expression in rustic and trellis work of all sorts, from the delicate to the robust, frequently used to establish a division between different parts of the garden. The use of hedges as boundary markers increased with the interest in gardening, and with the growing number of plants introduced from overseas which could be used for this purpose. Lilac, rhododendron, laburnum and other shrubs were sometimes used in preference to railings and fences, or in addition to them.

Right: A fine iron gate between overgrown brick and stone pillars sets the scene for the mature garden that lies beyond it.

ARBOURS, GAZEBOS AND SUMMER HOUSES

The Victorians brought to garden architecture a lightness of touch which was often absent in the house itself. If we want to see them in a really unbuttoned mood we must look to their arbours and summer houses, verandahs and winter gardens, and above all the enchanting detail of their ironwork and rustic wood.

Following the example of the early 18th century, the Victorians continued to build gazebos, temples and garden houses, albeit without the same style or sensitivity of landscaping as their predecessors. Naturally the garden buildings of the early part of the century echoed classical themes from the immediate past, but as medievalism took hold, the picturesque movement was gradually translated into the rustic, and burred wood, bark, unsawn branches and thatch replaced the previous stone and stucco, a transformation to be regretted as so many garden structures have consequently disappeared.

Sometimes these rustic buildings were erected in the branches of a tree, with simple stairs or a ladder for access, where they provided wonderful rooms for children. Similar buildings incorporated dovecots, whose occupants were bred for their enhancement of lawns and gravel walks, and no longer, as hitherto, for the pot.

The humbler outbuildings, the garden sheds and lean-to's (kept out of sight from the house windows) were functional affairs of simple brick or shiplap boarding. Woodwork was painted green, doors were plain boarded, and roofs tiled or slated according to local custom. Windows were often simple mullions puttied with overlapping sections of left-over greenhouse glass. Floors were brick or stone-flagged. There is a timeless quality about these buildings: their silent interiors stacked with pots, sacks, tools and accumulated rubbish can defy, if only for a moment, the restlessness of another century.

Below: The open structure of this elaborate pergola is designed to support a profusion of climbing plants which will eventually create a 'room' roofed and walled in leaves and flowers – a living summer house.

Below right: A delightful *trompe l'oeil* effect is achieved by attaching carefully constructed trellis work to a flat wall, bringing a garden image into a covered space.

One of the functions of a summer house or gazebo is to provide a space and atmosphere that is quite different from the interior of a house. The use of untrimmed timber and thatch produces an intensely rustic look, well complemented by an informal woodland garden.

This summer house derives all its character from the triptych of pointed arches, demonstrating that the Gothic style works remarkably well in intimate buildings.

CONSERVATORIES

The history of protecting plants through European winters goes back almost two thousand years; in Pompeii translucent sheets of marble were used in frames. However, the development of the glasshouse as we would recognize it today began in Renaissance times when new glass technology coincided with exotic plant introductions from warmer climates.

One of the earliest and most fashionable of these plants was the orange, known to have arrived in Europe by the 14th century. By the 15th and 16th centuries sophisticated ways of keeping orange trees alive in winter had been devised. In southern European climates, subject only to occasional frost, the trees could be left outside, but covered. Further north, the trees were grown in tubs; during the summer months they would decorate the terraces and take in the sun, but for the winter they would be wheeled into garden rooms specially boarded up for the purpose. So the earliest winter gardens were born.

It was not until about 1700 that glass manufacture had developed sufficiently to produce flat panes big enough for the double-hung sash windows of the period, replacing the old leaded lights and bottle glass. The first greenhouses appear at this time in illustrations. They consisted of sloping windows facing towards the south (great attention was paid to obtaining the best angle for average penetration of sunlight) and backed against brick or stone walls. The wall warmed up during the day and gave back heat at night.

Around 1800, as panes of glass grew larger in size and cheaper to make, so the ridged greenhouse was born, with pitched glazing on two

Opposite: The primary function of many conservatories today is to provide an additional living space. The charm of this one derives from the massed collage effect of stained glass and printed textiles. The roof blinds, with a William Morris design, compensate for a comparatively restrained amount of planting.

Left: Traditional details, such as the decorated ridge and the tracery in the fan lights, lighten the effect of an otherwise geometric modern design.

Above: The design of the tracery in this new, purpose-built conservatory takes its inspiration from the Gothic elements of the house to which it is attached, with the further embellishment of traditional roof crestings.

The roof space over an extension can provide an interesting site for a perched conservatory, with access from an upper floor. This kind of alteration, though it has a precedent in the natural-light studios built on by Victorian photographers, may however demand a cavalier attitude to the silhouette of the house.

sides. The southern orientation was no longer a critical factor. Stoves were replaced by hot water heating in pipes and improvements were made to ventilation. By the time Victoria came to the throne, huge structures of glass like those at Kew, Edinburgh and Chatsworth prepared for the culmination of the art in Paxton's Crystal Palace of 1851. Paxton, it will be remembered, started his working life as a gardener at Chatsworth and it was he who built the conservatory there, between 1836 and 1840.

Nobody had a greater influence in popularizing conservatories than John Claudius Loudon, both through his published works and through example. In 1824, at his own home in Porchester Terrace, Bayswater, he built a charming conservatory, which can still be seen today, consisting of a curvilinear dome seated on an Italianate stucco drum. From that time until the end of the century, as an adjunct even to quite modest houses, the conservatory enjoyed extraordinary popularity.

To ordinary Victorians the opportunity of bringing into their own homes the glamour of winter gardens seen at continental spas or at grand houses was irresistible. Glasshouse and conservatory builders quickly saw that the offer of a prefabricated product through catalogues had the additional benefit of keeping their carpenters and glaziers busy throughout the year.

A typical conservatory of the middle of the period might consist of a low brick wall all round, with glazing up to the level of the eaves, divided into narrow panes by vertical wooden mullions and incorporating open windows at the top. The roof would usually be of straight glass (curved glass was more expensive) decorated with iron crestings and provided with elaborate gable boards. Iron trusses and cross bars were used for larger spans and, if necessary, cast-iron columns provided intermediate support.

Conservatory floors were composed simply of iron grilles or of tiles with grilles over drainage and heating. Furniture, because of the all-pervading moisture, was generally in iron and came with loose cushions, if any. Indian and other oriental furniture also provided sensible and attractive seating and proclaimed the status of many a retired colonial civil servant. With this heritage also came the bungalow and verandah, two more overseas exotics now so much a part of our domestic architecture.

The conservatory flourished up to the Edwardian period. It was used primarily to provide hot-house plants and fruit for the breakfast table; bougainvillea, orange trees, passion fruit, figs and tomatoes enriched the Victorian diet and introduced a scent of the tropics in the northern climate of home. It declined when the cost of maintaining an ageing timber and glass structure became apparent. The conservatory has made a modest recovery recently. This is partly due to a revived appreciation of Victorian architecture but also to the discovery that the modern 'sun room', with its plate glass windows and uncompromising glare, is no substitute, particularly in winter, for a well designed conservatory with its lighting gently modified by glazing bars and a sensitive selection of plants.

As in Victorian times, off-the-peg conservatories are again available, mostly in a quasi-Victorian style which adopts some of the more obvious and coarser detailing of the period. Some of them use durable new materials such as aluminium in place of wood. The most appropriate for Victorian houses are purpose-built conservatories using good timber, preferably hardwood, putty and clear glass. Perspex and clear plastic can take curves and cannot be shattered like glass, but they are liable to scratching. It is certainly worthwhile to obtain estimates from builders to compare with those of specialist firms. As with built-in kitchens, prices can often be surprisingly competitive. Provided that the woodwork is painted every two or three years, the purpose-built look, however simple, may add just that extra difference to appearance and ultimate enjoyment.

The original conservatory to the right of this house is designed for the sole purpose of cultivating plants. None the less, care has been taken to see that it merges with the rest of the architecture, using the kind of detail that is so often omitted today. The later lean-to conservatory, though without ornament, also blends well.

Below: In warm climates the conservatory has its counterpart in the verandah which, though open to the elements, provides comparable opportunities for decorative treatment.

FURNISHING THE GARDEN

The furnishing of the Victorian garden was distinguished from that of previous eras in two notable ways. First, the cult of outdoor activities – from tea on the lawn to sports such as croquet and tennis – inspired the manufacture of movable chairs specifically designed for entertaining in the garden. Second, almost anyone with a plot of land devoted to ornamental gardening (as opposed to supplementing the diet) had in the mind's eye gardens on a grand scale: the challenge was to reproduce at least the atmosphere of these in a suburban small garden, and to this end statuary, urns and decorative vases became popular.

Garden statues and ornaments had originally been hand-carved or else painstakingly moulded in lead or terracotta. Towards the end of the 18th century the invention of Coade Stone (see pages 24–25) provided a means, albeit still comparatively expensive, to reproduce such ornaments on a large scale. When cheaper substitutes became available in the first half of the 19th century, manufacturers were inspired to produce an extraordinary variety and range of goods, impressively represented at the Great Exhibition in Hyde Park in 1851.

Outside furniture tends to be massive if it is to be left permanently in place or airily light if it has to be taken indoors at every shower of rain. Until the 19th century it was generally made of either stone or wood. Iron began to be used for exterior furniture around the beginning of the 19th century.

The Regency period introduced some delightful terrace furniture made of a cast-iron frame with wirework infilling, a fashion which lasted well into the century. The well known fern leaf and ivy designs have a sense of fun lacking in their parlour contemporaries. Some cast-iron seats incorporated painted wooden slats for sitting on and so formed the pattern for park

(continued on page 286)

Opposite: In a Victorian garden a heroic statue provided interest for visitors on a typically leisurely tour of the lawns and paths, as did sundials, stone seats, quiet arbours, topiary and fountains.

Far left: A monumental plant holder has been created by recruiting an elegant 'found' piece of architectural sculpture to support a moulded concrete pot.

Left: During the Victorian period classical reference, pleasingly interpreted in this lead urn, was if anything more widespread in the garden than in interior decoration.

This fine marble carving, placed in a rough-hewn basin, revives the mood of the Victorian era, the Indian summer of the angel and the cherub.

Below: The statue at the axis of this herb garden is the focus of the layout, bringing a sense of formality to the very informal planting.

Below right: The Egyptian theme of a sphinx is taken up rather ingeniously by the pyramidal forms of the topiary.

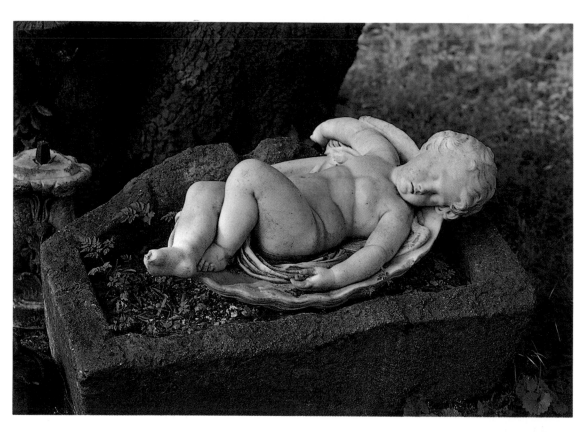

Arches at the entrance of the garden help to emphasize the feeling of passing from one distinct space into another, as well as to frame a first impression. This arch brings a touch of chinoiserie to an informal layout of lawn and borders.

Far left: The weathered look of the cherub has an agreeable correspondence with the silver-leaved senecio and the darker foliage to the rear.

Left: This garden, lying in the shadow of a large house, shows an effective combination of Victorian elements: ironwork, topiary in a formal layout around a statue, offset by the informal shapes of the trees.

and municipal outdoor furniture for the next few decades. With the Queen Anne and Arts and Craft Movements, wood returned to favour as a material to be used on its own, sometimes in Gothic designs, sometimes in oriental.

Some 19th-century moulds for iron furniture have survived and excellent originals – one can hardly call them reproductions – are still obtainable from traditional iron founders. On the cheaper side, a current favourite is the imitation of cast iron in cast aluminium. Not only do these aluminium chairs appear obviously thin to the eye, but somehow their very lightness when moved is disconcerting.

Outside lighting in Victorian times was mostly achieved by lanterns, traditionally of iron and glass. Japanese stone lanterns came in around the turn of the century along with more ephemeral variants in wood and paper, lit by candles. Authenticity today presents difficulties; the wiring up of old lamp posts for garden use is an affront to purists; reproduction fittings frequently only succeed in looking twee, too brassy or too curly. Tin lanterns which take candles are available from smart decorating firms; if these are thought too expensive, reproductions can be made up quite easily by a competent metal worker from sheet steel, after which they can be galvanized or simply painted with good quality paint, preferably matt. Outside as well as in, reproduction fittings are generally best when they follow simple designs.

Right: Concealed in an intimate corner beneath a rose-covered arbour, a seat of split timber displays the rustic effect typical of much Victorian garden furniture.

Far right: This is a fine example of the intricate patternwork of Victorian cast iron, combined with a comfortable wooden slatted seat.

Left: Defying time and the elements, stone seats are one-offs: no modern method can reproduce them at a viable cost.

Above: A simple wooden seat of Chinese-influenced geometric design has been invitingly hidden away.

Above left: This stone urn has seen better days, but is delightfully planted with a limited palette of yellow and white.

Above: The lavish ironwork of the seat and huge Victorian open-work urn is complemented by its sugary selection of plants and the clean lines of the box hedges.

Above and above right: Old clay chimney pots can have a new life in the garden – ideal for the informal, kitchen-garden style of layout.

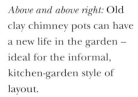

Left: Containers can be quite non-descript if adequately covered by plant material.

Right: A terracotta pedestal container has been planted for winter using evergreens, including the orange-fruiting 'winter cherry'.

287

Chapter Eight

KEEPING FAITH WITH THE PAST

Many Victorian houses have lost much of their original charm and character during ill-considered alterations made by succeeding generations of owners. It is only too easy to destroy the visual appeal of a Victorian house by installing an aluminium-framed picture window, but not all modifications have to clash: adding a well designed extension may enhance the original architecture. The key to a successful alteration or repair, no matter how small, is to follow the original.

All Victorian houses will inevitably have suffered the ravages of the climate on the outside and general wear and tear on the inside. In the average mid- to late-Victorian house, the original roof will probably have reached the end of its useful life. The brickwork may have deteriorated. The rain-water gutters and downpipes, if not regularly maintained, are likely to leak. Damaged plasterwork will need attention. Windows, doors, porches, verandahs and conservatories may have reached the stage where replacement is more cost effective than patching and mending.

Once the moment of replacement arrives, the decision has to be made whether to install a cheaper, readily available alternative or attempt to match the original work. Correct reinstatement can be expensive, but this minor act of homage to the past adds to the value of a property and helps to improve the neighbourhood to the advantage of everyone, including future householders. The ownership of an old house does not confer unlimited property rights. Legal restrictions are imposed by building and planning regulations, and moral restrictions are increasingly recognized and accepted; as householders, we not only inherit the work of past generations, we are trustees for posterity, and we ought to discharge that duty at the same time as securing our own comfort. A respect for Victorian architecture should encourage us to make the outlay necessary to preserve it in recognizable form.

Sometimes major alterations are necessary. It is always a shame to cut up an old house, but the owner may have no alternative. Even in the heyday of Victorian development, conversion became a practical necessity if the speculator had misjudged an area and his houses failed to find good families. The first sign of an estate going down was the notice in the window saying 'Rooms to let'. Multi-occupation was the simplest form of conversion: a change of use with the minimum change of facilities.

The recent rise in home ownership to historically unprecedented proportions has brought with it both new standards of convenience and new dangers to the fabric of old houses: plasterboard partitions, flush doors at the bottom of stairs, cramped front lobbies and truncated mouldings where new rooms meet old. In this chapter I have provided for sympathetic conversions: if the job has to be done, let it be done as well as possible. A little care taken over detailing and finish will pay for itself handsomely in pleasure and capital appreciation. The same principles will also serve the owner of a badly converted house who wants to repair the damage and improve the appearance of the property.

Some conversions do not affect more than one part of the house – making a separate flat in the basement, for example, or knocking two rooms into one. Other projects that are more disruptive require sensitive handling, including the conversion of whole houses, loft conversions and extensions. Finally in areas of high property values where family houses are not only hard to find but are likely to be prohibitively expensive, the prospective householder may be able to buy only a corner of a once-grand house: a side entrance hall perhaps, with an awkward opening cut through to what was once the servants' quarters; a couple of large rooms requiring conversion into reception-room, bedroom, kitchen and bathroom; a maisonette on two floors where a new internal staircase is needed. In such cases, an understanding of architectural detail and a bit of flair with paint, wallpaper and finishing touches can produce satisfying results.

Before starting any work that will affect the structure or appearance of a house, seek professional advice from an architect.

THE BASIC SURVEY

Roofs and chimney stacks

For anyone about to restore, repair or modernize a Victorian house, the first task is to assess its condition. The full professional survey of a house undertaken on behalf of buyers, either for their own information or as a condition of a mortgage, can be a useful diagnostic tool. Its aim is to establish what faults a house may have and what remedial action is necessary. Neither potential householders nor existing owners will be able to manage anything of this scope without employing an architect or a surveyor. The pages which follow identify key areas where faults commonly occur both inside and out. They are not intended in any sense as a substitute for a professional survey. Never rely on a valuation survey as a diagnostic tool.

Unlike most other external features, the roof is very difficult to examine closely. An old roof can appear sound when viewed from the ground but can in fact hide many small but significant problems. Most faults stem from poor maintenance and shoddy craftsmanship and materials, or sometimes just from age. Re-roofing can create its own problems. Roof timbers designed to support a covering of slates may sag under the extra weight of modern concrete tiles. Badly laid loft insulation can reduce ventilation from the eaves, allowing condensation, rot and damp to occur. Where slates or tiles meet the chimney stack, the usual lead or copper flashing may have been replaced by a cheaper mortar fillet.

External walls

The Victorians generally used cement-lime mortar for greater plasticity, allowing walls to shift and settle slightly without cracking. In the absence of building regulations, there was no common practice governing depth of foundations or even the inclusion of a damp proof course, walls being generally dry only if the site on which the house stood was well drained. Original damp proof courses are usually a layer of overlapping slates lying horizontally across the width of the wall, one or two bricks above ground.

Subsidence and bulging walls are a major problem and unless tackled immediately can lead to serious damage. They necessitate the services of a professional builder or structural engineer.

Drainage

The Victorian rain-water gutter was generally made of cast iron and emptied by way of a swan-neck, rain-water head and downpipe to a gulley or drain. Soil (sewage) is disposed of direct to an underground soil drain by means of a stack. Waste water from sink or bath can be fed directly into the stack but when rain-water is discharged into the soil drain it is not uncommon to see bath or sink outflow feeding into the rain-water head.

If walls remain damp over several years, due to a faulty drainage system, structural problems can arise. There may be frost penetration of bricks and the resulting dampness within the house can lead to dry rot, wet rot and flaking plaster. A cracked underground drain may cause part of the foundation to become waterlogged, resulting in localized subsidence. A blocked or broken soil drain is obviously a health hazard.

External woodwork

Surprising quantities of Victorian woodwork still survive. Top quality pine, oak, deal and other woods were used. These woods were well seasoned and mature, their resinous sap acting as a water-repellent preservative. They compare extremely favourably with the timbers used today which are often unseasoned kiln-dried woods, requiring treatment with artificial preservatives. Original woodwork should be kept wherever possible. Preventative work or partial repair should always be considered before replacement.

THE EXTERNAL SURVEY

1   Slates and tiles
Missing or slipped. Cracks, also worrying, are almost impossible to spot from ground level.

2   Ridge tiles
Missing or not firmly bedded in.

3   Moss
This indicates that water is not running off the roof as it should. Tiled roofs may have deposits of soot or wind-blown dust trapped beneath the tiles, encouraging moss to develop. Trapped water may be sucked up under the tiles by capillary action.

4   Delaminated or painted slates
Frost may cause slates to lose their outer layers and water may consequently find its way into the roof. Slates painted with tar, or tar with hessian underneath, indicate a problem that has only been temporarily cured.

5   Mortar fillet to a party wall
Mortar is not as flexible as lead flashing and may become dislodged over time. A soft mortar fillet is preferable to a hard one as it will resist cracking under extreme temperatures.

6   Hollows that collect water
Lead and zinc go brittle with age and are susceptible to hairline cracks. Any water that does not run straight off the roof may seep through it.

7   Patches and signs of temporary repair
The only effective way to stop water coming through a flat roof is to replace the covering completely.

8   Leaning chimney stack
Most stacks need repointing, being more exposed to the action of wind, rain and frost than any other part of the house. A stack that has been left unpointed for many years may develop a slight lean as the mortar between the brick courses decays and turns to powder.

9   Old flashing
Examine from the top of a ladder. If flashing has never been replaced, it will be brittle and liable to leak. Points of weakness are the gutter at the back of some chimneys and corroded soakers – overlapping protective zinc or lead plates tucked beneath the roof covering where it meets the chimney stack.

10   Wall plates
A sign that a bulging wall has been tied. If the house is sited on land liable to subsidence, for example on a hill or in a mining area, then the problem may recur.

11   Bulging walls
Easily overlooked. Compare the external walls with a strong perpendicular line such as a drainpipe or the wall of an adjoining house.

DEFECTIVE RAIN-WATER GOODS
1.   Hopper
2.   Rain-water downpipe has broken above bracket, causing damp in wall behind
3.   Rain-water gutter has broken away from the bracket

DETAIL OF WINDOW SILL DRIP
1.   Timber sill
2.   Water drip
3.   Window-frame
4.   Brick wall

FLASHING TO CHIMNEY
1.   Brick parapet on party wall
2.   Mortar fillet
3.   Lead flashing and soaker
4.   Ridge tile
5.   Haunching

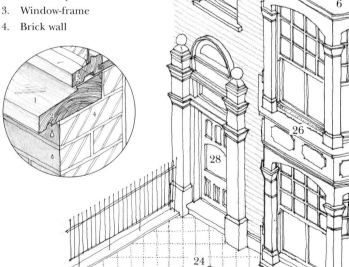

POINTING
1. Flush (correct)
2. Weathered or struck (incorrect)
3. Bucket handle (acceptable)
4. Recessed (acceptable)

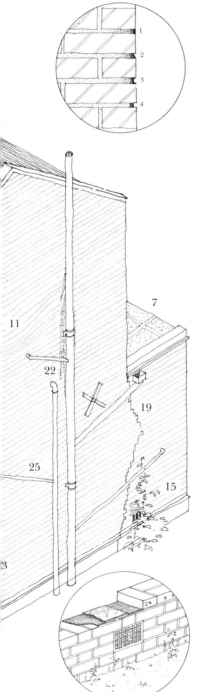

DAMP PROOFING
1. Old slate damp proof course
2. Holes bored for the injection of a damp proof course
3. Ventilation to void under suspended wooden floor

12 Cracks in brickwork and arches or lintels out of alignment

Often caused when the wooden sills, lintels and joists that support brickwork have warped or rotted. The most common place to find subsidence is a bay window.

13 Damp walls

These are often difficult for the amateur to spot, particularly in a damp climate. It is wise to hire a damp specialist to take accurate readings with a meter.

14 Damp proof course (DPC)

Scrape away mortar between the courses of bricks nearest the ground to look for evidence of a slate DPC. Earth from the garden may have piled up above the DPC, concealing it and conducting moisture up the wall. Even if a slate damp proof course appears intact, slight settlement could have caused cracking in some of the slates, allowing water to rise up the wall through capillary action. A series of holes filled with mortar indicate that a chemical DPC has been injected into the walls.

15 Blocked air bricks or vents

Air bricks are essential for under-floor ventilation. They combine with a DPC to keep walls dry. Sometimes Victorian builders put in too few air bricks, and often earth and leaves have been allowed to obstruct them. Houses that have a floor below ground level tend to have 'periscope vents' which serve the same purpose as air bricks.

16 Bad pointing

When a wall has been repointed, all too often there has been no attempt to reproduce the same lime/mortar mix as the original pointing. Mortar the wrong colour and strength will not merely look ugly, it can also split away from the brickwork in frosty weather, taking part of the brick's surface with it.

17 Painted walls

A brick wall keeps dry by 'breathing' and when a wall has been painted or covered with stone cladding, moisture will be unable to escape. A painted or clad wall with rising damp will far more easily transfer moisture to the inside of a house.

18 Cut bricks

Attempts to clean brickwork with a cutting tool or abrasive disc will remove the outer layer of the brick, making it more porous and more susceptible to damp and frost damage.

19 Extensions

Where an extension has been added to a house, its foundations may have settled causing the old and new brickwork to part company with each other. Sometimes cracks are obvious but occasionally they are tiny hairline fissures. Remedial work may not be drastic.

20 Damp patches beneath guttering

Since holes and cracks are usually found in the backs of gutters, damp patches may be the only visible sign of damage.

21 Uneven or sagging guttering

Weak joints and broken gutter clips or brackets may cause the gutter to sag and prevent water from draining properly. In rainy weather a sagging gutter will overflow.

22 Damp patches behind downpipes

Cracks or holes caused by corrosion or frost damage often occur where cast-iron pipes have been fixed so close to the wall that they cannot be painted.

23 Absence of water seal in rain-water gulley

If no water is visible at the bottom of a gulley, this means the stoneware trap is cracked, allowing water to seep into the ground around the foundations.

24 Bad-smelling main drain

The inspection chamber under the manhole cover may be inadequately rendered or the drain-pipes themselves may have cracked.

25 Disorganized pipework

Changes in plumbing over the years may have led to an unsightly tangle of exterior pipes. Pipework can be rationalized by feeding it directly into the stack. Seek the advice of a well established builder.

26 Uneven surface on window-sills and bottom rails of sashes

These are the most likely places for wet rot to occur since they are the most exposed. The surest way of finding rot is to prod the wood with a bradawl or small screwdriver. Uneven paintwork may indicate shoddy filling of rotted wood. Unless areas of rot have been cut back to the solid wood and then treated with a preservative, the rot fungus will continue to spread.

27 Flaking paintwork

This indicates shoddy or old work that has to be stripped to the bare timber. A primer, undercoat and, if possible, more than one top coat should be applied in sequence.

28 Replacement doors and windows

Many of the replacement doors and windows installed in Victorian houses between 1950 and the present are unsuitable, and appropriate joinery should be reinstated. Window conversions can be reversed if the sash boxes have been left in position. Rotten sashes can easily be copied and replaced with identical new ones.

THE INTERNAL SURVEY

Plumbing

For the Victorians it was standard to use lead piping throughout a house. The advantage was that joints could be easily soldered. The low melting point of lead also allows plumbers to 'sweat in' copper pipes to connect with modern fittings.

By the late-Victorian period, hot water was provided by coal-fired back boilers sited in the kitchen. Their mild steel pipes were often adapted when central heating was fitted. Besides being large and ugly, mild steel pipes can cause air locks if they have been clumsily connected to copper piping.

Modern balanced-flue boilers can be sited on any external wall either upstairs or down, wherever the connecting pipework causes least inconvenience.

The vogue for antique bathroom fittings has arrived too late to save all but a few examples of the genuine articles. Many so-called antique fittings were made in the 1930s and have had their chromium plating removed with spirit of salts.

Gas

Most Victorian houses were lit by gas (see page 168), evidence of which is often found when lifting floorboards or looking in the loft. Whereas much electric wiring was carried in mild steel conduits of no great strength, small bore gas piping used much thicker steel. Sometimes gas pipes were chased into the plaster of walls, ending in wooden roses which originally supported swan-necked light fittings. Old gas fittings of this kind can easily be adapted as electric light fittings, but they must be rewired and earthed. Brass bayonet bulb-holders can then be inserted in place of the gas mantle and a period or reproduction shade fitted. It may be possible to run new electrical cables inside old gas piping.

Electricity

A small number of houses built at the end of the Victorian era were wired for electricity and sometimes vulcanized, fabric-covered wiring, or even lead-sheathed cable, may be found when making repairs or alterations. Such wiring is potentially lethal if it is connected to the mains. It is unwise to tamper unnecessarily with the electrics. If in any doubt, call in a qualified electrician to check the system over.

Late-Victorian or Edwardian light fittings are highly collectable and will add to the atmosphere of a house if put back into use. They must be converted for modern wiring.

LATH AND PLASTER

1. Brace studding
2. Stud
3. Wooden laths
4. Plaster
5. Cornice

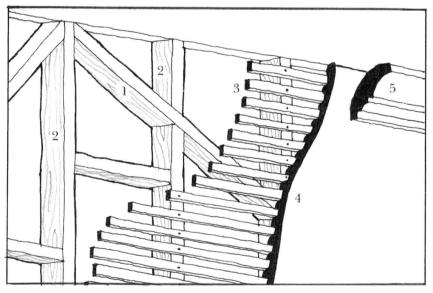

Plaster

The Victorians rendered their walls with a lime/horsehair plaster mix applied to bare bricks or laths. Only when wallpaper is completely stripped off can the state of the plaster beneath be seen and judged. When several layers of heavy wallpaper have been allowed to build up, stripping the paper can pull the skim coat of plaster off the wall. Cracks or bulges point to unsound areas of plaster which can be easily dislodged with a sharp hand tool such as a stripping knife. When investigating unsound plaster, it is best to adopt a radical approach; rather than repair isolated patches with filler, it is just as easy, and cheaper in the long run, to put a skim coat over a large area. Damp may be the cause of flaking or unsound plaster. This possibility should be investigated and, if necessary, put right before replastering. Dampness can usually be prevented by rendering a bare wall with a mortar mix of one part of cement to six parts of sand before the finishing coats of plaster are applied. If the plaster is undamaged, a slightly damp wall can be prepared for papering by hanging it with pitch paper, one side of which is coated with bitumen. Tin or aluminium strips, glued and rolled on to a wall before paper is applied, can also be used to isolate dampness. It is worth remembering that the plasterwork of Victorian builders was seldom exact, so the final finish should not be mirror smooth.

Ceilings

Original Victorian ceilings are of lath-and-plaster construction, usually papered over to help prevent cracking. But a combination of settlement and bomb damage during the Second World War has left many city ceilings a little shaky.

In cases of cracking, ceiling paper should be carefully stripped off and cracks cleaned out and filled with a flexible proprietary filling compound. Alternatively, a strip of thin gauze scrim will hold fresh finish plaster over the cracks, preventing them from opening up again. Once the cracks have been dealt with, the ceiling can be repapered.

Where water has found its way through a ceiling from burst pipes or a leaking water tank, areas of plaster may separate from the laths. If the sag is extreme, it is best to remove both plaster and laths and nail extra thick plasterboard to the joists before redecorating. If the sag is only slight, then it may be possible to contain both laths and plaster by lining the ceiling with plasterboard, securely nailed in place with long galvanized clouts.

Staircases

The staircase of the standard terraced house was made of timber. The underside should be well ventilated to prevent dry rot and the pillars (newel posts) that support the handrails should be securely anchored to the floor joists.

Wood rot

Wet rot in the main attacks external timbers; internal outbreaks tend to be localized and easily eradicated. Dry rot, on the other hand, can cause a great deal of damage within the house. This makes it the principal antagonist.

Dry rot – *Merulius lachrymans* – is a fungal growth which, despite its common name, thrives in warm, damp, unventilated conditions. Tiny spores of the fungus settle on moist wood and rapidly develop into a fruiting body which feeds off the wood, breaking it down. As the fungus takes hold, it sends out filaments which spread the rot to nearby wood. One reason why dry rot is so deadly is that these filaments can travel across concrete, bricks or even steel joists in their search for damp timber. It is so virulent that it can penetrate a wall 3 feet (1m) thick in days. Eradication is particularly difficult since it involves the destruction or sterilization of all building materials that have come into contact with it.

Dry rot is thought to have been introduced into Victorian houses by domestic coal. Wooden pit props in damp mines were a breeding ground for the fungus and spores were present in coal which was stored in such damp spots as cellars or under the stairs. Today's dry rot spores are probably wind-borne or have been lying dormant in timbers, awaiting the right conditions for growth.

The fact that outbreaks are sometimes only local when they do occur stands as a tribute to the enduring quality of the timber used in Victorian houses. Most of this was cut down when fully mature and consisted of dense, close-ringed heartwood which has a natural resistance to fungal attack. Today's pine, mostly sapwood, is more vulnerable.

Dry rot can develop unseen behind skirting-boards, under floorboards and in roof spaces, and it is often only detected when it has already caused a great deal of damage. It has a damp musty smell and affected wood breaks up into small cubes. For obvious reasons, it should be treated as quickly as possible. To prevent dry rot, keep potentially damp areas, like the loft, cellar and bathroom, well ventilated, and cure plumbing leaks immediately.

Treatment of dry rot

Although many people prefer to use specialist firms which offer a guarantee, a good builder will also be able to tackle dry rot without great expense. The builder may himself use a specialist firm if large areas have to be treated. In either case, the technique is to cut back timbers and expose affected brickwork or masonry beyond the limit of fungal growth. The exposed brickwork will then be treated with a flame gun or blowlamp. Dry rot dies after exposure to oxygen. The affected area should therefore be left exposed until it has fully dried out. All timbers removed from the site should be burned promptly as there is a danger of spores spreading. However, if dry rot has infected carved or decorated woodwork, the timber may be sterilized in a drying kiln before being pressure-impregnated with a preservative.

Treatment of wet rot

Wet rot is another fungus that attacks damp timber, particularly door- and window-frames. It often develops underneath cracked paintwork and it can go undetected for some time. Affected timber is invariably discoloured and spongy when wet, powdery when dry.

The cause of the damp should be cured before cutting away the damaged timber. The wood can then be painted with a preservative before being patched up with filler and redecorated.

Woodworm

The presence of woodworm, or furniture beetle, is indicated by large numbers of small holes in wood. The larvae eat their way through wood, creating bore holes. Finally, they emerge as fully-grown beetles through larger flight holes. Structural timbers should be inspected regularly for any tell-tale signs. Flight holes appear in the summer months and will show up bright in contrast to the dull or dusty surface of the timber. Flight holes give off a fine dust when the wood is tapped. Left untreated, affected timber can be both weakened and disfigured.

STRUCTURAL ALTERATIONS

Sometimes the original design of a Victorian house does not satisfy current requirements. A dingy room at the back of the house may feel claustrophobic, or a modest house may become too small for a growing family. Several options are available to people who want to open up, adapt or expand the existing living space, but most of them involve making major decisions that will affect the appearance and nature of the house permanently.

The disadvantages of open-plan living are better appreciated now than they were 10 or 15 years ago. Noise, smells and draughts all circulate more freely, other people's mess is more evident and personal space harder to obtain in a house where walls and doors have been removed. The architectural integrity of the building may be compromised by inappropriate styles of opening, and structural problems will almost certainly be encountered.

Major alterations must comply with the Building Regulations and may require planning permission before work goes ahead. Because of the legal and technical difficulties, it pays to call in professional advice at the earliest stage.

Planning permission

In England, Wales and Northern Ireland planning restrictions exist to control the siting and appearance of buildings and extensions. The regulations vary from district to district and are occasionally governed by local bye-laws.

Buildings listed by the Department of the Environment as being of historic or environmental interest always require planning permission before alterations are made. In certain towns, there are conservation areas where permission must be sought for external alterations. It is always wise to check with the local council if planning permission is required. It

would be foolhardy to extend a loft space, add an extension or make material alterations to a listed building if it meant that you fell foul of the law. In Scotland there is the requirement to notify adjoining proprietors.

Building Regulations

Any structural alteration to a building in England, Wales and Northern Ireland must comply with the Building Regulations, which are enforced to safeguard health, safety and stability the of a building. Before starting any major work, check that your plans comply with the appropriate regulations. Scotland has its own Building Standards and a building warrant must be obtained before alterations are made.

Professional advice

Anyone wishing to adapt or change the structure or appearance of a house should call in a specialist familiar with design, building construction and the law. An architect will assist you in drawing up detailed plans and obtaining necessary approvals. He will advise you on the selection of an appropriate contract and a builder to carry it out, and will inspect the job periodically while it is in progress. For alterations with no design implication, and which do not affect the character of the building or the rooms within, a surveyor should be well acquainted with what is necessary. Specialist firms, such as those that convert lofts, may offer a free consultation and survey but they lack the independence and objectivity of a professional.

Builders, electricians and plumbers work best when they have plans to follow, preferably drawn up by an architect. Many architects will recommend tradesmen. However, the client should always have a direct contract with builders and other contractors.

KNOCKING THROUGH

'Knocking through', the opening up of a wall between two rooms – often the wall between a ground-floor front room and a back room – is the most important and most common alteration made to Victorian houses by modern residents (see page 111).

Internal walls

The interior walls or partitions in a Victorian house are generally load-bearing, which means that they act as supports for the timber floor or ceiling joists above and also contribute to the structure and solidity of the external walls. Additionally, they may act as a support for staircases. Many are built in brick. Others may be timber-framed and still be of load-bearing specification, in which case they will be supported by a brick sleeper wall beneath floor level. Many timber-framed walls are hollow. Others are filled with rough brickwork called nogging. It is never easy to tell those that are load-bearing from those that

are not; this is where an expert's opinion is essential. Opening up a non-load-bearing wall is comparatively simple; removing a load-bearing wall is dangerous.

When demolishing or opening up a load-bearing wall, an RSJ (rolled steel joist) or UB (universal beam) will have to be positioned above the opening to take the weight of the floors above and supply the rigidity that would otherwise be lost. The first step towards this end is to demolish the wall section by section, temporarily inserting adjustable steel bars to bear the load. When the opening is the right size, brick or breeze block piers are built to support either end of the RSJ or UB, and the new joist or beam is inserted. Never attempt to do this job yourself.

The scars left to the walls after knocking through can be finished off by replastering; if appropriate, a new double door frame, complete with architraves, can be installed.

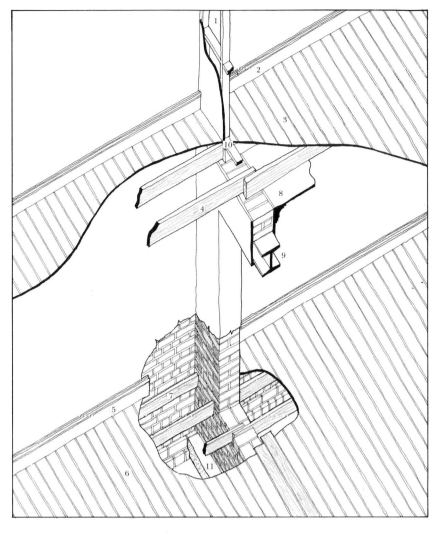

OPENING BETWEEN ROOMS
1. Stud wall with plasterboard
2. Skirting to first floor
3. Floorboards to first floor
4. First-floor joists
5. Skirting to ground floor
6. Floorboards to ground floor
7. Ground-floor joists
8. Plaster ceiling and cornice
9. New RSJ to support first-floor joists
10. New floorboards in location of former wall
11. Foundation to new pier

Cornices

The point at which the wall meets the ceiling is usually modified by a cove, moulding or length of decorated plaster cornice (see page 128).

When knocking through a pair of rooms with high ceilings and cornices, it may be better to take the opening below the line of the picture rail to avoid damage to the cornice above. However, where ceilings are low the cornices in both rooms will

have to be removed to allow the RSJ to be positioned. A mould can be taken from a piece of cornice left in place and lengths of fibrous plaster cornice made up off-site by a specialist firm. If cornices are in bad repair generally, it may be advisable to replace them (for stockists, see page 308).

Skirting

One side-benefit of knocking through is that skirting will be left over

from the base of the dividing wall. This can be used for making good and should be carefully removed with a crow-bar.

Refitting it is not easy. The ends have to be mitred and the wood itself may be brittle, making it difficult to nail in place.

Floorboards

Once the wall has been demolished, floorboards will have to be laid across the space it occupied. If the floorboards in the two

main rooms have been stripped, it is obviously sensible to put old floorboards in the new floor area. Architectural salvage companies may be able to supply old flooring (see page 308). If you are tempted to rescue old wood from a demolition site or skip, do check for woodworm and dry rot. If in the slightest doubt, paint the boards with a preservative. When fixing them down, make sure the new supports beneath

them are well secured to existing joists and that they bring the new boards to the exact level of the existing floor.

Relocation of services

The demolition of a dividing wall will probably entail the relocation of power points. The upheaval caused by such a major building project will in any case provide an opportunity to resite power points or to install a new wiring system.

CONVERSIONS

Basement conversions

Many older Victorian houses were built with cellars or basements where the ceilings are too low for the rooms to be used for anything but storage. Prone to dampness and poorly ventilated, these spaces are often uninhabitable. They are, however, natural candidates for improvement. It is often possible to lower the floor and improve the lighting at front and rear by installing, say, windows at the front and french windows at the rear. The space gained could provide not just extra living room but even a self-contained garden flat with its own kitchen and bathroom.

The building work involved, however, is complex and can prove expensive. Professional advice is definitely required. The floor will generally need to be lowered below that of the existing foundations of the house. This means either strengthening the foundations or underpinning the whole house. A newly excavated cellar will almost certainly have to be 'tanked' with waterproof membranes around the walls as well as under the floor in order to exclude ground water. This job is best left to a reputable specialist company.

As an alternative, a basement can be brought into the main body of the house by opening it from the top to create an unusual living area, full of height and the sensation of space. Where two ground-floor reception-rooms have been knocked into one, the floor of the rear room can simply be removed, with access provided to the basement floor by a spiral staircase. The opening must be made safe with balusters and handrail, creating the effect of a balcony within the drawing-room.

Creating new rooms

It is sometimes possible to achieve a more effective use of space by moving or adding walls – easy enough if they are mere partitions, not load-bearing. A run of three bedrooms could be converted into a suite of two bedrooms and two bathrooms. If there are only two bedrooms, both rather large, the wall dividing them could be

ROOM CONVERSIONS

BEFORE:	AFTER:
1. Kitchen	1. Day room
2. Dining-room	2. Kitchen
3. Lounge	3. Hall
4. Hall	4. Living-room
5. Parlour	

BEFORE:	AFTER:
1. Kitchen	1. Day room 2. Dining-room
2. Dining-room 3. Bathroom	3. Shower/WC 4. Utility room

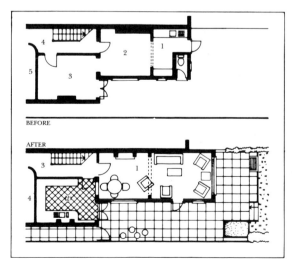

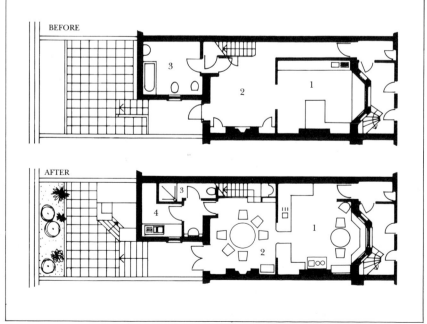

removed and its place taken by two stud walls 6 feet (2m) apart. This would create two slightly smaller bedrooms with a narrow slip between them, which could be split into two tiny rooms, with access from each bedroom. One could become a walk-in wardrobe (see page 266), while the other might become an en-suite bathroom.

An average-sized room can be made into a grand room by moving the back wall further back, and making the thinner room behind into a kitchen or bathroom. An extra sense of spaciousness can be achieved by styling the doorway to look like partition doors leading to another reception-room.

Loft conversions

One of the simplest ways to gain space in a house is to convert the loft, generally into bedroom, study or storeroom. When considering a loft conversion in a Victorian house, great attention needs to be given to making sure that changes respect the intentions of the original architecture and the general quality of the streetscape. All too easily, a row of fine houses can be spoiled by a single, insensitively designed dormer window conversion. This really is a case where the modern owner is honour-bound to try to keep faith with the past, regardless of the latitude extended by the responsible authorities.

External considerations

The use of skylights allows the profile of an existing roof to be retained where it is important to do so. If dormers have to be added to give ceiling height and views, then these should be in keeping with the style of the building. Similarly, skylights should be carefully chosen so that they do not conflict with the character of the house. Proprietary large double-glazed units may damage the appearance of a roof just as much as a picture window in a decorative facade.

On dormer roofs, or on any part of the main roof that has to be rebuilt, care should be taken to obtain a cladding material which matches that

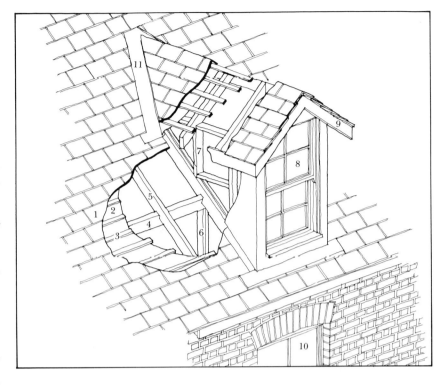

of the original roof. Second-hand slates may sometimes be available, but they need careful checking. New slates are now very expensive. A cheaper but effective substitute is found in the many modern types of resin-bonded composition slates or fibre cement slates. On tiled roofs, second-hand stock is again a suitable answer, with the local builder's merchant a likely source or, failing that, an architectural salvage company. Modern tiles can also be found to match the colour of old tiles darkened by soot and grime, but it is often impossible to match for size. In the case of a new dormer, however, size may not be as important as colour because new tiles will not be laid side by side with old ones.

Many 19th-century houses in the USA and some in Britain were roofed with cedar shingles. With these, it is advisable to check the condition of the whole roof. Shingle roofs were steeply pitched to throw off water but isolated damage or missing shingles lead to rain-water penetration and the rapid spread of rot. Even so, a shingle roof can last more than 50 years. Wood shingles present more of a fire hazard than other forms of roofing, but they can be treated with a chemical fire retardant.

DORMER WINDOW
1. Slates
2. Sarking felt
3. Battens
4. Purlin to main roof
5. Rafter to main roof supported on purlin and external wall
6. Additional studs to support end of purlin
7. Studwork to side of dormer
8. Sash window
9. Bargeboard
10. Existing window with brick arch
11. Valley gutter

Internal considerations

Victorian roofs were built on site by skilled joiners. The roof timbers were supported by hangers, struts and purlins which occupy the loft space; in order for it to be used as a room, this inconvenient but essential timber framing has to be moved and replaced by new structural beams capable of supporting the weight of the roof. Usually this means adding two large wooden beams from which stud frames are built up to support the roof timbers and any new dormers that may be required.

A floor has to be laid in a converted loft space and it is unlikely that the existing ceiling joists are of sufficient size to support it. Thicker, stronger joists have to be laid alongside existing timbers and their ends need support from new cross-members – either steel girders bolted together in sections or floor beams brought in through an open section of the roof. The dimensions of the new flooring joists will depend on the distance between them as well as on the floor area to be supported. The Building Regulations, available for consultation at local libraries, contain tables of joist sizes, spacing and floor loadings.

The head height in new rooms is an important consideration in any loft conversion. Up to 1985, British Building Regulations insisted on a minimum of 7 feet (2.3m) over at least half the total floor area. Since then, the regulations have been relaxed a little and the amount of headroom required is left to the discretion of the local Building Inspector. Even so, it is wise to try for as much height as possible.

Although the Building Regulations in England, Wales and Northern Ireland allow a loft ladder to be used, access to a loft conversion is best provided by a permanent staircase. From a design and space-saving perspective, this should generally be sited over the well of the existing staircase. Ideally, it should follow the same detailing as the staircase below with matching hand-rail and balusters.

Fire regulations governing the installation of staircases, particularly where these extend the original stairwell, are troublesome in terms of design, even though very important for safety. The problem is that a stairwell creates a natural draught that sucks a fire up through the middle of a house, causing it to spread rapidly to all floors. Local fire regulations vary but it is likely that all doors opening on to the stairwell may be required to be fireproofed, including existing ones, and each door may have to be self-closing. It is also often necessary to increase the fire

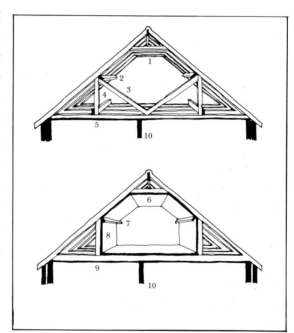

LOFT CONVERSION
1. Collar
2. Purlin
3. Purlin struts
4. Vertical struts
5. Ceiling joists
6. Attic ceiling
7. Retained or strengthened purlins
8. Plaster walls on additional struts
9. Additional deeper joists
10. Spine wall

resistance of the floor and ceiling; the flooring should be able to resist a fire for up to half an hour – floor-grade chipboard or tongue-and-groove boarding are the most suitable materials for this purpose.

In the event of a fire, a person could easily be trapped in an attic bedroom with no means of escape. Fire regulations allow for the provision of an escape route, for example over a flat roof via a large opening window. Where a route is provided, it is possible some of the other restrictions may be relaxed. Places such as store-rooms or bathrooms are classed as non-habitable and are accordingly exempt from fire regulations.

Services

Loft conversions require wiring circuits for power and light. They also necessitate re-arranging the plumbing within the original roof space. Many loft conversions are intended as extra bedrooms and it is often desirable to provide an en-suite bathroom or shower-room or, at the least, a wash basin. Domestic hot water is supplied from the cold water tank in the roofspace via a boiler. The tank must be higher than the outlets to maintain adequate pressure. Since it may not be feasible to site the tank higher than the new loft rooms, a shower or wash basin can successfully be fitted with an individual electric water heater and a cold water supply direct from the rising main.

If the central heating is extended to the loft, then probably a larger central heating boiler will be necessary. Thermostatically controlled electric heating is often better for a single room and much cheaper to add than altering the central heating.

Converting into flats

Converting a basement or loft into a self-contained flat is comparatively simple compared to dividing up a large Victorian house into a number of separate living spaces. Stringent regulations often dictate how the final design should or should not look. It is essential to have an architect draft detailed drawings.

FLAT CONVERSION
BEFORE: 1. Bedroom, 2. Bedroom, 3. Bathroom, 4. Bedroom.
AFTER: 1. Living-/dining-room/kitchen, 2. Bedroom, 3. Bathroom.

FLAT CONVERSION
BEFORE: 1. Hall, 2. Parlour, 3. Store, 4. Store, 5. Lobby, 6. Scullery, 7. WC.
AFTER: 1. Entrance hall, 2. Hall, 3. Bedroom, 4. Bathroom, 5. Kitchen, 6. Living-/dining-room.

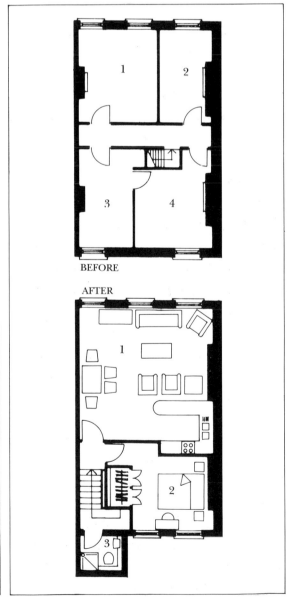

EXTENSIONS

Later Victorian terraced houses were often built with extensions at the rear, for kitchen, scullery, occasionally a bathroom and sometimes a servant's room. A grander extension could almost be a self-contained service wing.

It is possible to build out over an existing extension, but a number of questions have to be resolved and planning permission sought before any work commences. For example, can the existing walls take the extra load? How will the new addition be insulated? Will it connect with the stairs and corridors of the existing house? Similarly, an extension over a garage may require under-floor insulation. There is also the vital issue of matching the addition to the existing house. If strengthening of the original brickwork is required, the work could involve underpinning. Where ground-floor doors and windows are being resited, it may be simplest to knock down the original structure and start again. Alternatively, it may be possible to reduce the load to a manageable level by constructing the second storey with single skin walls of thermalite blocks, topped with a flat roof. A flat roof weighs much less than a pitched slate or tile roof, but will only be visually appropriate to a limited range of buildings. Cheaper flat roofs have a distressingly short life – probably no more than 10 to 15 years.

When a new back extension is to be built, an architect should specify the type and size of the foundations needed and give details on how they are to be tied in to the existing footings. Drains and inspection chambers may have to be moved or provision made for them inside the new building. The walls of most new extensions will have a cavity between the inner and outer 'leaves'. This type of construction provides improved insulation, but the brickwork bonding needs to be matched to the original pattern (for typical patterns, see page 301).

When adding an extension, it is advisable to use recycled building materials. Alternatively, if the roof of the main house is in a state of disrepair, the construction of an extension could be a good moment for renewing all the roofing of the house so that the pitched roof of the new addition exactly matches the main roof.

New extensions need to follow detailing of existing doors, windows, lintels and cornices; these should be covered by the architect's brief. Make sure to get the proportions right, especially the size of the windows. If they are too small, they will make the new part of the house look inferior to the old; if they are too big, they will swamp the original architecture.

Conservatories

Conservatories are by far the cheapest means of adding to a house. They are capable of giving great pleasure but do substantially alter the atmosphere of the room to which they are added, making it feel, paradoxically, a good deal more indoors, and affecting the amount and quality of natural light reaching it.

NEIGHBOURLY EXTENSION
1. New rear extension
2. Adapted dormer window
3. New clerestory window
4. New windows
5. New french windows
6. Original windows

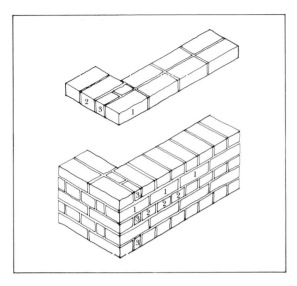

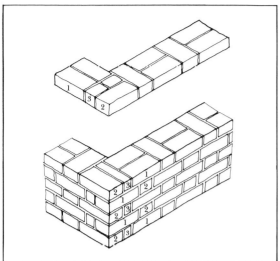

Right:
ENGLISH BOND
BRICKWORK
1. Stretcher
2. Header
3. Queen closer

Far right:
FLEMISH BOND
BRICKWORK
1. Stretcher
2. Header
3. Queen closer

Many pre-fabricated Victorian-style conservatories are available, and manufacturers will assemble them on site to specifications. These often look acceptable, last well and require little maintenance, but may cost more than a custom-made conservatory constructed of wood and glass in the traditional manner. A conservatory should be double-glazed and well ventilated in order to prevent condensation and remain cool in summer.

HEATING AND INSULATION

CENTRAL HEATING

Victorian central heating systems were often vast and inefficient but the same basic type is the only sort of central heating practicable today in a Victorian house – a 'wet' system run by the circulation of hot water through pipes and radiators. The modern, 'dry' alternative of ducted air is normally installed when a house is built, and only becomes an option in an old house when the building is being thoroughly reconstructed.

Those moving into Victorian houses still devoid of central heating have the advantage that they will be able to install a boiler that meets their known requirements and if applicable, one that can meet possible future demands such as a loft conversion or an extension.

Before installing a new system or upgrading an existing one, it is a wise precaution to call in a heating engineer who will calculate the boiler size and radiator output that is required.

Gas-fired central heating
On grounds of cost and flexibility, gas is generally the preferred fuel, wherever it is available. Most modern gas-fired boilers have balanced flues which enable air to be sucked in and burnt gases expelled through the same aperture in the wall. There are limitations on where the flue can be sited – for example, it must not go underneath a window – and local bye-laws may prevent it from being positioned on the front facade of a house where it could be an eyesore. For this reason it is always best to consult a surveyor or architect before installation. In larger houses a floor-standing model may be required. This can be sited in a fireplace, and the flue ducted up the chimney. To prevent acid residues from destroying the inside of the chimney, the stack has to be lined with non-corrosive material and a special cowl must be placed on top.

Oil-fired central heating
When gas is not available, particularly in the country, oil is often the best alternative. It has one major disadvantage: the need for lorry access to the oil-storage tank, which must be concealed where possible outside the house.

Pipe runs and radiators

The Victorians made a virtue of their central heating systems, siting large and elaborately decorated radiators in prominent positions. Some people living in Victorian houses may wish to echo this fashion (see page 113), at least in rooms where an imposing effect is wanted. However, most householders prefer their central heating to be more discreet.

The Victorians were perfectly prepared to run their horizontal pipes along the top of skirting-boards. In general the modern householder will want to run them under the floor. This poses few problems in the case of a suspended wooden floor, but it may be necessary to stick to the skirting-board position in some instances: for example, to avoid damage to tiles or where there is a solid concrete floor.

Any pipework laid against these surfaces should be carried in insulated trunking.

Vertical pipes running from ground level to upper floors also need to be concealed. Many late-Victorian houses were built with fitted cupboards in the kitchen, on landings or in bedrooms, and pipes can run inside them. Otherwise, pipes will have to be boxed in or chased into the plaster with insulated metal trunking.

Boxing in offers an opportunity for elaboration into a column, complete with capital, if the general style of the house will accept it.

The siting of radiators calls for efficiency as much as for discretion. In living areas, wall-mounted radiators are best placed under windows, close to the point of maximum heat loss. The cool air from the window is lifted and flows across the room more efficiently. In bedrooms, where slightly cooler temperatures may be desired, an internal wall is often more economical; some cool airflow from the windows will be felt, however. It is best to avoid siting a radiator against a panelled window recess – not only will the panelling be concealed but it could also become charred.

Heat loss from a radiator on an external wall can be cut down by putting reflective foil behind the radiator. Fitting a radiator shelf will help throw heat out into the room.

There will probably be awkward spots where radiators are hard to site due to lack of wall space. Instead, a hot water convector can be installed at skirting-board level or even above a door. Convectors are particularly useful in kitchens or bathrooms where work surfaces or fitted units take up most of the wall space.

ENERGY CONSERVATION

Whether a house is heated by gas, oil, electricity or coal fires, a heating system will be more efficient if heat loss can be minimized. Of all forms of heating, an open coal fire is the least efficient, as around 80 per cent of the heat is lost up the chimney. Even so, a coal fire is still the best source of radiant heat, felt intensely at close quarters.

Draughts

The Victorians stoically accepted draughts as a fact of life. Rather than cure them, they went to great lengths to avoid them. The sitting-room and the bedrooms often contained screens, and doors were hung with a thick velvet or chenille *portière*, a curtain suspended from a brass rail which was hinged to open with the door.

Today there are a number of products available to help the energy-conscious householder. Draughts around external doors can be prevented by a self-adhesive foam draught-excluder or, more attractively, a sprung brass weather-strip. A threshold seal consisting of a tightly packed brush held by an aluminium or nylon strip can be fixed to the bottom of the door.

A more radical, and more effective, solution to cure front-door draughts is to build an enclosed porch. The Victorians themselves were considerable porch builders but generally left them open so that they provided little more than shelter against rain. Sometimes it is possible to fit an external door with glazed surrounds within the framework of an original Victorian porch. This is easiest when the porch is a simple recess in the front of the building. The original external door can be brought forward and fitted into a new frame while an internal vestibule door can be fitted into the old frame. Even if there is no original porch, it is generally possible to have an architect design one that is in keeping with the house, and he will check planning regulations (see page 294).

Fireplaces can be a major source of heat loss even when unlit. Warm air in the room simply disappears up the flue. Cast-iron register grate fireplaces may be blocked off by pulling down the iron plate above the grate.

Unused fireplaces are often removed, most commonly to save bedroom wall space and at the same time to cut down on draughts. This can be a very messy operation as soot and rubble will be

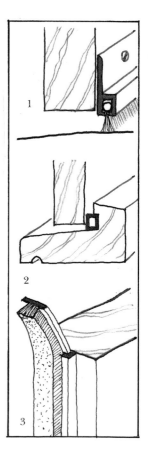

DRAUGHT EXCLUDERS
1. Brush draught excluder
2. Vinyl-sheathed urethane foam seal
3. Plant-on seal with removable brush

dislodged from behind the grate. When bricking up and plastering over the opening, it is important to provide space for an air vent and it is equally important to leave the top of the chimney uncapped. Any fireplace that has been completely closed off will cause condensation in the flue and this could leach out through the walls,

causing problems of damp, flaking plaster and possibly dry rot.

Floorboards at ground-floor level can also be a source of draughts. Suspended floors are ventilated from beneath through airbricks. If the floorboards are not close-fitting, and there is no floor covering, a ground-floor room can become

distinctly breezy. As a remedy, the floorboards may be relaid closer together or the cracks may be filled with a proprietary filling compound or home-made *papier mâché*, a cheap but effective filler.

The war against draughts, however, should have limits. Gas and coal fires need oxygen to burn and must have some

draught, however small. A fire can be made to draw better by providing grilles either side of the hearth which can be opened when the fire is lit, allowing air to be drawn up from the crawl space beneath the floor rather than across the room. When the fire is out, the grilles may be closed. A slight draught will prevent stuffiness and the

moisturizing effect will benefit antique furniture. Central heating is the enemy of old timber, drying out the air and causing splitting and warping. In rooms where sealing has been too effective, well watered plants and radiator humidifiers will help restore the moisture balance.

Loft insulation

Because it involves no structural alteration but merely the laying down between the joists of a material such as fibreglass roll or expanded polystyrene granules, loft insulation is the cheapest and most cost-effective form of household insulation to install. Where houses have no loft insulation, grants are sometimes available.

There are a number of rules to observe when insulating a loft. When laying fibreglass, for instance, it is best not to

take it all the way to the edge of the eaves but instead to leave a space of at least 6 inches (15cm). Most old roofs are ventilated from below the eaves, and reduced ventilation here could lead to condensation, dampness and, all too swiftly, dry rot. Because heat is prevented from passing upwards through the ceiling below, an insulated loft will be much colder than before. This makes it essential to lag all pipes and water tanks in the loft. It is best not to lay insulation under water tanks, allowing them

to receive some heat from below.

If the loft has been converted for use as a habitable room, then insulation should have been incorporated in the building materials used. The loft's ceiling and walls will probably have been constructed from thermal plasterboard incorporating a foil vapour barrier to ensure that timbers on the other side stay free from moisture. In addition, the spaces between the roof timbers should have been packed with insulating material.

Wall insulation

Thermally insulated plasterboard can help minimize heat loss through walls provided they are dry. Its use is problematic, however, in rooms where there are original plaster cornices and skirtings to be preserved. Here it is much easier to coat the walls with a wafer-thin layer from a roll of polystyrene. This will provide effective insulation and will double as a lining paper, evening out pitted or bumpy plaster and providing an easy base for wallpapering.

Floor insulation

Floor insulation is a great deal more radical than merely sealing the floorboards against draughts, but luckily it is rarely essential. The job entails taking up the boards and fitting expanded polystyrene blocks between the exposed joists. Battens are nailed along the sides of the joists allowing the polystyrene to sit flush with the top of the joists. It is important that no gaps be left where stagnant air might encourage condensation and dry rot.

Double glazing

Since only ten per cent of a house's heat loss is by way of windows, double glazing is scarcely the remedy for high fuel bills that salesmen's rhetoric often claims. In addition the appearance of many Victorian houses has been ruined by inappropriate aluminium frames. Some companies have begun to offer windows that retain the original lines of the sashes or glazing bars; and sometimes they can be fitted into existing Victorian frames.

Quotations for factory-made windows should be compared with the cost of employing a local joinery firm to make new wooden sashes suitable for double glazing.

Secondary glazing

When window frames and sashes are in good repair, it is worth considering secondary glazing: the fitting of another set of windows inside or even outside the existing frames. The greater distance between outer and inner panes makes

secondary glazing particularly effective in reducing noise but the drawback is the lack of a vacuum seal between the two layers of glass; unless some form of ventilation is provided, condensation may develop.

The frames or clips that support the new panes of glass can also look out of sorts with a Victorian interior.

Other solutions

The Victorians themselves had a range of simple forms of insulation which

can still be used today.

Almost all windows of early houses were fitted with folding pine internal shutters. These were usually made in the form of two or even three doors, hinged in the middle. When not in use they were folded back into recesses in the wall. Some still survive unrecognized under so many layers of paint that they appear to be a form of panelling. Rescued and unfolded, they are a delightful feature.

The Victorians also

made use of heavy, lined curtains to cut heat loss at night. On large windows these can hang right to the ground (see page 198). Deep ruffled pelmets above the curtain rail help prevent heat loss from the top of windows.

ADAPTING VICTORIAN FIXTURES AND FITTINGS

In Britain, particularly during the 1950s and 1960s, many original fixtures and fittings were removed from Victorian houses and replaced by substitutes which now appear unsuitable, if not cheap and nasty. Detail gave way to flat, easily cleaned surfaces. Fireplaces were removed and thrown away. Balusters were hidden beneath hardboard panelling and the mouldings on doors were hacked away or covered over with hardboard.

The many companies now specializing in reproduction or original fittings (see page 308) are an enormous help in reversing this trend. There should be no difficulty in obtaining anything from a doorknocker to a roll-top bath in a style suitable to the period of a house. The first step is to know what is missing. If in doubt about the nature of the original fittings, check for references in the body of this book. Neighbours are also a useful resource, since it may often happen that another house in the same street still has many of its original fixtures.

Reproduction fittings need to be scrutinized with care. Some are a weak pastiche of Victorian style, made in inferior materials and likely to look out of place. Others can be extremely good. For those with a scavenging instinct and a sharp eye for a bargain, it is still possible to buy original Victoriana at a price not very much higher than reproduction pieces.

Doors

Replacement Victorian or Victorian-style doors will be required in badly modernized houses.

The first step is to measure the frame into which the new door is to be inserted. Victorian joinery was made up on site and doors can vary by as much as 6 inches (150mm).

Old doors will need to be stripped, either to reveal the original wood, or as preparation for repainting. Generally, the caustic soda bath should be avoided – it dries out the timber, causing the wood to bleach and crack; and it also wreaks havoc with glued joints. Some companies offer a less drastic stripping service. If a door does come back bleached, it is possible to restore the natural shine and colour of the wood by repeated application of teak oil.

For home-stripping – a foul, messy, astringent and time-consuming affair – use a hot air stripper or a flame gun. Remove the remaining vestiges of paint with wire wool pads soaked in a strong chemical paint stripper and wear rubber gloves. To avoid being poisoned by old lead-based paint, work outside if possible or have all the windows open.

Original windows

Victorian windows are virtually impossible to find. The only way to reinstate correct windows is to have them made by a specialist joinery company. (See page 100 for styles.)

Restoring light fittings

Antique electric light fittings are likely to be Edwardian. Some of the best were made by the Ediswan Company, responsible not only for fixed, pendant light fittings but also for magnificent brass or silvered electroliers.

An original light fitting bought in a specialist shop will probably have been rewired and earthed in the process of restoration. Sometimes, however, it is possible to come across dusty old light fittings in markets and junk shops; these will need cleaning, polishing and re-wiring, best done professionally.

Brass fittings

With luck, a door salvaged from a skip or builder's yard will have all its fittings. A hunt around antique shops and junk yards is often worthwhile, but as a last resort, you can buy reproduction brass fittings coated with varnish which in time will wear off; a genuine patina will follow.

Victorian door locks that work are unusual and in most cases a modern mortice lock is a better option, especially for a front or back door.

Restoring a tarnished brass fitting requires elbow grease, 000 gauge wire wool and brass polish. Rub the fitting gently with wire wool dipped in the polish, remembering that brass is a comparatively soft metal and easily scratched. Avoid using chemicals as these can cause the metal to oxidize.

Antique taps or sanitary fittings can prove difficult to adapt. Victorian plumbers used to hand-cut the threads of pipe connections, so if part of a fitting is missing it will normally be impossible to find an exact replacement. In addition, 19th-century fittings were made for imperial, not metric pipe sizes. It is important to ensure that a Victorian fitting comes with a length of its original piping, to which a suitably sized copper pipe can then be joined. The alternative to joining different gauges of pipe is to adapt the fitting itself, which is a job for an engineer.

China fittings

Original china fittings – door knobs, lavatory chain pulls and finger-plates – are hard to find because they are easily broken. Again, reproductions are readily available, but it is worth seeking out those that follow the Victorian style faithfully.

Fireplaces

The Clean Air Act of 1958 enforced the use of smokeless fuels and led to the devastation of the Victorian fireplace, which was either removed or boarded up. A fresh wave of destruction occurred in the 1970s when central heating began to come within reach of the average householder. However, it gradually became clear that fireplaces have symbolic functions for which there is no good substitute and nowadays, with smokeless fuels more realistically priced, fireplaces are back in fashion (see page 146).

If the chimney breast has not been removed, then somewhere inside, the old hearth will probably have survived. The plaster on the lower part of the chimney breast should be opened up and it will then be possible to see where the hearth has been bricked up. The top of the original opening was generally finished with a brick arch supported by an iron strip called a water bar.

Remove the bricks or breeze blocks under this arch and dispose of rubble. There may be a small pile of more ancient rubble at the back of the hearth and this should be left. Its purpose was to sit behind the cast-iron fireplace, making sure it did not move and helping to cut down heat loss.

Once the fireplace has been revealed it is possible to measure the size of the opening and begin the search for a similarly sized fireplace. The cast-iron back plate should overlap the sides and top of the hearth opening to prevent smoke escaping.

Cast-iron fireplaces were moulded and cast in separate parts that bolt together. The fire-basket is bolted to the back plate; the bars to the grate bolt from behind; the riddle and chimney plate are adjustable and loose fitting to allow cleaning. The

REGISTER GRATE 1. Elevation 2. Section

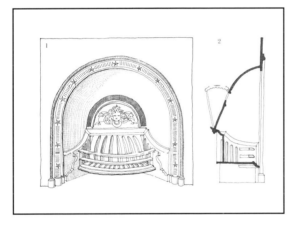

fireplace itself is held in position by the mantelpiece which is either nailed or screwed to the wall.

Before fitting the new fireplace, check that the chimney flue is in good condition and has not been capped. The fireplace should stand flush with the chimney breast, with the original pile of rubble found in the hearth now placed between the fire-basket and the chimney back. Whereas register grate fireplaces were constructed totally of iron, tiled fireplaces had firebrick cheeks and a fireback held in place by a metal band bolted across the back of the grate. The inset tiled panels were held from the back by a bolt-on metal frame. This was filled with plaster to hold the tiles in place. Reasonable care must be taken when handling either kind of fireplace: cast iron is brittle and decorative tiles are hard to match.

Sometimes cast-iron fireplaces with plain tiles can be bought cheaply. The plain tiles can be removed by unscrewing the nuts at the back of the tile frames, loosening the plaster and gently prising them out. Victorian decorative tiles bought at an antique fair or street market can then be inserted. They are almost all of standard size so there should be no problem in fitting them. On some large fireplaces, however, extra height is gained when standard tiles are alternated with spacing tiles. A set of tiles is usually ten in number. Eight of these should always match exactly but the two middle tiles in each frame are likely to be of different design, providing a 'feature'. When fitting a new set of tiles, wedge them in their frame with small blocks of wood. This will hold them firm until they can be set in plaster.

Mantelpieces

Mantelpieces were made in slate, marble, wood and cast iron (see page 146).

They are made up of sections which were assembled dry and held together in wooden frames. Blobs of quick-drying Keene's cement were often used to fix the pieces together.

The surfaces of antique marble mantelpieces will undoubtedly have deteriorated over the years. Sometimes they will have been given one, or several coats, of paint. This should be removed as carefully as possible with a weak solution of chemical paint stripper and a blunt stripping knife. Being porous, marble stains easily; stubborn stains can be removed with vinegar but this should not be left on the surface of the marble for longer than two minutes. Marble can be polished by rubbing on beeswax with a pad of 000 grade wire wool.

Some slate mantelpieces had imitation marble panels painted on them. Often these were surrounded by an incised border. If this kind of mantelpiece has been painted over it will be necessary to work very carefully indeed, stripping the paint a little at a time to see the effect on the surface below. When stripped, slate can be polished with a soft cloth and a household beeswax polish.

Missing pieces of marble or slate or any cracks can be repaired by using a hard, inert, resin-based filler of the type used to repair the bodywork of cars. When dry, the repair can be rubbed down to profile and carefully touched in with matt enamel paint mixed so that it resembles the colour of the surrounding surface.

Cast-iron mantelpieces are often covered in many coats of paint, mainly because they are difficult to strip. The heat of a hot air stripper or a flame gun is diffused by the cast iron and the surface paintwork remains unaffected. The quickest and most effective method is to have cast iron shot-blasted. Firms specializing in this kind of work will insist on having the fireplace brought to them but some tool and equipment hire companies hire out shot-blasting equipment.

After a fireplace has been stripped to the bare metal it can be polished with black lead paste.

Plasterwork

Reproduction cornices, ceiling roses, pillars and mouldings can be bought fairly cheaply from stores. However, many of these companies have a set of standard moulds and they do not necessarily suit all Victorian houses. If at all possible, it is best to take a diagram or, better still, a remnant of the original plasterwork to a specialist company, so that they can produce a replica. This, of course, costs money; the cheaper option is to restore or patch up damaged plasterwork *in situ*.

CARE AND MAINTENANCE

Plaster mouldings

Before attempting to clean or repair a large section of plaster moulding, it is important to experiment first on a small area which is not vital. Most ceiling mouldings are clogged with water-based emulsion or distemper and these paints can quite literally hold the plaster together.

The most effective way of removing thick layers of paint from intricate mouldings is to apply a layer of paint stripping paste over the top. Wear rubber gloves and be sure to work the paste into crevices and cracks. After spreading on the paste, cover it with polythene sheeting to prevent it from drying out and leave it for 24 hours.

After it has had time to do its work, remove the stripper with a blunt scraper and quantities of cold water. Various improvised tools, like a toothbrush and a spoon, are useful for getting the stripper out of deep or curved mouldings. It is important to wear gloves and goggles when removing the stripper – it can burn skin and is particularly nasty if it gets into the eyes.

Once the job is complete and all the paint and distemper has been washed out, the colour of the underlying plaster should be an attractive creamy colour.

Sash windows

A box-framed sash window (see page 100) has an upper and a lower sash each counterbalanced by two cast-iron weights. They run up and down inside the hollow box-sections of the frame when the sashes are opened and closed. The weights are supported by cords which run over pulleys at the top of the box frame. The sashes run in separate grooves and are divided by a parting bead. They are held in place by the edge of the frame on the outside and by staff beading on the inside. The staff beading should fit tightly around the frame and when closed the top rail of the lower sash and the bottom rail of the top sash should fit together to exclude draughts.

Attractive and practical though they are, sash windows are vulnerable to damage and misuse: rot, broken sash cords and layers of impenetrable paint can make them difficult, if not impossible, to operate.

Rotten windows

Wet rot is the scourge of sash windows. It is likely to attack the base of the bottom sash rail and can quickly affect the frame itself. Flaking paint and soft wood indicate wet rot and the only truly effective solution is to replace the damaged sections of wood. This is a task best left to a skilled joiner who may be able to salvage the frame if not the affected sash. In extreme cases, the entire window and its frame may have to be replaced.

There are two common reasons why wet rot latches on to sash windows. The first is that the paint covering may have cracked, letting in water and encouraging the fungus to develop. The second is a blocked drip groove on the underside of the sill (see pages 290-291). The purpose of the groove is to encourage rain-water to drain free of the sill and the wall beneath. If it gets blocked with dirt and cobwebs, water tends to run back to the wall and damp is the inevitable result.

Before repainting a window, it is imperative that all signs of wet rot have been eradicated, otherwise the problem will continue to spread. There is something of an art to repainting a sash window; it is only too easy to leave one or two surfaces uncoated and it is equally easy to allow wet paint surfaces to meet with the result that they stick together.

Broken sash cords

Sash cords tend to break either because they are old and have become rotten or because they have been painted over and have consequently become brittle. Replacing a broken cord is a fiddly business, especially if it holds the upper sash. The securing beadings have to be removed, followed by the sashes themselves. Then the weights have to be lifted out from their pockets and new cords attached to them.

Traditional hemp cords look more at home in a Victorian house than nylon cords but the latter last almost indefinitely.

Security

An original Victorian sash window secured by a solitary fitch latch is an invitation to burglars and it pays to secure all windows with special locks. The commonest type of secure sash bolt is an extremely hard steel screw that passes through the bottom sash into the top sash, one on each side, preventing the sashes from being opened. They are excellent value for money.

Internal woodwork

If painted, panelling is easily scuffed and, although the simple remedy is to repaint it, a more satisfying solution may be to strip it back to bare wood. This is best done with a hot air stripper or a chemical solvent. Both options require care: hot air strippers can scorch wood and chemicals can produce dangerous fumes.

Panelling that has buckled or 'blown' from a wall may need special attention. Buckling usually indicates that the wood is damp and has expanded, so tackle the cause before attending to the panelling itself; if the panelling is on an outside wall, suspect damp rising from the ground or penetrating through the walls.

Panelling is usually fixed by nails driven into wooden plugs or battens embedded in the wall. Loose panelling usually means that the plugs or battens have worked free of the masonry. The only solution is to fit new wooden supports in the wall and to renail the boards in place.

DOUBLE-HUNG SASH WINDOW Painting sequence

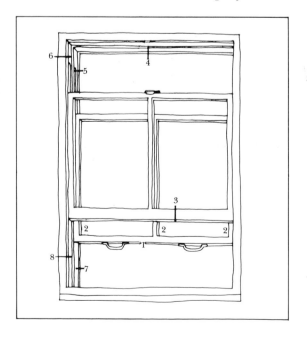

BIBLIOGRAPHY

The list of books, magazines and catalogues consulted during the preparation of this volume is too long to be included in full. What follows is a shortlist of those books used most frequently, arranged in date order.

John Claudius Loudon: *An Encyclopedia of Cottage, Farm, and Villa Architecture and Furniture,* (London) 1833.

Thomas Webster and Mrs Parkes: *An Encyclopedia of Domestic Economy,* Longmans (London) 1844.

Charles Eastlake: *Hints on Household Taste,* (London) 1868.

Mrs Orrinsmith: *The Drawing-Room,* Macmillan & Co. (London) 1878.

Mrs Loftie: *The Dining Room,* Macmillan & Co. (London) 1878.

Lady Barker: *The Bedroom and the Boudoir,* Macmillan & Co. (London) 1878.

Rhoda and Agnes Garrett: *Suggestions for House Decoration,* Macmillan & Co. (London) 1879.

Robert W. Edis: *The Decoration and Furniture of Town Houses,* Kegan Paul (London) 1881.

Lewis F. Day: *Some Principles of Everyday Art,* Batsford (London) 1890.

Hermann Muthesius: *Das Englische Haus,* (Berlin) 1904.

Mark Girouard: *Sweetness and Light: The Queen Anne Movement 1860–1900,* Yale (New Haven and London) 1977.

Peter Thornton: *Authentic Decor: The Domestic Interior 1620–1920,* Weidenfeld & Nicolson (London) 1984.

Gail Caskey Winkler and Roger W. Moss: *Victorian Interior Decoration; American Interiors 1830–1900,* Henry Holt & Co. (New York) 1986.

Jeremy Cooper: *Victorian and Edwardian Furniture and Interiors,* Thames & Hudson (London) 1987.

ACKNOWLEDGEMENTS

The authors, contributors and editors have relied heavily on the help, goodwill and enthusiasm of a large number of people. We are enormously grateful to them all for their support. In particular we would like to thank:

Elizabeth Aslin, Joanna Banham, Mrs Chris Base, Sarah Bevan, Kit Boddington, Roger and Sandy Boulanger, John Brandon-Jones, Asa Briggs, Angela Burgin, Alexandra Carlier, Elaine Clifton, Julia Courtney, Bob Crayford, Kathryn Cureton, Penny David, Fenella Dick, Caroline Eardley, Brent Elliott, Ray Evans, Mrs David Fenwick, John Fidler, Fergus Fleming, Jennifer Freeman, Charlotte Gere, Barbara Gold, Christophe Gollut, Ian Gow, Ian Grant, John Griffiths, John Hardy, Hugh Harris, Vicky Hayworth, Ian Hedley, Bridget Heal, Chris Hesford, Stephen Hoare, Gabrielle Hopkins, Jane Howell, Sinclair Johnston, Charyn Jones, Bernard Kaukas, Todd Longstaff-Gowan, Debbi Loth, Mr and Mrs A. Lyle, Francis Machin, Richard Man, David and Sue Milton, Barbara Morris, Mr and Mrs Trevor Nunn, Mimi O'Connell, Stanley Paine, Ruth Prentice, Paul Robinson, David Rodgers, Alistair Service, David Seaton, Liz Sheriff, Professor Jack Simmons, Keith Sugden, Nicole Swengley, Jasmine Taylor, Robert Thorne, Susanne Togna, Clive Wainwright, Mr and Mrs Bernard Weatherill, Sally Weatherill, Antony Wells-Cole, Robert and Josyane Young.

SUPPLIERS OF GOODS AND SERVICES

Despite the rapid proliferation of firms supplying original and reproduction Victorian fixtures, some materials and services can still be difficult to find. The yellow pages may not be enough if you are looking for someone to re-enamel a Victorian bath or make new tiles to match an old design, or for a specialist painter or joiner.

The table on the right will help you to identify the firms supplying the product or service you are looking for; the alphabetical directory on the following pages will give you their address and telephone number.

This is a selective list. It does not include general building services, such as damp-proofing and plumbing, which can be found in the local yellow pages. Nor does it include every stripped-pine and fireplace shop, every street market and bric-a-brac emporium; readers will have their own favourite hunting grounds.

We have been extremely careful in the selection of the companies in this directory, and have excluded those that did not come up to standard. Such a list needs regular updating, and readers are invited to submit the names and addresses of any reputable companies they have come across that are not included here.

If you still have trouble, a number of organizations that may be able to help are listed at the end of the directory, on page 313.

Company	A Restoration and interior decoration works	B Exterior architectural detail	C Garden furniture and structures (including conservatories)	D Architectural salvage	E Glass (etched, sandblasted, stained, leaded lights)	F Tiles/marble/stone	G Woodwork (mouldings, millwork, window frames and staircases)	H Plasterwork (mouldings, roses, cornices, etc.)	I Wall finishes (paper, fabric, decorative paint finishes)	J Door and window furniture	K Sanitary ware and fittings	L Fireplaces and stoves	M Light fittings (reproduction and renovation)	N Restoration and interior decoration advice
ACQUISITIONS	a	b		d		f						l		n
W. ADAMS & SON											k			
ALBION DESIGN OF CAMBRIDGE LTD	a	b												
ALNO							g							
ALSCOT RENOVATION SUPPLIES				d							k	l		
AMDEGA LTD			c											
A. ANDREWS & SON												l		
WILLIAM ANELAY LTD		b				f	g							
THE ANTIQUE FIREPLACE WAREHOUSE												l		
ARCHITECTURAL AND INDUSTRIAL GRP			c					h			k		m	n
ARCHITECTURAL ANTIQUES		b	c	d	e	f	g			j	k	l	m	
ARCHITECTURAL CASTINGS LIMITED		b				f		h						
ARCHITECTURAL CERAMICS LIMITED		b	c											
ARCHITECTURAL COMPONENTS			c							j	k	l	m	n
ARCHITECTURAL COMPONENTS-LOCKS & HANDLES										j				
ARCHITECTURAL HERITAGE	a		c	d	e							l		
ARCHITECTURL RECYCLING COMPANY		b	c	d										
THE ART TILE CO. LTD	a			d		f						l		n
ASHBURTON MARBLES												l		
ASHBY & HORNER LTD	a					f	g		i			l		n
B.L. PATTERN & FOUNDRY CO.		b												
BAILEYS ARCHITECTURAL ANTIQUES						f	g			j	k	l		
G.P. & J. BAKER LTD									i					
BALLANTINE BO'NESS IRON COMPANY		b	c											
BARBER WILSONS & CO. LTD											k			
NIGEL BARTLETT												l		
BATH RE-ENAMELLING COMPANY											k			
THE BATHROOM WAREHOUSE											k			
BEARDMORE ARCHITECTURAL IRONMONGER	a			d						j			m	
BETA LIGHTING LTD													m	
BISQUE	a													
BRAMBLEY GARDEN FURNITURE			c											
BRASS ARTCRAFT BIRMINGHAM LTD										j			m	
BRASS TACKS HARDWARE										j	k			
BRIDGWATER RECLAMATION				d								l		
BRIGHTON ARCHITECTURAL SALVAGE		b	c	d	e		g			j	k	l		
BRITANNIA ARCHITECTURAL METALWORK RESTORATION		b												
T.F. BUCKLE LTD												l		
BURLINGTON SLATE CO.		b				f								
CANTABRIAN ANTIQUES				d							k	l		n
CHAPEL HOUSE FIREPLACES												l		
CHELSOM LTD													m	
CHESHIRE RECLAIMED BUILDING MATERIALS		b												
CHILSTONE GARDEN ORNAMENTS		b	c											
CHILTERNHURST DESIGNS											k			
CHRISTOPHER WRAY'S LIGHTING EMPORIUM				d	e					j			m	
CIVIL ENGINEERING DEVELOPMENT LTD						f								
CLASSIC FURNITURE GROUP			c									l		
CLIFTON LITTLE VENICE		b	c									l		
COALBROOKDALE												l		
COMYN CHING										j				
CONSERVATION BUILDING PRODUCTS	a	b		d	e	f	g			j	k			
COUNTERPARTS DEMOLITION		b		d								l		
PETER COX												l		
CRADLEY CASTINGS LTD			c									l		
CROWTHER	a	b	c			f	g							n
T. CROWTHER			c				g							
DANICO BRASS LTD										j	k			
C.S.L. DAVEY & JORDAN							g					l		
DELABOLE SLATE DIVISION	a	b	c			f						l		
DENNIS RUABON LTD	a					f			i			l		
DERNIER & HAMLYN LTD													m	
THE DESIGN AND DECORATION BUILDING														n
END OF DAY LIGHTING COMPANY LTD													m	
J.W. FALKNER LTD	a													
DAVID FILEMAN ANTIQUES													m	
FIRED EARTH		b		d		f								
FIRST CHOICE DISTRIBUTION											k			
FLORIAN STUDIOS	a					f			i					
FRITZ FRYER ANTIQUE LIGHTING													m	
THE FURNITURE CAVE		b	c	d	e	f	g	h		j	k	l		
G. & H. PRODUCTS													m	
GLASS SCAPES					e									
GLOVER & STACEY		b	c	d	e	f	g			j	k	l		
GODDARD & GIBBS STUDIOS					e									
GRAHAMSTON IRON COMPANY			c									l		
GRANDISSON INTERNATIONAL			c				g					l		
J.W. GREAVES & SONS		b	c			f	g					l		
H.R. (DEMOLITION) SALES LTD		b		d	e	f	g				k	l		
HALLIDAYS							g					l		
CHRISTOPHER HARTNOLL			c											
HATHAWAY PINE FURNITURE	a					f			i		k	l		n
HAVENPLAN'S ARCHITECTURAL EMPORIUM	a	b	c	d	e	f	g	h		j	k			
C.M. HEMMING		b					g							
HERITAGE WOODCRAFT				d			g							
E.A. HIGGINSON & COMPANY							g							
HILL HOUSE ANTIQUES						f	g				k			
THE HOUSE HOSPITAL										j		l		
HOUSE OF BRASS										j	k			

	A Restoration and interior decoration works	B Exterior architectural detail	C Garden furniture and structures (including conservatories)	D Architectural salvage	E Glass (etched, sandblasted, stained, leaded lights)	F Tiles/marble/stone	G Woodwork (mouldings, millwork, window frames and staircases)	H Plasterwork (mouldings, roses, cornices, etc.)	I Wall finishes (paper, fabric, decorative paint finishes)	J Door and window furniture	K Sanitary ware and fittings	L Fireplaces and stoves	M Light fittings (reproduction and renovation)	N Restoration and interior decoration advice
HOUSE OF STEEL ANTIQUES		b	c				g					l		
IBSTOCK BUILDING PRODUCTS LTD		b												
ILLUMIN GLASS STUDIO					e								m	
THE ILLUSTRATED GLASS COMPANY					e									
INTER TRADE NETWORK LTD										j	k		m	
IRONBRIDGE GORGE MUSEUM TRUST	a	b	c				g	h				l		n
H. & R. JOHNSON TILES						f								
JONES LIGHTING													m	
JUNCKERS (LONDON) LTD							g							
KENTISH IRONCRAFT LTD		b					g							
LANGHAM ARCHITECTURAL MATERIALS		b	c	d	e							l		
B. LILLY & SONS LTD										j				
MATTHEW LLOYD STAINED GLASS STUDIO					e									
THE LOFT SHOP	a													n
LONDON ARCHITECTURAL SALVAGE COMPANY		b	c	d	e	f	g			j	k	l	m	
LONDON DOOR COMPANY					e		g							
LONDON PANELLING COMPANY							g							
THE LONDON STOVE CENTRE												l		
LYN LE GRICE									i					
MACHIN DESIGNS			c											
M. & A. MAIN ARCHITECTURAL ANTIQUES	a			d	e		g			j	k	l		n
MALVERN STUDIOS	a							h		j			m	n
PETER METCALFE LAMPS AND LAMPSHADES													m	
ARNOLD MONTROSE LTD													m	
MR JONES	a					f			i					
D. J. NICHOLLS	a								i					
BERTRAM NOLLER						f						l		
THE ORIGINAL CHOICE					e							l		n
OSBORNE & LITTLE									i					
OXFORD ARCHITECTURAL ANTIQUES	a	b	c	d	e	f				j	k	l	m	
PAGEANT ANTIQUES		b										l		
PARDON SCHOOL OF SPECIALIST DECORATION									i					
PARNDON MILL FORGE		b												
PATRICK'S OF FARNHAM						f						l		
PETIT ROQUE LTD						f						l		
STAN PIKE		b										l		
H.W. POULTER												l		
PREEDY GLASS					e									
D.A. & A.G. PRIGMORE		b										l		
RICHARD QUINELL LTD		b								*				
RAINFORD HOUSE OF ELEGANCE	a	b						h				l	m	n
RATTEE & KETT LTD	a		c			f	g		i					n
A.L. RATTRAY ARCHITECTURAL RECYCLING COMPANY			c	d	e	f	g			j	k	l	m	n
RECLAIMED MATERIALS		b										l		
REDBANK MANUFACTURING CO. LTD		b				f								
REDLAND ROOF TILES		b				f								
RELIC ANTIQUES		b	c		e	f	g	h		j		l	m	n
MARK RIPLEY ANTIQUES & FORGE		b										l		
ROGER'S DEMO & DISMANTLING SERVICE		b	c	d	e	f	g	h		j	k	l		
ROMAN WAY									i					
RYE TILES						f								
A. SANDERSON & SON									i					
SENSATION LIMITED	a								i					
SIBLEY & SON					e		g							
W. SITCH & COMPANY	a									j			m	
SITTING PRETTY											k			
ANNIE SLOAN									i					
H. & E. SMITH LTD	a	b				f						l		n
SMITH & WELLSTOOD LTD												l		
SOLENT FURNITURE							g							
SOLOPARK LTD	a	b	c	d	e	f	g			j	k	l		
STARLITE CHANDELIERS LTD													m	
STEETLEY BRICK & TILE LIMITED		b												
STENCIL DESIGNS LTD									i					
STOREY DECORATIVE PRODUCTS									i					
STUDIO TWO INTERIOR DESIGN LTD	a						g							n
SUGG LIGHTING LTD			c										m	
PAUL TEMPLE LTD	a													n
ROBERT THOMPSON CRAFTSMEN							g							
A. THORNTON		b		d	e	f						l	m	
THURTON FOUNDRIES		b	c									l	m	
A TOUCH OF BRASS										j				
TOYNBEE-CLARKE INTERIORS LTD									i					
M. TUCKEY JOINERY						f	g	h			k	l	m	
TURN ON THE LIGHT													m	
VERINE PRODUCTS							g	h				l		
VICTORIAN STAINED GLASS CO.					e									
VICTORIAN TILE CO.						f								
WALCOT RECLAMATION		b	c	d	e						k	l		
SUSAN WARD	a								i					n
WATTS & CO.									i					
WHEATLEY ORNAMENTAL PLASTERERS LTD								h				l		
WHITEWAY & WALDRON LTD		b	c	d	e	f	g					l	m	
D.W. WINDSOR LTD		b	c	d									m	
WING & STAPLES		b	c							j			m	
WOOD WORKSHOP							g							
WOODSTOCK FURNITURE LTD	a													
ANNA WYNER						f								
ZOFFANY									i					

SUPPLIERS' ADDRESSES

ACQUISITIONS
269 Camden High St
London NW1 7BX
Tel: 071 485 4955

W. ADAMS & SON
Westfield Works
Spon Lane
West Bromwich
West Midlands B70 6BM
Tel: 021 553 2161

ALBION DESIGN OF
CAMBRIDGE LTD
Unit F
Dales Manor Business Park
Babraham Road
Swanston
Cambridge CB2 4TJ
Tel: 0223 83 6128

ALNO
Unit 10 Hampton Farm
Industrial Estate
Hampton Rd West
Hanworth
Middx TW13 6DB
Tel: 081 898 4781

ALSCOT RENOVATION
SUPPLIES
The Stable Yard
Alscot Park
Preston-on-Stour
Stratford-on-Avon
Warwickshire CV37 8BL
Tel: 0789 87861

AMDEGA LTD
Faverdale
Darlington DL3 0PW
Tel: 0325 468522

A. ANDREWS & SON
324 Meanwood Rd
Leeds
Yorks LS7 2JE
Tel: 0532 624751

WILLIAM ANELAY LTD
Murton Way
Osbaldwick
York YO1 3UW
Tel: 0904 412624

THE ANTIQUE
FIREPLACE
WAREHOUSE
194-196 Battersea Park
Road
London SW8
Tel: 071 627 1410

ARCHITECTURAL AND
INDUSTRIAL GRP
562 Kingston Road
Raynes Park
London SW20 8DR
Tel: 081 543 9533

ARCHITECTURAL
ANTIQUES
Savoy Showroom
New Road
South Molton
Devon
Tel: 0769 57 3342

ARCHITECTURAL
CASTINGS LIMITED
64 The Arches
59 New Kings Road
London SW6 4RR
Tel: 071 731 7172

ARCHITECTURAL
CERAMICS LIMITED
Unit 120
Building A
Faircharm Industrial Estate
Creekside
London SE8 3DX
Tel: 081 692 7287

ARCHITECTURAL
COMPONENTS
4-8 Exhibition Road
London SW7 2HF
Tel: 071 581 2401

ARCHITECTURAL
COMPONENTS - LOCKS
& HANDLES
4-10 Exhibition Road
London SW7 2HF
Tel: 071 584 6800

ARCHITECTURAL
HERITAGE
Taddington Manor
Taddington nr Cutsdean
Cheltenham
Glos GL54 5RY
Tel: 038673 414

ARCHITECTURAL
RECYCLING COMPANY
The Garden House
Craighall
Blairgowrie
Perthshire
Tel: 0250 4749

THE ART TILE CO. LTD
Etruria Tile Works
Garner Street
Etruria Stoke-on-Trent
Staffs ST4 7SB
Tel: 0782 21 9819

ASHBURTON MARBLES
Great Hall
North Street
Ashburton
Devon TQ13 7QU
Tel: 0364 53189

ASHBY & HORNER LTD
58-62 Scrutton Street
London EC2A 4PH
Tel: 071 377 0266

B. L. PATTERN &
FOUNDRY CO.
37 Churton Street
London SW1
Tel: 071 834 1073/7486

BAILEYS
ARCHITECTURAL
ANTIQUES
The Engine Shed
Ashburton Industrial
Estate
Ross-on-Wye
Herefordshire HR9 7BW
Tel: 0989 63015

G. P. & J. BAKER LTD
P.O. Box 30
West End Road
High Wycombe
Bucks HP11 2QD
Tel: 0494 471155

BALLANTINE BO'NESS
IRON COMPANY
Links Road
Bo'ness
West Lothian Scotland
EH51 9PW
Tel: 0506 822721

BARBER WILSONS & CO.
LTD
Crawley Road
Westbury Avenue
London N22 6AH
Tel: 081 888 3461

NIGEL BARTLETT
67 St Thomas Street
London SE1
Tel: 071 378 7895

BATH RE-ENAMELLING
COMPANY
Victoria Works
Pall Mall
Nantwich
Cheshire CW5 6BN
Tel: 0270 626554

THE BATHROOM
WAREHOUSE
Unit 3 Wykeham Estate
Moorside Rd Winnal
Winchester
Hants SO23 7RX
Tel: 0962 62554

BEARDMORE
ARCHITECTURAL
IRONMONGER
3/5 Percy Street
London W1P 0EJ
Tel: 071 637 7041

BETA LIGHTING LTD
383-387 Leeds Rd
Bradford
Yorkshire BD3 9LZ
Tel: 0274 721129

BISQUE
15 Kingsmead Square
Bath BA1 2AE
Tel: 0225 46 9600

BRAMBLEY GARDEN
FURNITURE
Crittall Drive
Springwood Industrial
Estate
Braintree
Essex CM7 7QX
Tel: 0376 20210

BRASS ARTCRAFT
BIRMINGHAM LTD
76 Attwood Street
Lye Stourbridge
West Midlands DY9 8RY
Tel: 0384 89 4814

BRASS TACKS
HARDWARE
50-54 Clerkenwell Rd
London EC1M 5PS
Tel: 071 250 1971

BRIDGWATER
RECLAMATION
Monmouth Street
Bridgwater
Somerset TA6 5EJ
Tel: 0278 424636

BRIGHTON
ARCHITECTURAL
SALVAGE
33 Gloucester Road
Brighton
Sussex BN1 4AQ
Tel: 0273 681656

BRITANNIA
ARCHITECTURAL
METALWORK
RESTORATION
5 Normandy Street
Alton
Hants GU34 1DD
Tel: 0420 84427

T. F. BUCKLE LTD
427 Kings Road
London SW10 0LR
Tel: 071 352 0952

BURLINGTON SLATE
CO.
Cavendish House
Kirkby-in-Furness
Cumbria LA17 7UN
Tel: 022 989 661

CANTABRIAN ANTIQUES
16 Park Street
Lynton
North Devon EX35 6BY
Tel: 0598 53282

CHAPEL HOUSE
FIREPLACES
Netherfield House
St Georges Road
Scholes Holmfirth
West Yorks
Tel: 0484 682275

CHELSOM LTD
Heritage House
Clifton Road
Blackpool
Lancs FY4 4QA
Tel: 0253 791344

CHESHIRE RECLAIMED
BUILDING MATERIALS
Trafford Point
Westinghouse Road
Trafford Park
Manchester M17 1PY
Tel: 061 872 1352

CHILSTONE GARDEN
ORNAMENTS
Sprivers Estate
Horsmonden
Kent TN12 8DR
Tel: 089272 3553

CHILTERNHURST
DESIGNS
48 Coldharbour Lane
Harpenden
Herts AL5 4UR
Tel: 0582 76 0281

CHRISTOPHER WRAY'S
LIGHTING EMPORIUM
600 Kings Road
London SW6 2DX
Tel: 071 736 8434

CIVIL ENGINEERING
DEVELOPMENT LTD
728 London Road
West Thurrock
Grays
Essex RM16 1LU
Tel: 0708 867237

CLASSIC FURNITURE
GROUP
Audley Avenue
Newport
Shropshire TF10 7DS
Tel: 0952 825 000

CLIFTON LITTLE
VENICE
3 Warwick Place
London W9
Tel: 071 289 7894

COALBROOKDALE
Glynwed Consumer
Building Products Ltd
P.O. Box 30
Ketley Telford
Salop TF1 1BR
Tel: 0952 43 2522

COMYN CHING
19 Shelton Street
London WC2H 9JN
Tel: 071 379 3026

CONSERVATION
BUILDING PRODUCTS
Forge Works
Forge Lane Cradley Heath
Warley
West Midlands B64 5AL
Tel: 0384 64219

COUNTERPARTS
DEMOLITION
Station Yard
Topsham
Exeter
Devon EX3 0EF
Tel: 039 287 5995

PETER COX
The Heritage House
234 High Street
Sutton
Surrey SM1 1NX
Tel: 081 642 9444

CRADLEY CASTINGS LTD
Mill Street
Cradley
Halesowen
West Midlands B63 2UB
Tel: 0384 60601

CROWTHER
Syon Lodge
Busch Corner
London Road
Isleworth
Middlesex TW7 5BH
Tel: 081 560 7978

T. CROWTHER
282 North End Road
London SW6
Tel: 071 385 1375

DANICO BRASS LTD
31 Winchester Road
London NW3 3NR
Tel: 071 722 7992

C.S.L. DAVEY & JORDAN
The Forge
Kernick Industrial Estate
3 Jennings Road
Penryn
Cornwall TR10 9DQ
Tel: 0326 37 2282

DELABOLE SLATE
DIVISION
RTZ Mining and
Exploration Ltd
Pengelly House
Delabole
Cornwall PL33 9AZ
Tel: 0840 212242

DENNIS RUABON LTD
Hafod Tileries
Ruabon
Wrexham
Clwyd LL14 6ET
Tel: 0978 842283

DERNIER & HAMLYN
LTD
47-48 Berners Street
London W1P 3AD
Tel: 071 636 0122

THE DESIGN AND
DECORATION
BUILDING
107A Pimlico Road
London SW1W 8PH
Tel: 071 730 2353

END OF DAY LIGHTING
COMPANY LTD
54 Parkway
London NW1 7AH
Tel: 071 267 5239

J. W. FALKNER LTD
24 Ossory Road
off Old Kent Road
London SE1 5AP
Tel: 071 237 8101

DAVID FILEMAN
ANTIQUES
Squirrels Bayards
Horsham Road
Steyning
W. Sussex BN4 3AA
Tel: 0903 813229

FIRED EARTH
Twyford Mill
Oxford Road
Addersbury
Oxfordshire OX17 3HP
Tel: 0295 812088

FIRST CHOICE
DISTRIBUTION
12 Nimrod
Elgar Road
Reading
Berkshire RG2 0EB
Tel: 0734 756646

FLORIAN STUDIOS
The Stables
Waterston Manor
Dorchester
Dorset DT2 7SP
Tel: 0305 848600

FRITZ FRYER ANTIQUE
LIGHTING
12 Brookend Street
Ross-on-Wye
Herefordshire HR9 7EG
Tel: 0989 67416

THE FURNITURE CAVE
533 Kings Road
London SW10
Tel: 071 352 4229

G. & H. PRODUCTS
Cowleigh Wholesale
Baldwin Road
Stourport-on-Severn
Worcs DY13 9AX
Tel: 0299 827034

GLASS SCAPES
18 Devonshire Place
Exeter Devon
Tel: 0392 43 6329

GLOVER & STACEY
Oaklands House
Solartron Road
Farnborough
Hants GU14 7QL
Tel: 0252 549334

GODDARD & GIBBS
STUDIOS
41-49 Kingsland Road
London E2 8AD
Tel: 071 739 6563

GRAHAMSTON IRON
COMPANY
P.O. Box 5
Gowan Avenue
Falkirk
Stirlingshire FK2 7HH
Tel: 0324 22661

GRANDISSON
INTERNATIONAL
The Old Hall
West Hill Road
Ottery St Mary
Devon EX11 1TP
Tel: 040481 2876

J. W. GREAVES & SONS
Llechwedd Slate Mines
Blaenau Ffestiniog
Gwynedd LL41 3NB
Tel: 0766 830522

H. R. (DEMOLITION)
SALES LTD
Fairwater Yard
Staplegrove Road
Taunton
Somerset TA1 1DP
Tel: 0823 337035

HALLIDAYS
28 Beauchamp Place
London SW3 1NJ
Tel: 071 589 5534

CHRISTOPHER
HARTNOLL
Little Bray House
Brayford
N. Devon EX32 7QG
Tel: 059 871 0295

HATHAWAY PINE
FURNITURE
Clifford Mill
Clifford Chambers
nr Stratford-upon-Avon
Warwickshire CV37 8HW
Tel: 0789 205517

HAVENPLAN'S
ARCHITECTURAL
EMPORIUM
The Old Station
Station Road
Killamarsh
Sheffield S31 8EN
Tel: 0742 489972

C. M. HEMMING
Thrashers Barn
Norchard Crossway Green
Stourport
Worcs DY13 9SN
Tel: 0299 250223

HERITAGE WOODCRAFT
Atherstone Industrial Estate
14 Carlyon Rd
Atherstone
Warwickshire CV9 1JE
Tel: 0827 714761

E. A. HIGGINSON &
COMPANY
Unit 1
Carlisle Road
London NW9 0HD
Tel: 081 200 4848

HILL HOUSE ANTIQUES
Rotunda Bldgs
Montpelier Exchange
Cheltenham
Gloucs GL50 1SJ
Tel: 0242 57 3787

THE HOUSE HOSPITAL
68 Battersea High Street
London SW11
Tel: 071 223 3179

HOUSE OF BRASS
122 North Sherwood Street
Nottingham
Notts NG1 4EF
Tel: 0602 475430

HOUSE OF STEEL
ANTIQUES
400 Caledonian Road
London N1 1DN
Tel: 071 607 5889

IBSTOCK BUILDING
PRODUCTS LTD
Leicester Road
Ibstock
Leicester LE6 1HS
Tel: 0530 60531

ILLUMIN GLASS STUDIO
82 Bond Street
Macclesfield
Cheshire SK11 6QS
Tel: 0625 613600

THE ILLUSTRATED
GLASS COMPANY
1 The Queach
Great Barton
Bury St Edmunds
Suffolk IP31 2PY1
Tel: 0359 32 148

INTER TRADE NETWORK
LTD
Unit 9
Spring Road Ettingshall
Wolverhampton
West Midlands WV4 6JT
Tel: 0902 404788

IRONBRIDGE GORGE
MUSEUM TRUST
The Wharfage
Ironbridge
Telford
Salop TF8 7AW
Tel: 0952 45 3522

H. & R. JOHNSON TILES
Highgate Tile Works
Tunstall Stoke-on-Trent
Staffordshire ST6 4JX
Tel: 0782 57 5575

JONES LIGHTING
194 Westbourne Grove
London W11
Tel: 071 229 6866

JUNCKERS (LONDON)
LTD
Unit 3-5
Wheaton Court
Commercial Centre
Wheaton Road
Witham
Essex CM8 3UJ
Tel: 0376 517512

KENTISH IRONCRAFT
LTD
Ashford Road
Bethersden Ashford
Kent TN26 3AT
Tel: 023 382 465

LANGHAM
ARCHITECTURAL
MATERIALS
Langham Farm
East Nynehead
Wellington
Somerset TA21 0DD
Tel: 0823 66 5897

B. LILLY & SONS LTD
Baltimore Road
Birmingham B42 1DJ
Tel: 021 357 1761

MATTHEW LLOYD
STAINED GLASS STUDIO
63 Amberley Road
London N13 4BH
Tel: 081 886 0213

THE LOFT SHOP
Progress Way
Croydon
Surrey CR0 4XD
Tel: 081 681 4060

LONDON
ARCHITECTURAL
SALVAGE COMPANY
Mark Street (off Paul
Street)
London EC2A 4ER
Tel: 071 739 0448

LONDON DOOR
COMPANY
165 St Johns Hill
London SW11 1TQ
Tel: 071 223 7243

LONDON PANELLING
COMPANY
13 Palace Road
London N8 8QL
Tel: 081 341 0339

THE LONDON STOVE
CENTRE
49 Chiltern Street
London W1M 1HQ
Tel: 01 486 5168

LYN LE GRICE
Bread Street
Penzance
Cornwall TR18 2EQ
Tel: 0736 69881

MACHIN DESIGNS
Ransome's Dock
35-37 Parkgate Street
London SW11 4NP
Tel: 071 924 2438

M. & A. MAIN
ARCHITECTURAL
ANTIQUES
The Old Rectory
Cerrig-y-drudion
Corwen
Clwyd
N. Wales
Tel: 0490 82491

MALVERN STUDIOS
56 Cowleigh Road
Malvern
Worcs WR14 1QD
Tel: 068 45 4913

PETER METCALFE
ANTIQUE LAMPS AND
LAMPSHADES
2 Parsifal Road
Hampstead
London NW6 1UH
Tel: 071 435 5025

ARNOLD MONTROSE
LTD
47-48 Berners Street
London W1P 3AD
Tel: 071 580 5316

MR JONES
175-179 Muswell Hill
Broadway
London N10 3RS
Tel: 081 444 6066

D. J. NICHOLLS
94 Brocks Drive
North Cheam
Surrey SM3 9UR
Tel: 081 644 3257

BERTRAM NOLLER
14A London Road
Reigate
Surrey RH2 9HY
Tel: 0737 242548

THE ORIGINAL CHOICE
1340 Stratford Road
Hall Green
Birmingham B28 9EH
Tel: 021 778 3821

OSBORNE & LITTLE
49 Temperley Road
London SW12 8QE
Tel: 081 675 2255

OXFORD
ARCHITECTURAL
ANTIQUES
The Old Depot
Nelson Street Jericho
Oxford
Tel: 0865 53310

PAGEANT ANTIQUES
122 Dawes Road
London SW6 7EG
Tel: 071 385 7739

PARDON SCHOOL OF
SPECIALIST
DECORATION
5 Frederick Mews
Kinnerton Street
London SW1X 8EQ
Tel: 071 245 1049

PARNDON MILL FORGE
Parndon Mill Lane
Harlow
Essex CM20 2HP
Tel: 0279 419410

PATRICK'S OF
FARNHAM
Guildford Road
Farnham
Surrey GU9 9QA
Tel: 0252 72 2345

PETIT ROQUE LTD
5A New Road
Croxley Green
Herts WD3 3EJ
Tel: 0923 779 291

STAN PIKE
Blacksmith's Shop
Wayland's Forge
Sook Hill
Haltwhistle NA49 9PS
Northumberland
Tel: 0434 3443 09

H. W. POULTER
279 Fulham Road
London SW10 9PZ
Tel: 071 352 7268

PREEDY GLASS
Lamb Works
North Road
London N7 9PA
Tel: 071 700 0377

D. A. & A. G. PRIGMORE
Mill Cottage
Mill Road
Colmworth
Beds MK44 2NU
Tel: 023 062 264

RICHARD QUINELL LTD
Rowhurst Forge
Oxshott Road
Leatherhead
Surrey KT22 0EN
Tel: 0372 375148

RAINFORD HOUSE OF
ELEGANCE
Wentworth Street
Birdwell
Barnsley
Yorkshire S70 5UN
Tel: 0226 350360

RATTEE & KETT LTD
Perbeck Rd
Cambridge CB2 2PG
Tel: 0223 248061

A. L. RATTRAY
ARCHITECTURAL
RECYCLING COMPANY
The Garden House
Craig Hall
Blairgowrie
Perthshire PH10 7JB
Tel: 0250 4749

RECLAIMED MATERIALS
Northgate
Whitelund Industrial
Estate
Morecambe
Lancs
Tel: 0524 69094

REDBANK
MANUFACTURING CO.
LTD
Measham
Burton-on-Trent
Staffordshire DE12 7EL
Tel: 05302 70333

REDLAND ROOF TILES
Redland House
Reigate
Surrey RH2 0SJ
Tel: 0737 242488

RELIC ANTIQUES
Brillscote Farm
Lea nr Malmesbury
Wilts SN16 9PF
Tel: 0666 822332

MARK RIPLEY ANTIQUES
& FORGE
Bridge Bungalow
North Bridge Street
Robertsbridge
Sussex TN32 5NY
Tel: 0580 880324

ROGER'S DEMO &
DISMANTLING SERVICE
1 Spring Close Scholing
Southampton
Hampshire
Tel: 0703 449173

ROMAN WAY
34 Lacy Road
London SW15
Tel: 071 789 0143

RYE TILES
The Old Brewery
Wisward Rye
Sussex TN31 7DH
Tel: 0797 223038

A. SANDERSON & SON
52 Berners Street
London W1P 3AD
Tel: 071 636 7800

SENSATION LIMITED
66 Fulham High Street
London SW6 3LQ
Tel: 071 736 4135

SIBLEY & SON
The Mayford Centre
Smarts Heath Road
Woking, Surrey GU22 0PP
Tel: 0483 724854

W. SITCH & COMPANY
48 Berwick Street
London W1 4JD
Tel: 071 437 3776

SITTING PRETTY
131 Dawes Road
London SW6 7EA
Tel: 071 381 0049

ANNIE SLOAN
Knutsford House
Park Street Bladon
Oxfordshire OX7 1RW
Tel: 0993 812590

H. & E. SMITH LTD
Britannic Works
Broom Street Hanley
Stoke-on-Trent ST1 2ER
Tel: 0782 281617

SMITH & WELLSTOOD
LTD
Bonnybridge
Stirlingshire FK4 2AP
Tel: 0324 812171

SOLENT FURNITURE
Pymore Mills Bridport
Dorset DT6 5PJ
Tel: 0308 22305

SOLOPARK LTD
The Old Railway Station
Station Road nr Pampisford
Cambridgeshire CB2 4HB
Tel: 0223 834663

STARLITE CHANDELIERS
LTD
127 Harris Way
Windmill Rd
Sunbury-on-Thames
Middlesex TW16 7EL
Tel: 0932 788686

STEETLEY BRICK & TILE
LIMITED
P.O. Box 3
Brampton Mill
Newcastle-under-Lyme
Staffs ST5 0QU
Tel: 0782 615381

STENCIL DESIGNS LTD
91 Lower Sloane Street
London SW1W 8DA
Tel: 071 730 0728

STOREY DECORATIVE
PRODUCTS
Southgate
Whitelund Morecambe
Lancs LA3 3DA
Tel: 0524 65981

STUDIO TWO INTERIOR
DESIGN LTD
The Old Beet House
Silver Street
Askrigg Wensleydale
N. Yorkshire DL8 3HS
Tel: 0969 506594

SUGG LIGHTING LTD
Sussex Manor Business
Park
Gatwick Road
Crawley
West Sussex RH10 2GD
Tel: 0293 540111

PAUL TEMPLE LTD
Holloway Lane
Harmondsworth
West Drayton
Middlesex UB7 0AD
Tel: 081 759 1437

ROBERT THOMPSON
CRAFTSMEN
Kilburn York
N. Yorks YO6 4AH
Tel: 03476 218

A. THORNTON
Architectural Antiques
Ainleys Industrial Estate
Elland
West Yorks HX5 9JP
Tel: 0422 37 5595

THURTON FOUNDRIES
Thurton Norwich
Norfolk NR14 6AN
Tel: 0508 480 301

A TOUCH OF BRASS
210 Fulham Road
London SW10 9PJ
Tel: 071 351 2255

TOYNBEE-CLARKE
INTERIORS LTD
95 Mount Street
London W1
Tel: 071 499 4472

M. TUCKEY JOINERY
20 Cherry Street
Warwick CV34 4LR
Tel: 0926 493679

TURN ON THE LIGHT
Camden Passage
116-118 Islington High
Street
London N1 8EG
Tel: 071 359 7616

VERINE PRODUCTS
Folly Faunts House
Goldhanger Maldon
Essex CM9 8AP
Tel: 0621 88611

VICTORIAN STAINED
GLASS CO.
The Studio
83 Stamford Hill
London N16
Tel: 081 800 9008

(continued on page 313)

MUSEUMS AND ASSOCIATIONS

(continued from page 312)

VICTORIAN TILE CO.
20 Smugglers Way
London SW18
Tel 081 870 0167

WALCOT
RECLAMATION
108 Walcot Street
Bath Avon
Tel: 0225 46 4057

SUSAN WARD
7 Brailsford Road
London SW2 2TB
Tel: 081 674 7082

WATTS & CO.
7 Tufton Street
London SW1P 3QE
Tel: 071 222 2893

WHEATLEY
ORNAMENTAL
PLASTERERS LTD
Avondale Studio
Workshops
Avondale Place
Batheaston
Bath
Avon BA1 7RF
Tel: 0225 859678

WHITEWAY & WALDRON
LTD
305 Munster Road
London SW6
Tel: 071 381 3195

D. W. WINDSOR LTD
Marsh Lane
Ware
Herts SG12 9QL
Tel: 0920 466 499

WING & STAPLES
The Forge
Motcombe nr Shaftesbury
Dorset SP7 9PE
Tel: 0747 5 3104

WOOD WORKSHOP
21 Canterbury Grove
London SE27 0NT
Tel: 081 670 8984

WOODSTOCK
FURNITURE LTD
23 Packenham St
London WC1 0LB
Tel: 071 837 1818

ANNA WYNER
Mosaic Artist
2 Ferry Road
London SW13 9RX
Tel: 081 748 3940

ZOFFANY
63 Audley Street
London W1Y 5BF
Tel: 071 629 92 62

ACANTHUS
ASSOCIATED
ARCHITECTURAL
PRACTICES
Vosey House
Barley Mow Passage
Chiswick
London W4 4PN
Tel: 081 995 1232

THE ARCHITECTURAL
ASSOCIATION
34-36 Bedford Square
London WC1
Tel: 071 636 0974

THE ART WORKERS
GUILD
6 Queen Square
London WC1N 3AR
Tel: 071 837 3474

THE BRITISH CERAMIC
TILE COUNCIL
Federation House
Station Road
Stoke-on-Trent
Staffordshire ST4 2RT
Tel: 0782 747147

THE BRITISH
DECORATORS
ASSOCIATION
6 Haywra Street
Harrogate
N. Yorks HG1 5BL
Tel: 0423 67292

THE BRITISH
INSTITUTE OF
INTERIOR DESIGN
1c Devonshire Avenue
Beeston
Nottingham NG9 1BS
Tel: 0602 221255

THE BROOKING
COLLECTION
Woodhay House
White Lane
Guildford
Surrey GU4 8PU
Tel: 0483 504555

THE BUILDING
CONSERVATION TRUST
Apt 39 Hampton Court
Palace
East Molesey
Surrey KT8 9BS
Tel: 081 943 2277

THE BUILDING
EMPLOYERS
CONFEDERATION
82 New Cavendish Street
London W1M 8AD
Tel: 071 580 5588

THE CIVIC TRUST
17 Carlton House Terrace
London SW1Y 5AW
Tel: 071 930 0914

THE CONSERVATION
BUREAU
Rosebery House
Haymarket Terrace
Edinburgh
Tel: 031 337 9595

THE CONSERVATION
UNIT
Museums & Galleries
Commission
7 St James's Square
London SW1Y 4JU
Tel: 071 839 9341

ENGLISH HERITAGE
Fortress House
23 Savile Row
London W1X 2HE
Tel: 071 973 3000

THE GUILD OF MASTER
CRAFTSMEN
170 High Street
Lewes
E Sussex
Tel: 07916 77374

HISTORIC HOUSES
ASSOCIATION
38 Ebury Street
London SW1W 0LU
Tel: 071 730 9419

HUTTON'S
ARCHITECTURAL
REGISTER
Netley House
Gomshall nr Guildford
Surrey GU5 9QA
Tel: 048641 3221

THE INCHBALD
SCHOOL OF DESIGN
7 Eaton Gate
London SW1 9BA
Tel: 071 730 5508

THE NATIONAL
REGISTER OF
CONSERVATION CRAFT
SKILLS IN THE
BUILDING INDUSTRY
7 St James's Square
London SW1
Tel: 071 839 9341

THE NATIONAL HOME
ENLARGEMENT
BUREAU
P.O. Box 67
High Wycombe
Bucks HP15 6XP
Tel: 0494 711649

THE NATIONAL
REGISTER OF
WARRANTED BUILDERS
33 John Street
London WC1N 2BB
Tel: 071 242 7583

THE NATIONAL TRUST
42 Queen Anne's Gate
London SW1H 9AS
Tel: 071 222 9251

THE ROYAL
COMMISSION OF
HISTORIC MONUMENTS
Edleston House
Queens Road Aberystwyth
Dyfed Wales SY23 2HP
Tel: 0970 4381

THE ROYAL
INCORPORATION OF
ARCHITECTS OF
SCOTLAND
15 Rutland Square
Edinburgh EH1 2BE
Tel: 031 229 7205

THE ROYAL
INSTITUTION OF
CHARTERED SURVEYORS
12 Great George Street
London SW1P 3AD
Tel: 071 222 7000

SAVE
68 Battersea High Street
London SW11 3HX
Tel: 071 228 3336

THE SCOTTISH
DEPARTMENT OF
HISTORIC BUILDINGS
20 Brandon Street
Edinburgh EH3 5RA
Tel: 031 244 2865

THE SCOTTISH CIVIC
TRUST
24 George Square
Glasgow G2 1EF

SOCIETY FOR THE
PROTECTION OF
ANCIENT BUILDINGS
37 Spital Square
London E1 6DY
Tel: 071 377 1644

THE TIMBER RESEARCH
AND DEVELOPMENT
ASSOCIATION
Stocking Lane
Hughenden Valley
High Wycombe
Bucks HP14 4ND
Tel: 024024 3091

THE VICTORIAN
SOCIETY
1 Priory Gardens
Bedford Park
London W4 1TT
Tel: 081 994 1019

THE WALLPAPER
HISTORY SOCIETY
Victoria & Albert Museum
South Kensington
London SW7 2RL
Tel: 071 589 6371

THE WILLIAM MORRIS
SOCIETY
26 Upper Mall
London W6
Tel: 081 748 5618

PICTURE CREDITS

Sources for the illustrations in this book are listed in order from the top of the left-hand column to the bottom of the right-hand column on each double spread.

Many of the photographs were specially commissioned. They were shot on location by Ken Kirkwood, Robin McCartney, Derry Moore, James Mortimer, George Ong and Peter Woloszynski. For reasons of space the commissioned photographers are identified by their initials as follows:
KK = Ken Kirkwood
RMcC = Robin McCartney
DM = Derry Moore
JM = James Mortimer
GO = George Ong
PW = Peter Woloszynski.

Front Cover/Back Cover - JM. Back Flap - JM. Endpapers - Sheldrake Press,courtesy of The House Of Commons. 1/5 - JM. 6/7 - RMcC. 8/13 - All by JM. 14/15 - Christopher Wood Gallery, London & The Bridgeman Art Library. 16/17 - Jon Bouchier; Alain Le Garsmeur/Impact Photos; RMcC; Hulton-Deutsch Collection; Edifice/Lewis.18/19 - Ray Joyce/Weldon Trannies; Campbell Smith & Co. 20/21 - Vernon Gibberd; Architectural Association/Cannon Parsons; George Wright; Alain le Garsmeur/Impact Photos; Mayotte Magnus. 22/23 - Andrew Lawson; Angelo Hornak; Timothy Woodcock Photolibrary; Mayotte Magnus; Charles McKean. 24/25 - Architectural Association/Valerie Bennett; Ray Joyce/Weldon Trannies; Andrew Lawson; John Bethell; Osborne House/The Bridgeman Art Library; Timothy Woodcock. 26/27 - KK. 28/29 - Robert Estall Photo Library; Sheldrake Press; Sheldrake Press. 30/33 - All artwork by Ann Winterbotham. 34/35 - Architectural Association/Colin Penn; The Design Archive, Arthur Sanderson & Sons Ltd; Mary Evans Picture Library; West Surrey College of Art & Design; Watts & Co; Woodmansterne Picture Library. 36/37 - Mary Evans Picture Library; Geoff Morgan; Studio Magazine; Architectural Association/Barry Capper. 38/39 - S.& O. Mathews Photography; Topham; Topham; Aldus Archives; Topham. 40/41 - Topham; Richard Bryant/Arcaid; Woodmansterne Picture Library; National Trust; Edifice/Darley. 42/43 - Robin Guild. 44/45 - Ray Joyce/Weldon Trannies; Andrew Lawson; S.& O. Mathews Photography. 46/47 - Jane Lewis/Robert Estall Photo Library; Edifice/Lewis; Michael Boys Syndication; Andrew Lawson. 48/53 - cut-away house drawings by Nigel Husband RIBA. 54/55 - Jon Bouchier. 56/57 - Angelo Hornak; Ray Joyce/Weldon Trannies; Jerry Harpur; The Garden Picture Library/G.Rogers; The Garden Picture Library/R.Sutherland. 58/59 - Robert Estall Photo Library; Jerry Harpur; Andrew Lawson; RMcC; Andrew Lawson; Robert Estall Photo Library; Robert Estall Photo Library; Robert Estall Photo Library. 60/61 - Edifice/Lewis; Edifice/Darley; Ray Joyce/Weldon Trannies. 62/63 - Jon Bouchier; Edifice/Lewis; Edifice/Lewis; Edifice/Lewis; George Wright; S.& O. Mathews Photography; Ann Kelly/Elizabeth Whiting Agency. 64/65 - Andrew Lawson; Ray Joyce/Weldon Trannies; Jon Bouchier; Edifice/Darley; Robert Estall Photo Library; Edifice/Darley; Jessica Strang; Edifice/Lewis. 66/67 - Robert Estall Photo Library; Robert Estall Photo Library; Andrew Lawson; Robert Estall Photo Library; Andrew Lawson. 68/69 - Robert Estall Photo Library; Peter Aaron/Esto; Robert Estall Photo Library; Robert Estall Photo Library; Ray Joyce/Weldon Trannies; Ray Joyce/Weldon Trannies; Andrew Lawson; Robert Estall Photo Library. 70/71 - Nigel Husband RIBA and Stephen Carpenter RIBA. 72/73 - Robert Estall Photo Library; Robert Estall Photo Library; Robert Estall Photo Library. 74/75 - Andrew Lawson; Edifice/Lewis; Richard Bryant/Arcaid; Edifice/ Lewis; Robert Estall Photo Library. 76/77 - Edifice/Lewis; Edifice/Lewis; Jon Bouchier; Timothy Woodcock Photolibrary. 78/79 - Lucinda Lambton/Arcaid; Robert Estall Photo Library; Edifice/Lewis; Robert Estall Photo Library; S.& O. Mathews Photography; George Wright; Robert Estall Photo Library; Robert Estall Photo Library; Sonia Halliday Photographs/Else Tricket; Robert Estall Photo Library. 80/81 - Nigel Husband RIBA and Stephen Carpenter RIBA. 82/83 - Gary Pownall. 84/85 - Dornsite Collection of The Victorian Society in America at the Athenaeum of Philadelphia; The Athenaeum of Philadelphia Collection; The Athenaeum of Philadelphia Collection. 86/87 - Edifice/Lewis; Michael Boys Syndication; Gary Pownall; Edifice/Lewis. 88/89 - Michael Boys Syndication; Edifice/Lewis; Edifice/Lewis; Spike Powell/Elizabeth Whiting Agency; all the rest Robert Estall Photo Library. 90/91 - Ray Joyce/Weldon Trannies; Andrew Lawson. 92/93 - Nigel Husband RIBA and Stephen Carpenter RIBA; Edifice/Lewis; Linda Burgess/Insight Picture Library; Robert Estall Photo Library; Edifice Lewis; Andrew Lawson. 94/95 - Ray Joyce/Weldon Trannies. 96/97 - Robert Estall Photo Library; S .& O. Mathews Photography; Andrew Lawson. 98/99 - Robert Estall Photo Library; Robert Estall Photo Library; Linda Burgess/Insight Picture Library; Lucinda Lambton/Arcaid; Robert Estall Photo Library; Jon Bouchier; KK. 100/101 - Nigel Husband RIBA and Stephen Carpenter RIBA 102/103 - Lucinda Lambton/Arcaid. 104/105 - Woodmansterne Picture Library; Christine Hanscomb; Richard Bryant/Arcaid. 106/107 - The Royal Incorporation of Architects in Scotland. 114/115 - Lucinda Lambton/Arcaid; Peter Aaron/Esto. 116/117 - Ray Joyce/Weldon Trannies; RMcC; RMcC. 118/119 - KK; Architectural Association/Ethel Hurwicz; KK; Michael Boys Syndication. 120/121 - DM; PW. 122/123 - Nigel Husband RIBA and Stephen Carpenter RIBA. 124/125 - RMcC; Lucinda Lambton/Arcaid. 126/127 - Ianthe Ruthven; KK; RMcC; KK; RMcC. 128/129 - Nigel Husband RIBA and Stephen Carpenter RIBA. 130/131 - Richard Bryant/Arcaid. 132/133 - KK. 134/135 - The National Trust; Woodmansterne Picture Library; KK. 136/137 - Nigel Husband RIBA and Stephen Carpenter RIBA. 138/139 - DM; Michael Dunne/Elizabeth Whiting Agency. 140/141 - DM; PW; Rodney Hyett/Elizabeth Whiting Agency. 142/143 - DM; PW. 144/145 - Nigel Husband RIBA and Stephen Carpenter RIBA. 146/147 - Christine Hanscomb; KK; Christine Hanscomb. 148/149 - Townsends,London; Richard Bryant/Arcaid. 150/151 - RMcC; RMcC; DM; Jessica Strang; Woodmansterne Picture Library; Mary Evans Picture Library. 152/153 - Nigel Husband RIBA and Stephen Carpenter RIBA. 154/155 - DM. 156/157 - Christine Hanscomb; all the rest Robert Estall Photo Library. 158/159 - Victoria & Albert Museum,London & The Bridgeman Art Library London; Aldus Archives; Ceramic Tile Design, London; Fine Art Society Catalogue and The Bridgeman Art Library; Woodmansterne Picture Library; E.T. Archive; private collection/The Bridgeman Art Library; Mary Evans Picture Library. 160/161 - RMcC. 162/163 - Charles Parsons, courtesy Susie Bower, Glasscapes; Ray Joyce/Weldon Trannies; Ray Joyce/Weldon Trannies; C.M. Swash; Ray Joyce/Weldon Trannies; Sonia Halliday Photographs; Pamla Toler/Impact Photos; Woodmansterne Picture Library. 164/165 - Sonia Halliday Photographs; RMcC. 166/167 - KK; GO. 168/169 - KK; The Design Council; by courtesy of the board of Trustees of The Victoria & Albert Museum,London; National Trust/ J. Gibson; The Design Council; Christopher Wray's Lighting Emporium, London; Christopher Wray's Lighting Emporium, London; The End of The Day Lighting Company; Christopher Wray's Lighting Emporium, London; Christopher Wray's Lighting Emporium, London; Christopher Wray's Lighting Emporium, London. 170/171 - Nigel Husband RIBA and Stephen Carpenter RIBA. 172/173 - KK; Ray Joyce/Weldon Trannies; Ray Joyce/Weldon Trannies; Lucinda Lambton/Arcaid. 174/175 - Nigel Husband RIBA and Stephen Carpenter RIBA. 176/177 - Harrogate Art Gallery/Robert Harding Picture Library; Aldus Archives. 178/179 - George Wright. 180/181 - All artwork by Ann Winterbotham. 182/183 - GO; Christine Hanscomb; JM; Christine Hanscomb. 184/185 - All by KK. 186/187 - all courtesy of Leonard Pardon, Principal of the Pardon Schools, London and New York. 188/189 - private collection/The Bridgeman Art Library; by courtesy of the board of Trustees of The Victoria & Albert Museum, London; The Victoria & Albert Museum, London, and The Bridgeman Art Library. 190/191 - The Design Archive, Arthur Sanderson & Sons Ltd; Sheldrake Press, courtesy of The House of Commons; Sheldrake Press, courtesy of The House of Commons; Sheldrake Press, courtesy of The House of Commons; Sheldrake Press, courtesy of The House of Commons; The Design Archive, Arthur Sanderson & Sons Ltd; Watts & Co; E.T. Archive; Watts & Co; The Victoria & Albert Museum, London, and The Bridgeman Art Library; The Design Archive, Arthur Sanderson & Sons Ltd; Watts & Co; RD 125 Anaglypta Original. 192/193 - The Victoria & Albert Museum, London and The Bridgeman Art Library; by courtesy of the board of Trustees of The Victoria & Albert Museum; William Morris Gallery, London and The Bridgeman Art Library; Lenoble by Charles Hammond; Palmyra by Charles Hammond; Osborne & Little Botanica Collection; The Victoria & Albert Museum and The Bridgeman Art Library; Osborne & Little Botanica Collection. 194/195 - E.T. Archive; Victoria & Albert Museum, London and The Bridgeman Art Library. 196/197 - private collection/The Bridgeman Art Library; National Trust/L & M Gayton. 198/199 - GO. 200/201 - JM; Mary Evans Picture Library; KK; KK. 202/203 - Nigel Husband RIBA and Stephen Carpenter RIBA. 204/205 - JM; all the rest courtesy of Bernard Thorp (Paris, London), Custom Weaving and Printing. 206/207 - Nigel Husband RIBA and Stephen Carpenter RIBA. 208/209 - GO. 210/211 - Spike Powell/Elizabeth Whiting Agency; JM; KK. 212/213 - KK; Jon Bouchier/Elizabeth Whiting Agency. 214/215 - JM; JM. 216/217 - GO; PW; KK. 218/219 - Lucinda Lambton/Arcaid; KK. 220/221 - Michael Boys Syndication; GO. 222/223 - Lucinda Lambton/Arcaid; Smithsonian Institution (National Museum of History and Technology), Washington; The Design Council. 224/225 - JM; JM; Woodmansterne Picture Library. 226/227 - National Trust/J.Bethell. 228/229 - Michael Nicholson/Elizabeth Whiting Agency; Michael Boys Syndication; National Trust. 230/231 - National Trust; PW. 232/233 - Spike Powell/Elizabeth Whiting Agency; JM. 234/235 - Ianthe Ruthven; Automobile Association Photo Library; DM; KK. 236/237 - Ianthe Ruthven; Smallbone; PW; JM. 238/239 - Michael Nicholson/Elizabeth Whiting Agency; KK; GO; KK; Smallbone. 240/241 - Rodney Hyett/Elizabeth Whiting Agency; Sheldrake Press; PW; Tim Street-Porter/Elizabeth Whiting Agency. 242/243 - KK; Pipe Dreams. 244/245 - Rodney Hyett/Elizabeth Whiting Agency; Michael Boys Syndication; Michael Dunne/Elizabeth Whiting Agency; GO; B.C. Sanitan; Traditional Bathroom Warehouses, London. 246/247 - KK; PW; PW; Michael Boys Syndication; KK. 248/249 - Rodney Hyett/Elizabeth Whiting Agency; Michael Boys Syndication. 250/251 - Michael Nicholson/Elizabeth Whiting Agency; Peter Aaron/Esto; Traditional Bathroom Warehouses, London; Nigel Husband RIBA and Stephen Carpenter RIBA; KK. 252/253 - DM. 254/255 - Mary Evans Picture Library; DM. 256/257 - KK. 258/259 - Woodmansterne Picture Library; DM; PW. 260/261 - JM; Richard Bryant/Arcaid; Michael Boys Syndication; KK. 262/263 - DM; DM. 264/265 - JM. 266/267 - Nigel Husband RIBA and Stephen Carpenter RIBA. 268/269 - Jerry Harpur. 270/271 - Ray Joyce/Weldon Trannies; Lucinda Lambton/Arcaid; Photograph courtesy of Fine Art Photographic Library. 272/273 - Neil Holmes; Neil Holmes; Jerry Harpur; KK. 274/275 - Paul Miles; The Garden Picture Library/G.Bouchet; Linda Burgess/Insight Picture Library; The Garden Picture Library/B.Carter. 276/277 - Jerry Harpur; George Wright; Andrew Lawson; Pamla Toler/Impact Photos. 278/279 - KK; Town & Country Conservatories. 280/281 - Linda Burgess/Insight Picture Library; George Wright; Ray Joyce/Weldon Trannies. 282/283 - Linda Burgess/Insight Picture Library; George Wright; Lucinda Lambton/Arcaid. 284/285 - George Wright; Jerry Harpur; Jerry Harpur; National Trust/P.Lacey; Linda Burgess/Insight Picture Library; Edifice/Lewis. 286/287 - George Wright; Eric Crichton Photos; Linda Burgess/Insight Picture Library; S.& O. Mathews Photography; Eric Crichton Photos; Linda Burgess/Insight Picture Library; Linda Burgess/Insight Picture Library; Eric Crichton Photos; Linda Burgess/Insight Picture Library; Linda Burgess/Insight Picture Library. 290/307 - All artwork by Sime/Baillie Lane/Architecture Environment.

INDEX

L

lancet doorways *13*, 65
lancet windows *45*, 100
land for building 16, 46-47
landings *10*, 105, 114-23, *118*, *120*, 141, 160
Lanhydrock, Cornwall: kitchen *226*
lanterns *56*, 286
larders 228, *241*
latches *133*, 134, *175*, 306
Late Regency 19, *22*, 54, *63*, 82, 90, 180, *210*
Late Victorian 19
lath-and-plaster, ceilings 293; internal
    partitions 50
lavatories, water closets 46-47, 102, *162*, 229,
    244, *245*, 248, *251*, 304
lawns *270*, 271, *271*, *285*
lead, in paints 84, 184, 304; pipes, gutters, etc.
    80, 106, 290, 292
leaded lights 65, 99, *100-101*, 160, 200
leather 206, 222, 264
leather-paper, *see* dadoes (paper)
Leighton House, Holland Park *118*
letter boxes (letter plates) *68*, 68, 90, *92*
Liberty's, London 34, 179
libraries *21*, *102*, 128-29, *153*; books and
    library furniture 138, 142, *144*, *206-07*,
    206, *222*, 222-24, *225*, *266*; false bookcase
    61
light fittings *102*, 113, *143*, 166-69, *170-71*,
    292, 304
light well *10*
lighting *126*, *166-71*, 166-71, 224; bathrooms
    248, *251*, 286; electric 112-13, *166*, *168*,
    169-70, *171*, 172, 292, 295, *298-99*; gardens
    286; gas 11, 106, 112, *126*, 126, *166*, *168*,
    168-70, *171*; kitchens *240*, 240, *241*; lamps
    71, *166*, 166-67, *168*, 168, *169*, *170-71*, 170;
    natural 160, 198, *200-01*, *213*, *see also* glass
    (fanlights, *etc.*); oil 166-67, *169*, *170-71*,
    170; shades *168*, 168, *169*, 169, *170-71*
Lindisfarne Castle, Northumberland:
    bedroom *40*
Lindley, John: report on Kew 268-70, *218*
linoleum 154, 240, 248, *255*, 264
lintels *16*, 50, 72, 100, 290
Little Thakeham, W. Sussex *40*
living-halls *116*, *181*
living-rooms *210*, 226; *see also* drawing-rooms;
    sitting-rooms
lobbies, *see* vestibules
lock-plates *145*, *172*, 172, *174*
locks 110, *174-75*, 304, 306
loft conversions 79, 122, 289, 297-99, 303 *210*,
    270-71, 280
Loudon, J. C. (1783-1843) 7, 31, 176, 198-200,
    210, 270-71, 280
Lutyens, Sir Edwin (1869-1944) 38, *40*, *41*, 41,
    229, 273
Lyncrusta 192, 248

M

Macdonald, Margaret 38, *39*, 41
Mackintosh, Charles Rennie (1868-1928) *38*,
    38-41, *39*, 160, *207*
Mackmurdo, Arthur H. (1851-1942) 38
malachite finishes (marbling) *187*
malthouse, converted *217*
mantelpieces *133*, *151*, 180, 305; mirrors *148*,

180
marble *4*, 154, 185, 271, *273*, 305; fireplaces
    151, *218*, fenders (kerbs) *150*, 152;
    surrounds 148-50, *150*, 152; wash-stands
    228, *229*, 244, 262, *266*
marbling 122, *182*, 182, 184-85, 186, *187*
Mark Twain House, Hartford *88*
match boarding (tongue-and-groove
    boarding) *130*, 130-35, 141, *234*, *238*, 240
matting 194, 197, 248, *255*; doormats 122
Mayborough, Queensland *270*
metal 67, 68, *70-71*, 118, *122-23*, 168, *174-75*,
    201, *251*; aluminium 286, 292; roofing
    tiles *76*, 79; tin 172, 286, 292; *see also* iron
mews, converted *217*
Minton tiles *157*, *159*
mirrors *148*, 168, *180*, 229, 267
Miss Cranston Tea Rooms, Glasgow 38-41
modern houses: dismal ornamentation 26
Modern Movement (International Style) 11,
    26, *37*, 38, *39*, 42, 68, 213
Moorish influence 20, 184
'mop-boards' 124
morning-rooms *179*, 218
Morris, William (1834-96) 6, 14, 28, *34*, 34-37,
    35, *38*, 41, 179, *206-07*; blinds *279*; carpets
    195, 196, *197*; fireplaces 146; gardens 272;
    living-halls 116; ornaments *59*; paper *34*,
    35, 130, 160, 180, 188, *189*, 190, *191*, 192,
    193, bathrooms *245*, bedrooms *258*; Red
    House *34*, 37, 228; stained glass 160, *163*;
    textile-design *35*, 37, 190; tiles 157; *see also*
    Arts and Crafts Movement
Morrison, Alfred *190*
mortar 25, 72-74, 290-91
mosaic floors 154
mouldings *102*, 102, *104*, 128-29, *136-37*, 142,
    230-32, 235, 288, 295, 305, 306
Munstead Wood, Surrey *40*, 273
murals 84, 192
Muthesius, Hermann 188, 192, 195-96, 248

N

nannies 257
Nash, Sir John (1752-1835) 20, *22*, 25, *25*
Nesfield, W.A. 272
newel posts *114*, 118, *122-23*, 170, 293
niches *13*, *124*, *141*, 143; *see also* alcoves
nickel bathroom fittings *251*
Norman Gothic 19-20
numbers *67*, 67
nurseries 252, *255*, 256-57, *264*, 264-66

O

oil-cloths 194, 197
Old English revival 20, 37, 41, 130, 179; *see*
    also Elizabethan; Tudor
Old Swan House, Chelsea Embankment 37,
    64
Oldham, Lancs.: terraced housing *16*
open-plan living *220*, *224*, 294
oranges 279
The Orchard, Chorleywood 37
oriental influence 20, *21*, *57*, 72, *76*, 194, 208,
    280, *285-86*, 286; bedrooms 252, 256, 264;
    see also Egyptian; Indian; Islamic; Japanese;
    Moorish
ornamentation *16*, 19, 25-26, 42, 44

ornaments, garden, *see* statuary and
    ornaments
Osborne & Little: paper *193*
Osborne House, Isle of Wight *24*
outbuildings 276
overthrow *56*
Oxford Museum: Ruskin's work 28
Oxford University Museum 90

P

paint, colour 33, *65*, *82*, 82-85, *84-90*, *93*;
    doors 65, 172, *240*; effects *182-87*, 182-87,
    240, *see also* graining; marbling; external
    60, *62*, *82-89*, 82-89, 291, 306; floors *154*,
    154; lead-based 84, 184, 304; panelling 84,
    135; removal and restoration 90, 108, 141,
    142, 305, 306; white 82, 84, 85, *146*; *see also*
    stencils
paintwork, damaged by gas burners 168
Palace of Westminster 22, *26*, *118*, *135*, 188,
    190, 201, 261
Palladian (or palazzo) style 20, 31, 76
panelling *104*, 130, *133*, *134*, *135*, 222, 224,
    261; kitchen 230-32, 240; linenfold 130;
    painted 84, 135, 306; restoration 110, *134-
    35*, 141, 306
pantries *236*, 236
paper *35*, 114, 176-81, 184, *188-93*, *189-93*,
    210-13, *222*, *234*; bathrooms *185*, *229*, 248;
    ceilings 126, 184, *191*, 192, 293; dadoes
    189, 192, 213, 248, 254, anaglypta (or
    leather-paper) 114, *116*, 126, 130, 190-92,
    191; flocked 190, *191*, 192, 220; friezes
    192, *214*, 266; hand-printed 190, 192;
    private rooms (bedrooms, *etc.*) 254, *255*,
    256, 258, 264-66; restoration 108, 292;
    translucent *185*; *see also* Morris
Parliament, *see* Palace of Westminster
parlours 105, 169, 170, 194, *213*, 218, 226
parquet floors *114*, *154*, 154, 196
parterres 271, 272, 273
passages *4*, 122, 158, 160, *182*
paths *57*, *58*, 58, 60, *273*, 273
pavilions 268
Paxton, Sir Joseph (1801-65) 14, 188, 280
pebbledash walls 33, 38, *39*
Peckover House, Cambs.: garden 268
pediments 42, *80*, 142
pelmets (or cornices) 198, *200*, 200, *202-03*,
    210, 303
pergolas 268, 276
Perpendicular Gothic 19-20, 100, *124*
Peto, Harold (1828-97): Queen Anne style 37
photographs 208, 218-20, 248, *259*
pictorialism 177, *179*, 188-90, *191*, *196*
picture rails *102*, 124, *137*, *141*
pictures *126*, 192, 214, 220, 222, 248; of
    glazed tiles 58, *59*; painted ceilings 105
'picturesque' style 19, 20, 22-25, 76, 274, 276
pilasters 112, 148
pillars 50, 112, *274*, 305
pipes 106, 112, 113, 232, 292, 302; downpipes
    79, *80-81*, 80, 288, 289, 291; water supply
    229, 246, 292, 293, 304
plants, indoor *213*, 268, 303
plaster 124-29, 130, 184, 288, 292; lath-and-
    plaster 50, 293; ornamentation *102*, 102,
    104, 105, *124*, 128-29, 192; restoration
    111-12, 305, 306; vaulting *20*; *see also*